Microsoft®
Excel 2000
Illustrated Second Course

Tara Lynn O'Keefe

COURSE
TECHNOLOGY

Thomson Learning™

ONE MAIN STREET, CAMBRIDGE, MA 02142

Australia • Canada • Denmark • Japan • Mexico • New Zealand • Philippines
Puerto Rico • Singapore • South Africa • Spain • United Kingdom • United States

Microsoft Excel 2000—Illustrated Second Course is published by Course Technology

Senior Product Manager:	Kathryn Schooling
Product Manager:	Rebecca VanEsselstine
Contributing Author:	Barbara Clemens
Associate Product Manager:	Emily Heberlein
Production Editor:	Jennifer Goguen
Developmental Editor:	India Koopman
Composition House:	GEX, Inc.
QA Manuscript Reviewers:	Jeff Schwartz, Alex White, John Freitas, Matt Carroll, Jon Greacen
Text Designer:	Joseph Lee, Joseph Lee Designs
Cover Designer:	Doug Goodman, Doug Goodman Designs

For more information contact:

Course Technology
One Main Street
Cambridge, MA 02142

Or find us on the World Wide Web at: www.course.com

Disclaimer
Course Technology reserves the right to revise this publication and make changes from time to time in its content without notice.

ISBN 0-7600-6063-0

Printed in the United States of America

1 2 3 4 5 6 7 8 9 BM 04 03 02 01 00

The Illustrated Series Offers the Entire Package for your Microsoft Office 2000 Needs

Office 2000 MOUS Certification Coverage

The Illustrated Series offers a growing number of Microsoft-approved titles that cover the objectives required to pass the Office 2000 MOUS exams. After studying with any of the approved Illustrated titles (see list on inside cover), you will have mastered the Core and Expert skills necessary to pass any Office 2000 MOUS exam with flying colors. In addition, **Excel 2000 MOUS Certification Objectives** at the end of the book map to where specific MOUS skills can be found in each lesson and where students can find additional practice.

Helpful New Features

The Illustrated Series responded to Customer Feedback by adding a **Project Files list** at the back of the book for easy reference, Changing the red font in the Steps to green for easier reading, and Adding New Conceptual lessons to units to give students the extra information they need when learning Office 2000.

New Exciting Case and Innovative On-Line Companion

There is an exciting new case study used throughout our textbooks, a fictitious company called MediaLoft, designed to be "real-world" in nature by introducing the kinds of activities that students will encounter when working with Microsoft Office 2000. The **MediaLoft Web site**, available at www.course.com/illustrated/medialoft, is an innovative Student Online Companion which enhances and augments the printed page by bringing students onto the Web for a dynamic and continually updated learning experience. The MediaLoft site mirrors the case study used throughout the book, creating a real-world intranet site for this chain of bookstore cafés. This Companion is used to complete the WebWorks exercise in each unit of this book, and to allow students to become familiar with the business application of an intranet site.

Enhance Any Illustrated Text with these Exciting Products!

Course CBT

Enhance your students' Office 2000 classroom learning experience with self-paced computer-based training on CD-ROM. Course CBT engages students with interactive multimedia and hands-on simulations that reinforce and complement the concepts and skills covered in the textbook. All the content is aligned with the MOUS (Microsoft Office User Specialist) program, making it a great preparation tool for the certification exams. Course CBT also includes extensive pre- and post-assessments that test students' mastery of skills.

SAM 2000

How well do your students *really* know Microsoft Office? SAM 2000 is a performance-based testing program that measures students' proficiency in Microsoft Office 2000. You can use SAM 2000 to place students into or out of courses, monitor their performance throughout a course, and help prepare them for the MOUS certification exams.

Create Your Ideal Course Package with CourseKits™

If one book doesn't offer all the coverage you need, create a course package that does. With Course Technology's CourseKits—our mix-and-match approach to selecting texts—you have the freedom to combine products from more than one series. When you choose any two or more Course Technology products for one course, we'll discount the price and package them together so your students can pick up one convenient bundle at the bookstore.

For more information about any of these offerings or other Course Technology products, contact your sales representative or visit our web site at:
www.course.com

Preface

Welcome to *Microsoft Excel 2000—Illustrated Second Course*. This highly visual book is a continuation of *Microsoft Excel 2000—Illustrated Introductory* and is designed for people who want even more hands-on coverage of Excel 2000 skills.

▶ Organization and Coverage

This text contains eight units that cover advanced Excel skills. In these units, students learn how to analyze list data, enhance charts and worksheets, use What-If Analysis, summarize data with PivotTables, create a worksheet for the Web, and program with Excel.

▶ About this Approach

What makes the Illustrated approach so effective at teaching software skills? It's quite simple. Each skill is presented on two facing pages, with the step-by-step instructions on the left page, and large screen illustrations on the right. Students can focus on a single skill without having to turn the page. This unique design makes information extremely accessible and easy to absorb, and provides a great reference for after the course is over. This hands-on approach also makes it ideal for both self-paced or instructor-led classes.

Each lesson, or "information display," contains the following elements:

Each 2-page spread focuses on a single skill.

Clear step-by-step directions explain how to complete the specific task, with what students are to type in green. When students follow the numbered steps, they quickly learn how each procedure is performed and what the results will be.

Concise text that introduces the basic principles discussed in the lesson. Procedures are easier to learn when concepts fit into a framework.

Excel 2000

Importing a Database Table

In addition to importing text files, you can also use Excel to import files from other programs or database tables. To import files that contain supported file formats, simply open the file, then you are ready to work with the data in Excel. ◀━━ Jim received a database table of CafeCorp's corporate customers, which was created with dBASE IV. He will import this table into Excel, then format, sort, and total the data.

Steps

QuickTip

You can also import information from a database outside Excel using the Excel Query Wizard. Click Data on the menu bar, point to Get External Data, then click New Database Query. Open the database with the information you want to retrieve. See the Excel help topic "Get external data by using Microsoft Query."

1. Click the **Open button** 📂 on the Standard toolbar, make sure the drive containing your Project Disk appears in the Look in box, click the **Files of type list arrow**, scroll down and click **dBase Files**, click **EX M-2**, if necessary, then click **Open**
   Excel opens the database table and names the sheet tab EX M-2. See Figure M-5. Before manipulating the data, you should save the table as an Excel workbook.

2. Click **File** on the menu bar; click **Save As**; make sure the drive containing your Project Disk appears in the Save in box; click the **Save as type list arrow**; scroll up, if necessary, and click **Microsoft Excel Workbook**; edit the File name box to read **CafeCorp - Corporate Customer Info**; click **Save**; then rename the sheet tab **Corporate Customer Info**
   The truncated column labels in row 1 are not very readable; they would look better if the text wrapped to two lines.

3. Edit cell A1 to read **COMPANY NAME** (no underscore), click cell F1, type **1994**, press **[Alt][Enter]** to force a new line, type **ORDER**, press Tab, type **1995**, press **[Alt][Enter]**, type **ORDER**, then press **[Enter]**
   Pressing [Alt][Enter] as you create cell entries forces the text to wrap to the next line. Columns F and G could be wider, and the column labels would look better if they were formatted.

4. Format the numbers in **columns F and G** using the Comma style with no decimal places, center and apply bold formatting to all the column labels, then widen the columns as necessary

QuickTip

If the Sort Descending button does not appear on the Standard toolbar, click the More Buttons button ➕ to view it.

5. Save the workbook, click cell G2, then click the **Sort Descending button** on the Standard toolbar
   Columns F and G need totals.

6. Select range F19:G19, click the **AutoSum button** Σ on the Standard toolbar, then format the range F19:G19 with the Comma style and no decimal places, add a border around it, then click cell A1
   Your completed worksheet should match Figure M-6.

7. Add your name to the worksheet footer, preview and print the list in landscape orientation, fit the list to one page if necessary, then save the workbook

---

Hints as well as trouble-shooting advice, right where you need it — next to the step itself.

Every lesson features large-size, full-color representations of what the students' screen should look like after completing the numbered steps.

Other Features

The two-page lesson format featured in this book provides the new user with a powerful learning experience. Additionally, this book contains the following features:

▶ **MOUS Certification Coverage**
Each unit opener has a ⌐MOUS¬ next to it to indicate where Microsoft Office User Specialist (MOUS) skills are covered. In addition, there is a MOUS appendix which contains a grid that maps to where specific skills can be found in each lesson and where students can find additional practice. Complete coverage of both Expert and Core MOUS skills can be found in *Microsoft Excel—Illustrated Complete*, 0-7600-6064-9.

▶ **Real-World Case**
The case study used throughout the textbook, a fictitious company called MediaLoft, is designed to be "'real-world" in nature and introduces the kinds of activities that students will encounter when working with Microsoft Excel 2000. With a real-world case, the process of solving problems will be more meaningful to students. Students can also enhance their skills by completing the Web Works exercises in each unit by going to the innovative Student Online Companion, available at **www.course.com/illustrated/medialoft**. The MediaLoft site mirrors the case study by acting as the company's intranet site, further allowing students to become familiar with applicable business scenarios.

▶ **End of Unit Material**
Each unit concludes with a Concepts Review that tests students' understanding of what they learned in the unit. The Concepts Review is followed by a Skills Review, which provides students with additional hands-on practice of the skills. The Skills Review is followed by Independent Challenges, which pose case problems for students to solve. At least one Independent Challenge in each unit asks students to use the World Wide Web to solve the problem as indicated by a Web Work icon. The Visual Workshops that follow the Independent Challenges help students develop critical thinking skills. Students are shown completed Web pages or screens and are asked to recreate them from scratch.

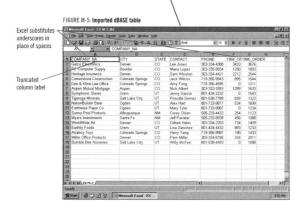

FIGURE M-5: Imported dBASE table

Excel substitutes underscores in place of spaces

Truncated column label

FIGURE M-6: Completed worksheet containing imported data

Adjusted and formatted column labels

Figures for 1995 arranged in descending order

New totals

Renamed sheet tab

Exporting Excel data
Most of the file types that Excel can import (listed in Table M-1) are also the file types to which Excel can export, or deliver data. Excel can also export Text and CSV formats for Macintosh and OS/2. To export an Excel worksheet, use the Save As command on the File menu, click the Save as type list arrow, then select the desired format. Saving to a non-Excel format might result in the loss of formatting that is unique to Excel.

Clues to Use boxes provide concise information that either expands on one component of the major lesson skill or describes an independent task that is in some way related to the major lesson skill.

The page numbers are designed like a road map. Excel indicates the Excel section, M indicates the thirteenth unit, and 7 indicates the page within the unit.

Instructor's Resource Kit

The Instructor's Resource Kit is Course Technology's way of putting the resources and information needed to teach and learn effectively into your hands. With an integrated array of teaching and learning tools that offers you and your students a broad range of technology-based instructional options, we believe this kit represents the highest quality and most cutting edge resources available to instructors today. Many of these resources are available at www.course.com. The resources available with this book are:

MediaLoft Web site   Available at **www.course.com/illustrated/medialoft**, this innovative Student Online Companion enhances and augments the printed page by bringing students onto the Web for a dynamic and continually updated learning experience. The MediaLoft site mirrors the case study used throughout the book, creating a real-world intranet site for this fictitious company, a national chain of bookstore cafés. This Companion is used to complete the WebWorks exercise in each unit of this book, and to allow students to become familiar with the business application of an intranet site.

Instructor's Manual   Available as an electronic file, the Instructor's Manual is quality-assurance tested and includes unit overviews, detailed lecture topics for each unit with teaching tips, an Upgrader's Guide, solutions to all lessons and end-of-unit material, and extra Independent Challenges. The Instructor's Manual is available on the Instructor's Resource Kit CD-ROM, or you can download it from **www.course.com**.

Course Test Manager   Designed by Course Technology, this Windows-based testing software helps instructors design, administer, and print tests and pre-tests. A full-featured program, Course Test Manager also has an online testing component that allows students to take tests at the computer and have their exams automatically graded.

Course Faculty Online Companion   You can browse this textbook's password-protected site to obtain the Instructor's Manual, Solution Files, Project Files, and any updates to the text. Contact your Customer Service Representative for the site address and password.

Project Files   Project Files contain all of the data that students will use to complete the lessons and end-of-unit material. A Readme file includes instructions for using the files. Adopters of this text are granted the right to install the Project Files on any standalone computer or network. The Project Files are available on the Instructor's Resource Kit CD-ROM, the Review Pack, and can also be downloaded from www.course.com.

Solution Files   Solution Files contain every file students are asked to create or modify in the lessons and end-of-unit material. A Help file on the Instructor's Resource Kit includes information for using the Solution Files.

Figure Files   Figure files contain all the figures from the book in bitmap format. Use the figure files to create transparency masters or in a PowerPoint presentation.

WebCT   WebCT is a tool used to create Web-based educational environments and also uses WWW browsers as the interface for the course-building environment. The site is hosted on your school campus, allowing complete control over the information. WebCT has its own internal communication system, offering internal e-mail, a Bulletin Board, and a Chat room.

Course Technology offers pre-existing supplemental information to help in your WebCT class creation, such as a suggested Syllabus, Lecture Notes, Figures in the Book / Course Presenter, Student Downloads, and Test Banks in which you can schedule an exam, create reports, and more.

Brief Contents

Contents

Excel 2000

Contents

Enhancing Charts and Worksheets   EXCEL J-1

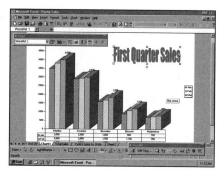

Using a What-If Analysis EXCEL K-1

Contents

Summarizing Data with PivotTables EXCEL L-1

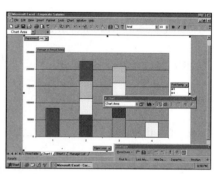

Exchanging Data with Other Programs

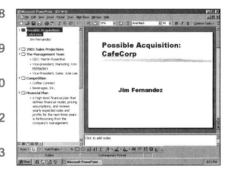

Contents

Sharing Excel Files and Incorporating Web Information

EXCEL N-1

Gaining Control over Your Work — EXCEL O-1

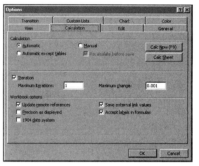

Contents

Analyzing
List Data

Objectives

- MOUS ▶ **Retrieve records with AutoFilter**
- MOUS ▶ **Create a custom filter**
- MOUS ▶ **Filter a list with Advanced Filter**
- MOUS ▶ **Extract list data**
- MOUS ▶ **Create subtotals using grouping and outlines**
- MOUS ▶ **Look up values in a list**
- MOUS ▶ **Summarize list data**
- MOUS ▶ **Use data validation for list entries**

There are many ways to **analyze**, or manipulate, list data with Excel. One way is to filter a list so that only the rows that meet certain criteria are retrieved. In this unit you will retrieve records using AutoFilter, create a custom filter, and filter a list using Excel's Advanced Filter feature. In addition, you will learn to insert automatic subtotals, use lookup functions to locate list entries, and apply database functions to summarize list data that meets specific criteria. You'll also learn how to restrict entries in a column using data validation. ✐ Jim Fernandez recently conducted a survey for the MediaLoft Marketing department. He mailed questionnaires to a random selection of customers at all stores. After the questionnaires were returned, he entered all the data into Excel, where he will analyze the data and create reports.

Retrieving Records with AutoFilter

The Excel AutoFilter feature searches for records that meet criteria the user specifies, and then lists those matching records. One way is to **filter** out, or hide, data that fails to meet certain criteria. You can filter specific values in a column, use the predefined Top 10 option to filter records based on upper or lower values in a column, or create a custom filter. For example, you can filter a customer list to retrieve names of only those customers residing in Canada. You also can filter records based on a specific field and request that Excel retrieve only those records having an entry (or no entry) in that field. Once you create a filtered list, you can print it or copy it to another part of the worksheet to manipulate it further. ◢━━━ Jim is now ready to work on his survey information. He begins by retrieving data on only those customers who live in Chicago, Illinois.

QuickTip

To return personalized tool-bars and menus to their default state, click Tools on the menu bar, click Customize, click the Options tab in the Customize dialog box, click Reset my usage data to restore the default settings, click Yes, click Close, then close the Drawing toolbar if it is displayed.

1. **Open the workbook titled EX I-1, then save it as Survey Data**
   The AutoFilter feature will enable you to retrieve the records for the report.

2. **Click Data on the menu bar, point to Filter, then click AutoFilter**
   List arrows appear to the right of each field name.

3. **Click the City list arrow**
   An AutoFilter list containing the different city options appears below the field name, as shown in Figure I-1. Because you want to retrieve data for only those customers who live in Chicago, "Chicago" will be your **search criterion.**

4. **In the filter list, click Chicago**
   Only those records containing Chicago in the City field appear, as shown in Figure I-2. The status bar indicates the number of matching records (in this case, 5 of 35), the color of the row numbers changes for the matching records, and the color of the list arrow for the filtered field changes. Next, you want to retrieve information about those customers who purchased the most merchandise. To do so, you must clear the previous filter.

5. **Click Data on the menu bar, point to Filter, then click Show All**
   All the records reappear.

Trouble?

If the column label in cell A1 covers the column headers, making it difficult to find the appropriate columns, select A2 before scrolling.

6. **Scroll right until columns G through N are visible, click the Purchases to Date list arrow, then click (Top 10 . . .)**
   The Top 10 AutoFilter dialog box opens. The default is to select the ten records with the highest value. You need to display only the top 2.

7. **With 10 selected in the middle box, type 2, then click OK**
   The records are retrieved for the two customers who purchased the most merchandise, $3,200 and $2,530. See Figure I-3.

8. **Click the Purchases to Date list arrow, click (All), press [Ctrl][Home], add your name to the right side of the footer, then print the list**
   You have cleared the filter and all the records reappear. Because you didn't make any changes to the list, there is no need to save the file.

FIGURE I-1: Worksheet showing AutoFilter options

City field

Click Chicago to filter by this city

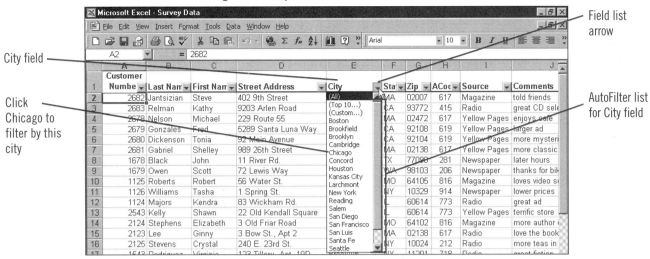

Field list arrow

AutoFilter list for City field

FIGURE I-2: List filtered with AutoFilter

Search based on this field

Note break in record numbers

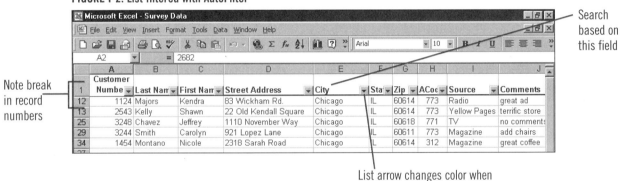

List arrow changes color when AutoFilter is in effect

FIGURE I-3: List filtered with Top 2 AutoFilter criteria

	F	G	H	I	J	K	L	M	N	O	F
1	Sta	Zip	ACo	Source	Comments	First Purcha	Purchases to Date	Income	Household Type		
23	CA	94108	510	Magazine	more events for kids	6/22/90	$ 3,200	$ 84,000	Couple		
28	NM	87505	505	TV	more bike racks	4/20/98	$ 2,530	$ 34,000	Single		

List filtered with two highest values in this field

Creating a Custom Filter

So far, you have used the AutoFilter command to filter rows based on an entry in a single column. You can perform more complex filters using options in the Custom AutoFilter dialog box. For example, you can filter rows based on two entries in a single column or use comparison operators such as "greater than" or "less than" to display only those records with amounts greater than $50,000 in a particular column. ◀▬▬ Jim's next task is to locate those customers who live west of the Rocky Mountains, who live in a "single" household, and who heard about MediaLoft through a magazine advertisement.

Steps 1 2 3 4

1. **Click the Zip list arrow, then click (Custom . . .)**
   The Custom AutoFilter dialog box opens. Because you know that all residents west of the Rockies have a zip code greater than 81000, you specify this criterion here. Because all the zip codes in the list were originally entered as labels with leading apostrophes, you need to include this apostrophe when entering the zip code value.

2. **Click the Zip list arrow, click is greater than, press [Tab], then type '81000**
   Your completed Custom AutoFilter dialog box should match Figure I-4.

3. **Click OK**
   The dialog box closes, and only those records having a zip code greater than 81000 appear in the worksheet. Now, you'll narrow the list even further by displaying only those customers who live in a single household.

4. **Scroll right until columns G through N are visible, click the Household Type list arrow, then click Single**
   The list of records retrieved has narrowed. Finally, you need to filter out all customers except those who heard about MediaLoft through a magazine advertisement.

5. **Click the Source list arrow, then click Magazine**
   Your final filtered list now shows only customers in single households west of the Rocky Mountains who heard about MediaLoft through magazine ads. See Figure I-5.

6. **Preview, then print the worksheet**
   The worksheet prints using the existing print settings—landscape orientation, scaled to fit on a single page.

7. **Click Data on the menu bar, point to Filter, click AutoFilter to deselect it, then press [Ctrl][Home]**
   You have cleared the filter, and all the customer records appear.

FIGURE I-4: Custom AutoFilter dialog box

Value includes
leading apostrophe

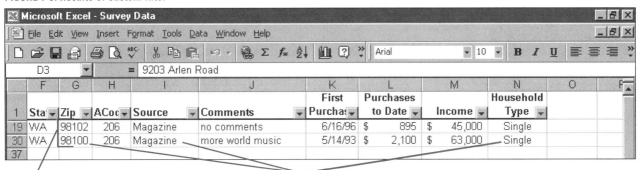

FIGURE I-5: Results of custom filter

	F	G	H	I	J	K	L	M	N	O	P
1	Sta	Zip	ACod	Source	Comments	First Purcha	Purchases to Date	Income	Household Type		
19	WA	98102	206	Magazine	no comments	6/16/96	$ 895	$ 45,000	Single		
30	WA	98100	206	Magazine	more world music	5/14/93	$ 2,100	$ 63,000	Single		
37											

Zip codes greater than 81000   Fields used in custom filter

And and Or logical conditions

You can narrow a search even further by using the And or Or buttons in the Custom AutoFilter dialog box. For example, you can select records for those customers with homes in California *and* Texas as well as select records for customers with homes in California *or* Texas. See Figure I-6. When used in this way, "And" and "Or" are often referred to as logical conditions. When you search for customers with homes in California *and* Texas, you are specifying an And condition. When you search for customers with homes in either California *or* Texas, you are specifying an Or condition.

FIGURE I-6: Using the Custom AutoFilter dialog box

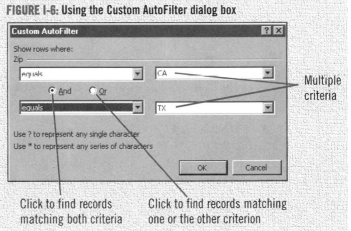

Multiple
criteria

Click to find records
matching both criteria

Click to find records matching
one or the other criterion

Filtering a List with Advanced Filter

The Advanced Filter command allows you to search for data that matches complicated criteria in more than one column, using And and Or conditions. To use advanced filtering, you must define a criteria range. A **criteria range** is a cell range containing one row of labels (usually a copy of the column labels) and at least one additional row underneath the row of labels that contains the criteria you want to match. ⟶ Jim's next task is to identify customers who have been buying at MediaLoft since before May 1, 1999, and whose total purchases are less than or equal to $1,000. He will use the Advanced Filter command to retrieve this data. Jim begins by defining the criteria range.

1. Select **rows 1 through 6**, click **Insert** on the menu bar, then click **Rows**; click cell **A1**, type **Criteria Range**, click cell **A6**, type **List Range**, then click the **Enter button** 🗹 on the formula bar

   See Figure I-7. Six blank rows are added above the list. Excel does not require the labels "Criteria Range" and "List Range," but they are useful because they help organize the worksheet. It will be helpful to see the column labels. (In the next step, if the column labels make it difficult for you to drag the pointer to cell N7, try clicking N7 first; then drag the pointer all the way left to cell A7.)

   ### Trouble?
   If the Copy button does not appear on your Standard toolbar, click the More Buttons button 🔽 to view it.

2. Select range **A7:N7**, click the **Copy button** 🗐 on the Standard toolbar, click cell **A2**, then press **[Enter]**

   Next, you need to specify that you want records for only those customers who have been customers since before May 1 and who have purchased no more than $1,000. In other words, you need records with a date before (less than) May 1, 1999 (<5/1/99) and a Purchases to Date amount that is less than or equal to $1,000 (<=1000).

3. Scroll right until columns H through N are visible, click cell **K3**, type **< 5/1/99**, click cell **L3**, type **<=1000**, then click 🗹

   This enters the criteria in the cells directly beneath the Criteria Range labels. See Figure I-8. Placing the criteria in the same row indicates that the records you are searching for must match both criteria; that is, it specifies an And condition.

4. Press **[Ctrl][Home]**, click **Data** on the menu bar, point to **Filter**, then click **Advanced Filter**

   The Advanced Filter dialog box opens, with the list range already entered. (Notice that the default setting under Action is to filter the list in its current location rather than copy it to another location. You will change this setting later.)

5. Click the **Criteria Range box**, select range **A2:N3** in the worksheet (move the dialog box if necessary), then click **OK**

   You have specified the criteria range. The filtered list contains 19 records that match both the criteria—their first purchase was before 5/1/99 and their purchases to date total less than $1,000. You'll filter this list even further in the next lesson.

FIGURE I-7: Using the Advanced Filter command

New rows ──

New labels ──

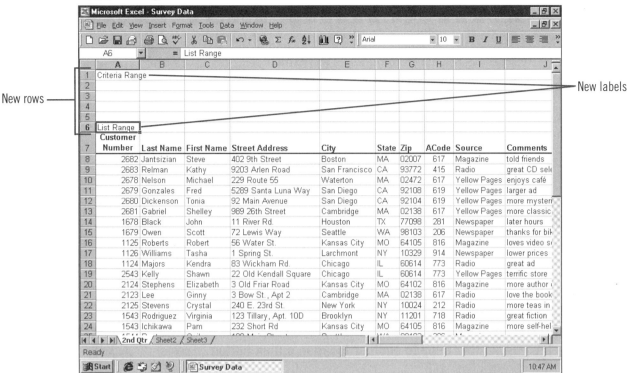

FIGURE I-8: Criteria in the same row

Subsequent filtered records will match these criteria

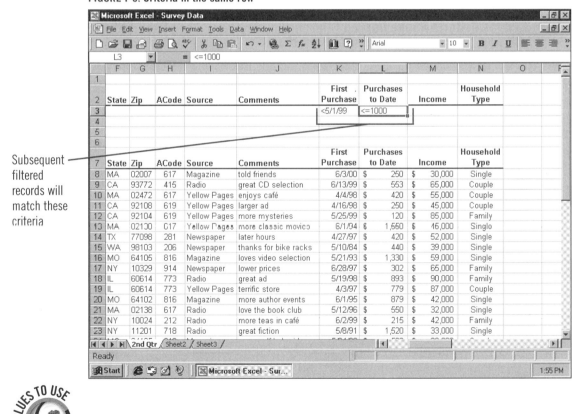

Understanding the criteria range

When you define the criteria range in the Advanced Filter dialog box, Excel automatically creates a name for this range in the worksheet (Criteria). The criteria range includes the field names and any criteria rows underneath the names.

Extracting List Data

Whenever you take the time to specify a complicated set of search criteria, it's a good idea to extract the matching records. When you **extract** data, you place a copy of a filtered list in a range you specify in the Advanced Filter dialog box. That way, you won't accidentally clear the filter or lose track of the records you spent time compiling. ◄━━━ Jim needs to filter the previous list one step further to reflect only those customers in the current filtered list who heard of MediaLoft through TV or a magazine ad. To complete this filter, he will specify an Or condition by entering two sets of criteria in two separate rows. He decides to save the matching records by extracting them to a different location in the worksheet.

Steps

1. **Click cell I3, type TV, then press [Enter]; in cell I4, type Magazine, click the Enter button ☑ on the formula bar, then copy the criteria in K3:L3 to K4:L4**
   See Figure I-9. This time, you'll indicate that you want to copy the filtered list to a range beginning in cell A50.

2. **Click Data on the menu bar, point to Filter, then click Advanced Filter; under Action, click the Copy to another location option button to select it, click the Copy to box, then type A50**
   The last time you filtered the list, the criteria range included only rows 2 and 3, and now you have criteria in row 4.

3. **In the Criteria Range box, edit the current formula to read $A$2:$N$4, click OK; then scroll down until row 50 is visible**
   You have changed the criteria range to include row 4. The matching records are copied to the range beginning in cell A50. The original list (starting in cell A7) contains the records filtered in the previous lesson. See Figure I-10.

4. **Select range A50:N61, click File on the menu bar, click Print, under Print what, click the Selection option button, click Preview, then click Print**
   The selected area prints.

5. **Press [Ctrl][Home], click Data on the menu bar, point to Filter, then click Show All**
   All the records in the range reappear. You return to the original list, which starts at its new location in cell A7.

6. **Save, then close the workbook**

FIGURE I-9: Criteria in separate rows

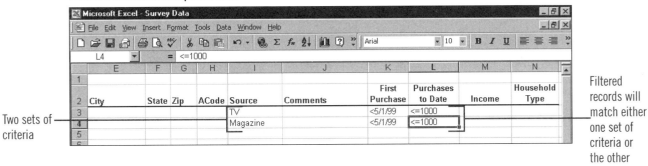

Two sets of criteria

Filtered records will match either one set of criteria or the other

FIGURE I-10: Extracted data records

Extracted records copied to the range starting at cell A50

	Street Address	City	State	Zip	ACode	Source	Comments	First Purchase	Purchases to Date	
50	Street Address	City	State	Zip	ACode	Source	Comments	First Purchase	Purchases to Date	
51	3 Old Friar Road	Kansas City	MO	64102	816	Magazine	more author events	6/1/95	$ 879	$
52	232 Short Rd	Kansas City	MO	64105	816	Magazine	more self-help videos	5/24/96	$ 530	$
53	100 Main Street	Seattle	WA	98102	206	Magazine	no comments	6/16/96	$ 895	$
54	123 Elm St.	Houston	TX	77098	281	Magazine	salespeople helpful	6/28/98	$ 320	$
55	1110 November Way	Chicago	IL	60618	771	TV	no comments	3/22/99	$ 250	$
56	42 Silver Street	Reading	MA	03882	413	TV	fun store	4/6/87	$ 420	$
57	921 Lopez Lane	Chicago	IL	60611	773	Magazine	add chairs	4/9/93	$ 480	$
58	900 Monument St.	Concord	MA	01742	508	Magazine	love the book club	6/15/97	$ 450	$
59	486 Intel Circuit	Houston	TX	77092	281	TV	very effective ad	5/26/96	$ 990	$
60	2318 Sarah Road	Chicago	IL	60614	312	Magazine	great coffee	4/29/97	$ 640	$
61	2120 Witch Way	Salem	MA	01970	508	Magazine	loves our staff	5/25/97	$ 820	$

Extracted records for customers with first purchase before 5/1/99 or purchases less than $1,000 and who heard about MediaLoft through TV or magazines

Understanding the criteria range and the copy-to location

When you define the criteria range and/or copy-to location in the Advanced Filter dialog box, Excel automatically creates names for these ranges in the worksheet (Criteria and Extract). The criteria range includes the field names and any criteria rows underneath them. The extract range includes just the field names above the extracted list. To extract a different list, simply select Extract as the copy-to location. Excel automatically deletes the old list in the extract area and generates a new list under the field names. Make sure the worksheet has enough blank rows underneath the field names for your data.

Creating Subtotals Using Grouping and Outlines

The Excel subtotals feature provides a quick, easy way to group and summarize data in a list. Usually, you create subtotals with the SUM function. You also can subtotal groups with functions such as COUNT, AVERAGE, MAX, and MIN. Your list must have field names and be sorted before you can issue the Subtotal command. ◢▬▬▬ Jim wants to create a list grouped by advertising source, with subtotals for purchases to date and household income. He starts by sorting the list in ascending order—first by advertising source, then by state, and, finally, by city.

Steps 1 2 3 4

1. Open the workbook titled **EX I-1**, then save it as **Survey Data 2**

2. Click the **Name Box** list arrow, click **Database**, click **Data** on the menu bar, then click **Sort**; click the **Sort by** list arrow, click **Source**, click the first **Then by** list arrow, click **State**, click the **Ascending option button** to set the Then by sort order; click the second **Then by** list arrow, click **City**, then click **OK**
   You have sorted the list in ascending order, first by advertising source, then by state, and, finally, by city.

Trouble?

You may receive the following message: "No list found. Select a single cell within your list and Microsoft Excel will select the list for you." If you do, this means that you did not select the list before issuing the Subtotals command. Click OK, then repeat Steps 2 and 3.

3. Press **[Ctrl][Home]**, click **Data** on the menu bar, then click **Subtotals**
   Before you use the Subtotals command, you must position the cell pointer within the list range (in this case, range A1:N36). The Subtotal dialog box opens. Here, you specify the items you want subtotaled, the function you want to apply to the values, and the fields you want to summarize.

4. Click the **At each change in** list arrow, click **Source**, click the **Use function** list arrow, click **Sum**; in the Add subtotal to list, click the **Purchases to Date** and **Income** check boxes to select them; if necessary, click the **Household☐Type** check box to deselect it; then, if necessary, click the **Replace current subtotals** and **Summary below data** check boxes to select them
   Your completed Subtotal dialog box should match Figure I-11.

5. Click **OK**, then scroll to and click cell **L41**
   The subtotaled list appears, showing the calculated subtotals and grand total in columns L and M. See Figure I-12. Notice that Excel displays an outline to the left of the worksheet showing the structure of the subtotaled lists.

6. Preview the worksheet, click **Setup** and place your name on the right side of the footer, then print the worksheet using the current settings

7. Press **[Ctrl][Home]**, click **Data** on the menu bar, click **Subtotals**, then click **Remove All**
   You have turned off the Subtotaling feature. The subtotals are removed, and the Outline feature is turned off automatically. Because you did not alter the worksheet data, there's no need to save the file.

FIGURE I-11: Completed Subtotal dialog box

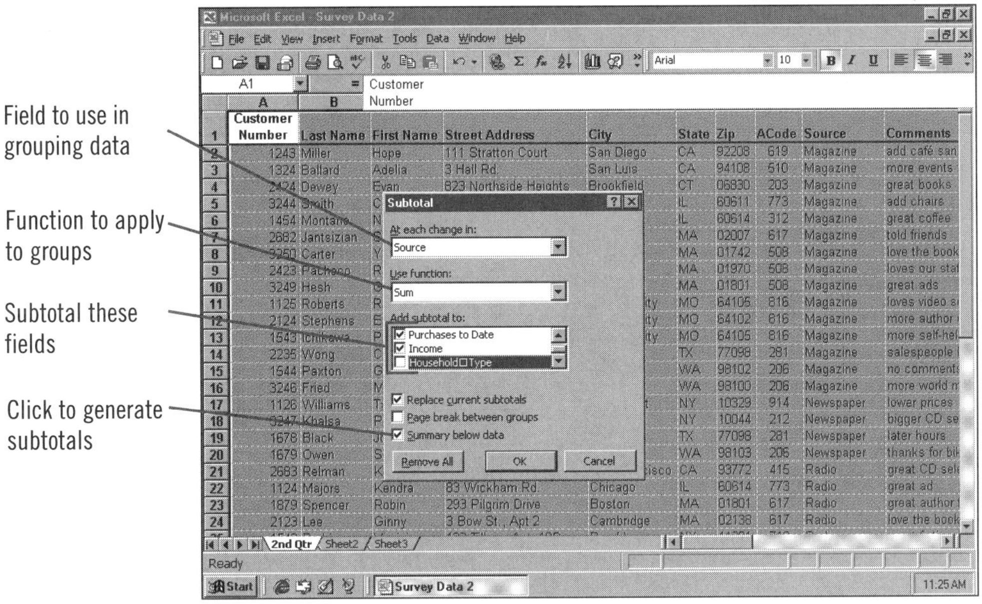

Field to use in grouping data

Function to apply to groups

Subtotal these fields

Click to generate subtotals

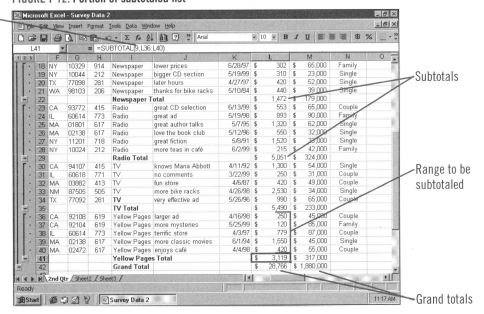

FIGURE I-12: Portion of subtotaled list

Number 9 indicates the SUM function

Subtotals

Range to be subtotaled

Grand totals

Show or hide details in an Excel outline

Once subtotals have been generated, all detail records are displayed in an outline. See Figure I-13. You can then click the Hide Details button ▬ of your choice to hide that group of records, creating a summary report. You can also create a chart that shows the summary data. Any chart you create will be automatically updated as you show or hide data. You can also click the Show Details button ➕ for the group of data you want to display. To show a specific level of detail, click the row or column level button for the lowest level you want to display. For example, to display levels 1 through 3, click ③.

FIGURE I-13: Subtotaled list with level 2 details hidden

Hide Details button

Show Details buttons

Row level symbols

Looking Up Values in a List

The Excel VLOOKUP function helps you locate specific values in a list. The VLOOKUP searches vertically (V) down the leftmost column of a list and then reads across the row to find the value in the column you specify. The process of looking up a number in a phone book uses the same logic as the Excel VLOOKUP function: You locate a person's name and then read across the row to find the phone number you are looking for. At times, Jim wants to be able to find out what type of household a particular customer lives in simply by entering his or her specific customer number. To do this, he uses the VLOOKUP function. He begins by creating a special list, or table, containing the customer numbers he wants to look up. Then he copies names to a separate location.

Steps 1 2 3 4

1. Click cell **C2**, click **Window** on the menu bar, then click **Freeze Panes**; scroll right until columns N through T and rows 1 through 15 are visible

2. Click cell **P1**, type **VLOOKUP Function**, click the **Enter button** on the formula bar; copy the contents of cell **A1** to cell **R1**, copy the contents of cell **N1** to cell **S1**, widen the columns as necessary to display the text, then click any blank cell
   See Figure I-14. Jim wants to know the household type for customer number 3247.

3. Click cell **R2**, type **3247**, then press [→]
   The VLOOKUP function in the Paste Function dialog box will let Jim find the household type for customer number 3247.

4. Make sure cell S2 is still selected, click the **Paste Function button** on the Standard toolbar, under Function category click **Lookup & Reference**, under Function name click **VLOOKUP**, then click **OK**
   The VLOOKUP dialog box opens. Because the value you want to find is in cell R2, that will be the Lookup_value. The list you want to search is the customer list, so its name ("Database") will be the Table_array.

5. Drag the **VLOOKUP dialog box** down so that at least rows 1 and 2 of the worksheet are visible; with the insertion point in the Lookup_value box, click cell **R2**, click the **Table_array box**, then type **DATABASE**
   The column you want to search (Household Type) is the fourteenth column from the left, so the Col_index_num will be 14. Because you want to find an exact match for the value in cell R2, the Range_lookup argument will be FALSE. (If you want to find only the closest match for a value, you enter TRUE in the Range_lookup box, as indicated in the bottom of the VLOOKUP dialog box.)

6. Click the **Col_index_num box**, type **14**, click the **Range_lookup box**, then type **FALSE**
   Your completed VLOOKUP dialog box should match Figure I-15.

7. Click **OK**
   Excel searches down the leftmost column of the customer list until it finds a value matching the one in cell R2. Then it finds the household type for that record ("Single") and displays it in cell S2. Now, you'll use this function to determine the household type for one other customer.

8. Click cell **R2**, type **2125**, then click
   The VLOOKUP function returns the value Family in cell S2.

9. Press **[Ctrl][Home]**, then save the workbook.

FIGURE I-14: Worksheet with headings for VLOOKUP

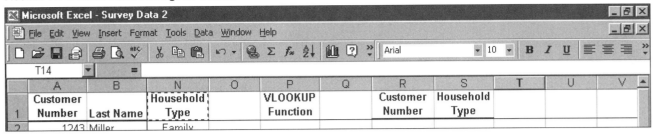

FIGURE I-15: Completed VLOOKUP dialog box

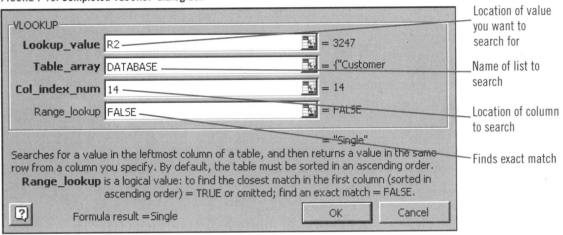

Location of value
you want to
search for

Name of list to
search

Location of column
to search

Finds exact match

Using the HLOOKUP function

The VLOOKUP (Vertical Lookup) function is useful when your data is arranged vertically in columns. The HLOOKUP (Horizontal Lookup) function is useful when your data is arranged horizontally in rows. HLOOKUP searches horizontally across the topmost row of a list until the matching value is found, then looks down the number of rows you specify. The arguments for this function are identical to those for the VLOOKUP function, with one exception. Instead of a Col_index_number, HLOOKUP uses a Row_index_number, which indicates the location of the row you want to search. For example, if you want to search the fourth row from the top, the Row_index_number should be 4.

Excel 2000

Summarizing List Data

Database functions allow you to summarize list data in a variety of ways. For example, you can use them to count, average, or total values in a field for only those records that meet specified criteria. When working with a sales activity list, for instance, you can use Excel to count the number of client contacts by sales representative or to total the amount sold to specific accounts by month. The format for database functions is explained in Figure I-16. ▰▰▰ Jim wants to summarize the information in his list in two ways. First, he wants to find the total purchases to date for each advertising source. He also wants to count the number of records for each advertising source. Jim begins by creating a criteria range that includes a copy of the column label for the column he wants to summarize, as well as the criterion itself.

Steps 1234

1. **With the panes still frozen, scroll down until row 31 is the top row underneath the frozen headings, then enter and format the five labels shown in Figure I-17 in the range: I39:K41**

   The criteria range in I40:I41 tells Excel to summarize records with the entry "Yellow Pages" in the Source column. The functions will be in cells L39 and L41.

QuickTip

You can use a column label, such as "City", in place of a column number. Type the text exactly as it is entered in the list and enclose it in double quotation marks.

2. **Click cell L39, type =DSUM(DATABASE,12,I40:I41), then click the Enter button ☑ on the formula bar**

   The result in cell L39 is 3119. For the range named Database, Excel totaled the information in column 12 (Purchases to Date) for those records that meet the criteria of Source = Yellow Pages. The DCOUNTA function will help you determine the number of nonblank records meeting the criteria Source = Yellow Pages.

Trouble?

If the result you receive is incorrect, make sure you entered the formula correctly, using the letter "I" in the criteria range address, and the number one (1) for the column number.

3. **Click cell L41, type =DCOUNTA(DATABASE,1,I40:I41), then click ☑**

   The result in cell L41 is 5, meaning that there are five customers who heard about MediaLoft through the Yellow Pages. This function uses the first field in the list, Customer Number, to check for nonblank cells within the criteria range Source = Yellow Pages. Jim also wants to see total purchases and a count for the magazine ads.

4. **Click cell I41, type Magazine, then click ☑**

   With total purchases of $13,634, it's clear that magazine advertising is the most effective way of attracting MediaLoft customers. Compare your results with Figure I-18.

5. **Press [Ctrl][Home], then save and close the workbook**

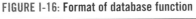
FIGURE I-16: Format of database function

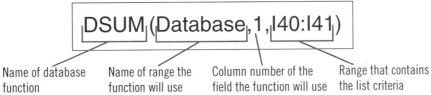

DSUM (Database, 1, I40:I41)

Name of database function | Name of range the function will use | Column number of the field the function will use | Range that contains the list criteria

FIGURE I-17: Portion of worksheet showing summary area

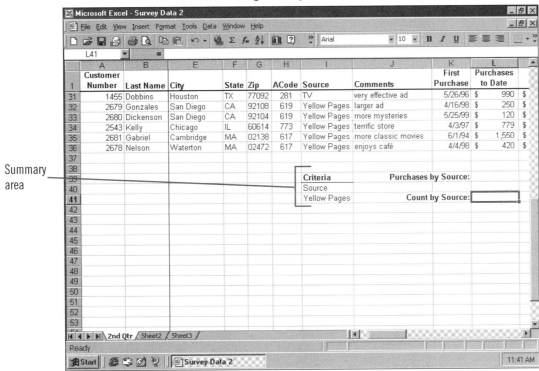

FIGURE I-18: Result generated by database function

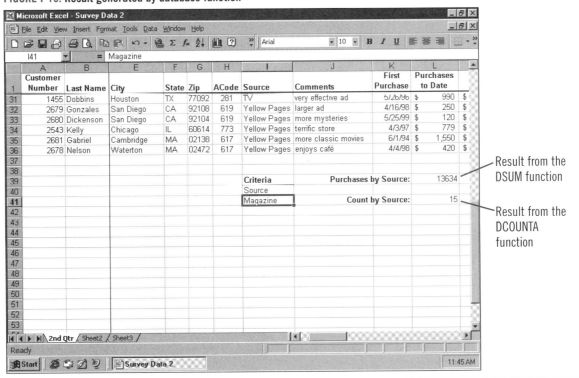

Excel 2000

Using Data Validation for List Entries

The Excel Data Validation feature allows you to specify what data is valid for a range of cells. You can restrict data to whole numbers, decimal numbers, or text, or you can set limits on entries. You can also specify a list of acceptable entries. Once you've specified what data is considered valid, Excel prevents users from entering any other data (considered invalid) except your specified choices. ▄▄▄ Jim wants to make sure that information in the Household Type column is entered consistently in the future. He decides to restrict the entries in that column to three options: Couple, Single, and Family. First, he selects the column he wants to restrict.

Steps

1. Open the workbook titled **EX I-1**, then save it as **Survey Data 3**

2. Scroll right until column N is displayed, then click the **Column N** column header
   The entire column is selected.

QuickTip

To restrict entries to decimal or whole numbers, dates, or times, select the appropriate option in the Allow list. To specify a long list of valid entries, type the list in a column elsewhere in the worksheet, then type the address of the list in the Source box.

3. Click **Data** on the menu bar, click **Validation**, click the **Settings tab** if necessary, click the **Allow** list arrow, then click **List**
   Selecting the List option enables you to type a list of specific options.

4. Click the **Source** box, then type **Couple, Single, Family**
   You have entered the list of acceptable entries, separated by commas. See Figure I-19. Jim wants the data entry person to be able to select a valid entry from a drop-down list.

5. Click the **In-cell Drop-down check box** to select it if necessary, then click **OK**
   The dialog box closes, and you return to the worksheet. The new data restrictions will apply only to new entries in the Household Type column.

6. Click cell **N37**, then click the **list arrow** to display the list of valid entries
   See Figure I-20. You could click an item in the list to have it entered in the cell, but Jim first wants to know what happens if you enter an invalid entry.

7. Click the **list arrow** to close the list, type **Individual**, then press **[Enter]**
   A warning dialog box appears to prevent you from entering the invalid data. See Figure I-21.

8. Click **Cancel**, click the **list arrow**, then click **Single**
   The cell accepts the valid entry. The data restriction ensures that new records will contain only one of the three correct entries in the Household Type column. The customer list is finished and ready for future data entry.

9. Save and close the workbook

FIGURE I-19: Creating data restrictions

Restricts entries to a list of valid options

List of valid options

Displays a list of valid options during data entry

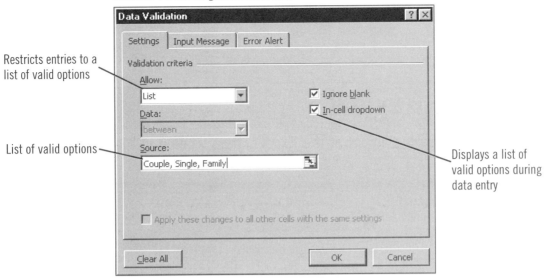

FIGURE I-20: Entering data in restricted cells

List appears when you click a restricted cell

Click on option to enter it in the cell

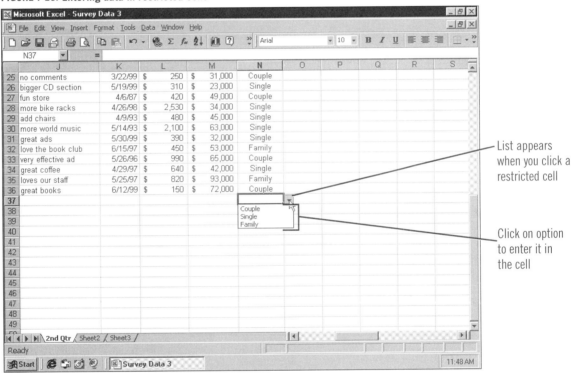

FIGURE I-21: Validation message

Click here to return to cell and enter a valid option

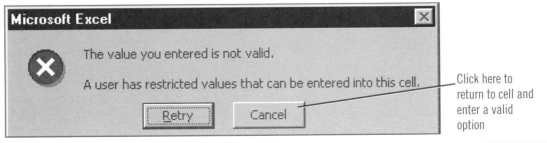

Practice

► Concepts Review

Explain the function of each element of the Excel screen labeled in Figure I-22.

FIGURE I-22

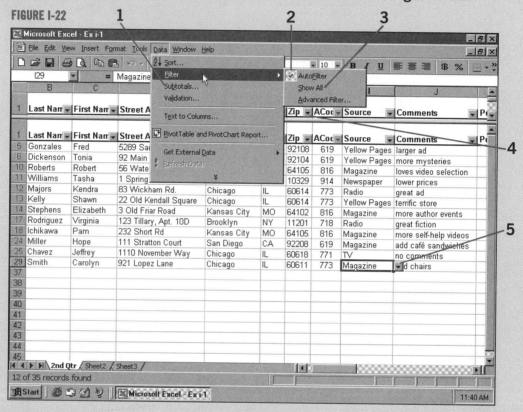

Match each term with the statement that describes it.

6. HLOOKUP
7. Extracted list
8. Data validation
9. Criteria range
10. List range

a. Cell range when advanced filter results are copied to another location
b. Range in which search conditions are set
c. Restricts list entries to specified options
d. Range used to specify a database in database functions
e. Function to use when data is arranged horizontally in rows

Select the best answer from the list of choices.

11. You might perform an AutoFilter and search for nonblank entries in order to
    a. Identify missing data.
    b. Find records with data in a particular field.
    c. Sum records with data in a particular field.
    d. b and c.

12. **What does it mean when you select the Or option when creating a custom filter?**
    a. Neither criterion has to be 100% true.
    b. Either criterion can be true to find a match.
    c. Both criteria must be true to find a match.
    d. Custom filter requires a criteria range.

13. **What must a list have before automatic subtotals can be inserted?**
    a. Enough records to show multiple subtotals
    b. Grand totals
    c. Column or field headings
    d. Formatted cells

► Skills Review

1. **Retrieve records with AutoFilter.**
    a. Open the workbook titled EX I-2, then save it as "Compensation Summary".
    b. Use AutoFilter to list records for employees in the Accounting department.
    c. Redisplay all employees, then use AutoFilter to show the three employees with the highest annual salary.
    d. Redisplay all the records.

2. **Create a custom filter.**
    a. Create a custom filter showing employees hired prior to 1/1/90 or after 1/1/94.
    b. Preview, then print the list in A1:J11.
    c. Redisplay all records.
    d. Turn off AutoFilter.

3. **Filter and extract a list with Advanced Filter.**
    a. You will retrieve a list of employees who were hired prior to 1/1/90 and earn more than $60,000 a year. Define a criteria range by copying the field names in range A1:J1 to cell A14.
    b. In cell D15, enter the criterion < 1/1/90, then in cell G15 enter >60000.
    c. Return to cell A1.
    d. Open the Advanced Filter dialog box.
    e. Indicate that you want to copy to another location, enter the criteria range A14:J15, then indicate that you want to copy to cell A18.
    f. If necessary, scroll so that rows 18 through 20 are visible to confirm that the retrieved list meets the criteria.
    g. Change the page setup to landscape orientation, then select and print only the extracted list in range A18:J20.
    h. Use the Edit menu to clear data and formats from the range A14:J20.

4. **Creating subtotals using grouping and outlines.**
    a. Move to cell A1. Sort the list in ascending order by department, then in descending order by monthly salary.
    b. Group and create subtotals by department, using the Sum function; select Monthly Salary in the Add Subtotal to list box, deselect Annual Comp., then click OK.
    c. AutoFit column E.
    d. Use the outline to display only the subtotals, preview, then print only the subtotaled list in landscape orientation fitting the data to one page.
    e. Remove the subtotals.

5. Look up values in a list.

   a. You will locate annual compensation information by entering a social security number. Scroll so that columns I through Q are visible.

   b. In cell N2, enter 556-53-7589.

   c. In cell O2, enter the following function: =VLOOKUP(N2,A2:J11,10,FALSE), then view the results.

   d. Enter another social security number, 356-93-2123, in cell N2 and view the annual compensation for that employee.

   e. Save your worksheet.

6. Summarize list data.

   a. You'll enter a database function to average the annual salaries by department, using the Marketing department as the initial criterion.

   b. Define the criteria area: In cell C14, enter "Criteria"; in cell C15, enter "Dept." (make sure you type the period); then in cell C16, enter "Marketing".

   c. In cell E14, enter "Average Annual Salary by Department:".

   d. In cell H14, enter the following database function: =DAVERAGE(Database,7,C15:C16).

   e. Test the function further by entering the text "Accounting" in cell C16. When the criterion is entered, cell H14 should display 58650 as the result.

   f. Save the workbook, then close it.

7. Use data validation for list entries.

   a. Open the workbook titled EX I-2 again, then save it as "Compensation Summary 2".

   b. Select column E.

   c. For the validation criteria, specify that you want to allow a list of valid options.

   d. Enter a list of valid options that restricts the entries to "Accounting", "Information Systems", and "Marketing". Remember to use a comma between each item in the list.

   e. Indicate that you want the options to appear in an in-cell dropdown list, then close the dialog box.

   f. Go to cell E12, then select "Accounting" in the dropdown list.

   g. Select column F.

   h. Indicate that you want to restrict the data entered to be only whole numbers.

   i. In the minimum box, enter 1000. In the Maximum box, enter 20000. Close the dialog box.

   j. Click cell F12, enter 25000, then press [Enter].

   k. Click Cancel, then enter 19000.50.

   l. Click Cancel, then enter 19000.

   m. Save, then close the workbook and exit Excel.

▶ Independent Challenges

1. Your neighbor, Phillipe, brought over his wine cellar inventory workbook file on disk and asked you to help him manipulate the data in Excel. Phillipe would like to filter the list to show two subsets: all wines with a 1985 vintage and Chardonnay wines with a vintage prior to 1985. He would also like to subtotal the list and show the total dollar value by type of wine as well as restrict entries in the Type of Wine column to eight possibilities.

To complete this independent challenge:

a. Open the workbook titled EX I-3, then save it as "Wine Cellar Inventory".

b. Use AutoFilter to generate a list of wines with a 1985 vintage. Preview, then print the list.

c. Use Advanced Filter to extract a list of Chardonnay wines with a vintage in or prior to 1985. Preview, then print the list.

d. Clear the filter, and insert subtotals for Total $ according to type of wine. (*Hint:* Make sure to sort the list by type of wine prior to creating the subtotals.) Print the subtotaled list. Turn off subtotaling.

e. Beginning in cell H1, type the list of eight wine types in column H. The list should include Cabernet, Champagne, Chardonnay, Muscat, Pinot Noir, Riesling, Sauvignon Blanc, and Zinfandel.

f. Select column B. Open the Data Validation dialog box, then click List in the Allow box. Enter the range address for the list of wine types in the Source box. Make sure the In-cell dropdown check box is selected. Close the dialog box.

g. Test the data validation by entering valid and invalid data in cell B31.

h. Type your name in the worksheet footer, then save, print, and close the workbook.

2. Your neighbor, Phillipe, was pleased when you delivered his filtered and subtotaled wine inventory list. After viewing your printouts, he asks you to help him with a few more tasks. He wants the list to be sorted by wine label. In addition, he wants to be able to type in the vintage year (starting with 1985) and get a total bottle count and average cost per bottle for that vintage. (*Hint:* You need to define a criteria area outside the list to contain the two database functions.) Finally, Phillipe wants you to provide him with some form of documentation on how to accomplish the summaries.

To complete this independent challenge:

a. Open the workbook titled EX I-3, then save it as "Wine Cellar Inventory 2".

b. Sort the list alphabetically by wine label.

c. Define an area either above or below the list with the label "Criteria". Add appropriate column labels and criteria. Use 1985 as the vintage year for the criterion.

d. Near the criteria area, type labels for the two database functions.

e. Enter the database functions to find total bottle count and average price per bottle for a particular vintage.

f. Save your work. Preview and then print the list. Display the worksheet formulas, add your name to the worksheet footer, then preview and print the criteria area. Hide the formulas again.

g. Create a separate worksheet that documents the functions you used: Format the two cells containing the database functions as text by adding leading apostrophes. Widen any columns as necessary. Print a second copy of the list with the two database functions. Change the page setup so that the gridlines and row and column headings are printed. Leave a valid entry in the cell.

h. Save, then close the workbook.

3. A few months ago, you started your own business, called Books 4 You. You create and sell personalized books for special occasions. You bought a distributorship from an established book company and the rights to use several of the company's titles. Using your personal computer, specialized software, and preprinted book pages, you create personalized books on your laser printer. All you need from a customer is the name of the book's "star," his or her special date if appropriate (usually a birth or anniversary date), and the desired book title. Using the software, you enter the data and generate book pages, which you later bind together. After several months of struggle, you are starting to make a profit. You decided to put together an invoice list to track sales, starting in October. Now that you have this list, you would like to manipulate it in several ways. First, you want to filter the list to retrieve only children's books ordered during the first half of the month (prior to 10/16). Next, you want to subtotal the unit price, sales tax, and total cost columns by book title. Finally, you want to restrict entries in the Order Date column.

To complete this independent challenge:

a. Open the workbook titled EX I-4, then save it as "Books 4 You, Invoice Database".

b. Filter the list to show children's books ordered prior to 10/16/00. Print the filtered list on a single page with gridlines and row and column headings. Clear the filter, then save your work.

c. Create subtotals in the Unit Price, Sales Tax, and Total Cost columns by book title. Print the subtotaled list on a single page without gridlines, row, or column headings. Clear the subtotals.

d. Use the Data Validation dialog box to restrict entries to those with order dates between 12/31/99 and 1/1/01. Select "Date" In the Allow list, then enter the appropriate dates in the Start date and End date boxes. Test the data restrictions by attempting to enter an invalid date.

e. Add your name to the worksheet footer, then save, print, and close the workbook.

f. Open the workbook titled EX I-4, then save it as "Books 4 You, Lookup".

g. Enter a VLOOKUP function to retrieve a customer's book title based on its invoice number. Enter a second VLOOKUP function to look up the order date. Format the cell displaying the date in a date format, then save your work.

h. Below the VLOOKUP area, and to the right of the invoice list, define an area in which to count the number of birthday books ordered on any given date. Save your work.

i. Add your name to the worksheet footer, then print the list on a single page, if possible.

j. Provide documentation for any functions used, then add your name to the range and print the worksheet functions with gridlines and row and column headings on a single page, if possible.

k. Save, then close the workbook.

WEB WORK

4. Each month, the MediaLoft Product department lists the top-selling book, video, and CD products on the MediaLoft intranet site. The department also keeps track of these products in an Excel list. As a new employee of the MediaLoft Corporate Headquarters, you have been asked to update the Excel list with the latest information on the intranet site and to then analyze the information using Excel.

To complete this independent challenge:

a. Connect to the Internet, then go to the MediaLoft intranet site at http://www.course.com/Illustrated/MediaLoft. Click the Products link, then click the Bestsellers of the month link. Print the page and disconnect from the Internet.

b. Open the file EX I-5 on your Project Disk, save it as "Bestsellers", and, referring to your printout, add the three top-selling items. (If there is more than one author/performer, choose only the first one.) Enter the date as 12/30/00.

c. Use AutoFilter to display only books.

d. Further filter the list to display only books that were on the bestseller list before 7/30/00.

e. Enter your name in the worksheet footer, then print the filtered list.

f. Clear the filter.

g. Create an advanced filter that retrieves, to its current location, records whose dates were before 9/1/2000 and whose dollar sales were greater than $2,000. Print only the cells containing the filtered list, then clear the filter and redisplay all the records.

h. Create another advanced filter that extracts products whose sales were $3,000 or more and places them in another area of the worksheet.

i. Print the range containing only the extracted list, centered horizontally on the page, with row and column headings.

j. Save and close the Bestsellers workbook.

k. Open the file EX I-5 and save it as "Bestsellers 2".

l. Subtotal the sales by category.

m. Use the outline to display only category names and totals. Enter your name in the worksheet footer and print the worksheet.

n. Redisplay the records and remove the subtotals.

o. Freeze the column headings and scroll to display several blank lines below the last line.

p. Use the DSUM function to let worksheet users find the total sales by category. Format the cell containing the function appropriately.

q. Use data validation to restrict category entries to CD, Book, or Video, then test an entry with valid and invalid entries.

r. Print, save, and close the worksheet.

Excel 2000

▶ Visual Workshop

Create the worksheet shown in Figure I-23. Save the workbook as "Commission Lookup" on your Project disk. (*Hints:* The formula in cell D5 accesses the commission from the table. Calculate the commission by multiplying the Amount of Sale by the Commission Rate. If an exact amount for the Amount of Sale does not exist, the next highest or lowest dollar value is used.) Add your name to the worksheet footer, then preview and print the worksheet.

FIGURE I-23

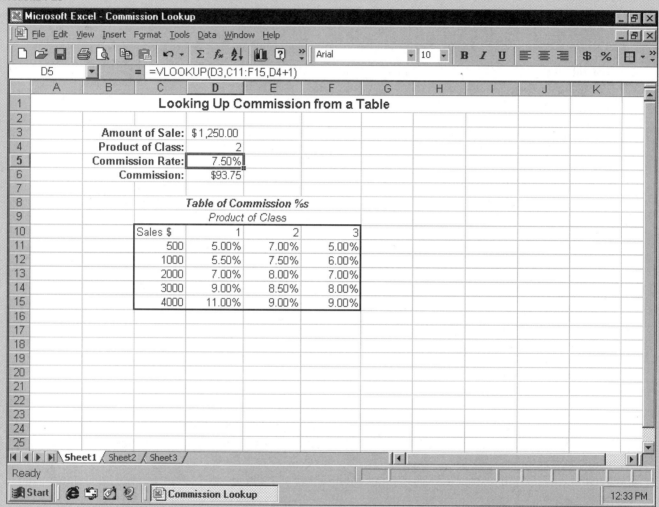

Enhancing
Charts and Worksheets

Objectives

► Select a custom chart type
► Customize a data series
► Format a chart axis
► Add a data table to a chart
► Rotate a chart
► Enhance a chart with WordArt
► Rotate text
► Map data

There are many ways to revise a chart or a worksheet to present its data with greater impact. In this unit, you enhance both charts and worksheets by selecting a custom chart type, customizing a data series, formatting axes, adding a data table, and rotating a chart. You also add special text effects and rotate text. Finally, you increase the impact of geographical data by plotting it on a map. Keep in mind that your goal in enhancing charts or worksheets is to communicate your data more clearly. Avoid excessive customization, which can be visually distracting. MediaLoft's director of café operations, Jeff Shimada, has asked Jim Fernandez to produce two charts showing the sales of café pastry products in the first two quarters. He encourages Jim to enhance the charts and the worksheet data to improve their appearance and make the data more accessible. Finally, he asks Jim to create a map illustrating pastry sales by state.

Selecting a Custom Chart Type

The Excel Chart Wizard offers a choice between standard and custom chart types. A **standard chart type** is a commonly used column, bar, pie, or area chart with several variations. For each standard chart type, you can choose from several subtypes, such as clustered column or stacked column. You can use the Wizard to add display options, and can later modify the formatting of any chart element. Excel supplies 20 built-in **custom chart types**, with special formatting already applied. You can also define your own custom chart type by modifying any of the existing Excel chart types. For example, you could define a company chart type that has the same title and then distribute it to other users in your office. ✐ Jim's first task is to create a chart showing the amount of each pastry type sold for the first quarter. To save time, he decides to use an Excel built-in custom chart.

Steps

1. Open the workbook titled **EX J-1**, then save it as **Pastry Sales**

   The first step is to select the data you want to appear in the chart. In this case, you want the row labels in cells A6:A10 and the data for January and February in cells B5:C10.

2. Select the range **A5:C10**

3. Click the **Chart Wizard button** 📊 on the Standard toolbar, click the **Custom Types tab** in the Step 1 Chart Wizard dialog box, then under Select from, click the **Built-in option button** to select it if necessary

   See Figure J-1. When the built-in option button in the Custom Types tab is selected, all of the Excel custom chart types are displayed in the Chart type box, and a sample of the default chart appears in the Sample box. Once you make a selection in the Chart type box, the default chart disappears and a preview of the selected chart type appears in the Sample box. If the Chart Wizard button does not appear on your Standard toolbar, click the More Buttons button 👐 to view it.

4. Click **Columns with Depth** in the Chart type box

   A preview of the chart appears in the Sample box. Notice that this custom chart type, with its 3-D bars and white background, has a more elegant appearance than the default chart shown in Figure J-1. Unlike the previous default chart, this chart doesn't have gridlines.

5. Click **Next**

6. Make sure = 'TotalSales'!A$5:$C$10 appears as the data range in the Data range box in the Step 2 Chart Wizard dialog box, then click **Next**

7. In the Step 3 Chart Wizard dialog box, click **Next**; if necessary, click the **As object in option button** in the Step 4 Chart Wizard dialog box to select it; then click **Finish**

   The completed chart appears, covering part of the worksheet data, along with the Chart tool-bar. The Chart toolbar can appear anywhere within the worksheet window. As you complete the following steps, you may need to drag the toolbar to a new location.

8. Scroll down the worksheet until **rows 13** through **28** are visible, click the **chart border** and drag the chart left and down until its upper-left corner is in cell **A13**, drag the **middle right sizing handle** right to the border between **column H** and **column I**, then check that its bottom border is between **rows 25** and **26**

   The new chart fills the range A13:H25, as shown in Figure J-2.

9. Save the workbook

FIGURE J-1: **Custom Types tab settings**

Custom Types tab

Custom chart types

Default chart

Default chart has only basic formatting

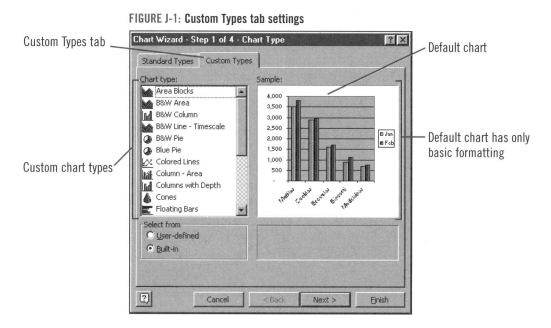

FIGURE J-2: **New chart**

Chart fills range A13:A25

Chart toolbar

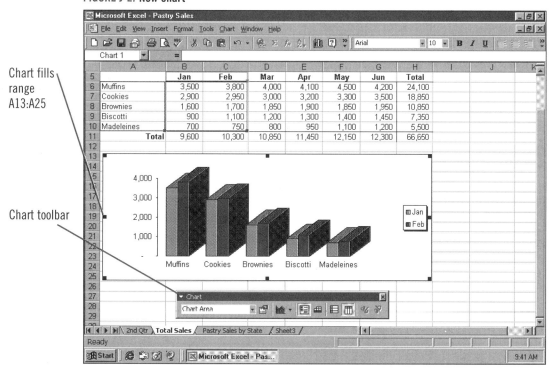

Creating a custom chart type

You can create your own custom chart type by starting with a standard chart and then adding elements (such as a legend, color, or gridlines) that suit your needs. After you've finished creating the chart, click it to activate the Chart menu on the menu bar, click Chart, click Chart type, click the Custom Types tab, then click User-defined. Click Add, then type a name for your chart type in the Name box. To use your custom chart type when creating additional charts, open the Chart Wizard dialog box, then click the User-defined button in the Custom Types tab.

Excel 2000

Unit J
Excel 2000

Customizing a Data Series

A **data series** is the information, usually numbers or values, that Excel plots on a chart. You can customize the data series in a chart easily by altering the spreadsheet range that contains the chart data *or* by entering descriptive text, called a **data label**, that appears above a data marker in a chart. As with other Excel elements, you can change the borders, patterns, or colors of a data series. Jim notices that he omitted the data for March when he created his first-quarter sales chart. He needs to add this information to make the chart accurately reflect the entire first-quarter sales. Also, he wants to customize the updated chart by adding data labels to one of the data series to make it more specific. Then he'll change the color of another data series so its respective column figures will stand out more. He starts by adding the March data.

Steps 1234

1. If necessary, click the **chart** to select it, scroll up until **row 5** is the top row in the worksheet area, select the range **D5:D10**, position the pointer over the lower border of cell D10 until it changes to ▱, then drag the selected range anywhere within the chart area

   The chart now includes data for the entire first quarter: January, February, and March. Next, you will add data labels to the March data series.

QuickTip

If you have difficulty identifying the Chart Objects list arrow, rest your pointer on the first list arrow to the left on the Chart toolbar until the name "Chart Objects" appears.

2. Click the **Chart Objects list arrow** in the Chart toolbar, then click **Series "Mar"**

   See Figure J-3. Selection handles appear on each of the columns representing the data for March. Now that the data series is selected, you can format it by adding labels.

3. Click the **Format Object button** 🖼 on the Chart toolbar, then click the **Data Labels tab** in the Format Data Series dialog box

   The Data Labels tab opens. You want the value to appear on top of each selected data marker.

QuickTip

The ToolTip name for the Format Data Series button 🖼 changes, depending on what is selected. In this book it is called the Format Object button.

4. Under Data labels, click the **Show value option button** to select it, then click **OK**

   The data labels appear on the data markers, as shown in Figure J-4. The February data series could stand out more.

5. Click the **Chart Objects list arrow** on the Chart toolbar, click **Series "Feb"**, click 🖼, then click the **Patterns tab** in the Format Data Series dialog box

   The Patterns tab opens. See Figure J-5. The maroon color in the Sample box matches the current color displayed in the chart for the February data series. You decide that the series would show up better in a brighter shade of red.

QuickTip

You also can click outside the chart to deselect it.

6. Under Area, click the **red box** (third row, first color from the left), click **OK**, press **[Esc]** to deselect the data series, press **[Esc]** again to deselect the entire chart, then save the workbook

   The February data series now appears in a brighter shade of red.

Columns represent
data for March

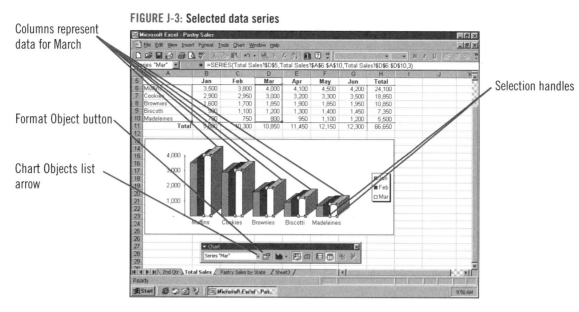

Selection handles

Format Object button

Chart Objects list
arrow

FIGURE J-3: Selected data series

FIGURE J-4: Chart with data labels

Data labels

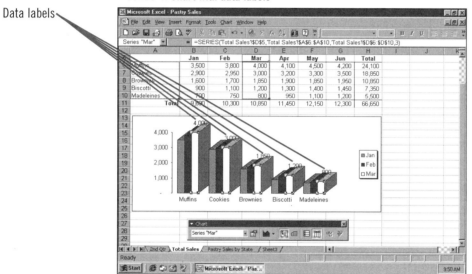

FIGURE J-5: Patterns tab settings

Bright red
color choice

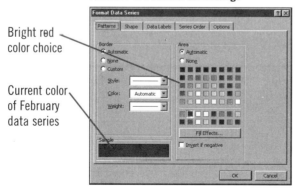

Current color
of February
data series

Removing, inserting, and formatting legends

To insert or remove a legend, click the Legend button on the Chart toolbar to toggle the legend on or off. To format legend text, click Legend in the Chart Objects list box of the Chart toolbar. Then click the Format Object button on the Chart toolbar and choose the options you want in the Font tab.

Unit J
Excel 2000

Formatting a Chart Axis

Excel automatically plots and formats all chart data and places chart axes within the chart's **plot area**. Data values in two-dimensional charts are plotted on the value (*y*) axis and categories are plotted on the category (*x*) axis. Excel creates a scale for the value (*y*) axis that is based on the highest and lowest values in the data series. Then Excel determines the intervals in which the values occur along the scale. In three-dimensional charts, like the one in Figure J-6, Excel generates three axes, where *x* remains the category axis but *z* becomes the value axis and *y* becomes the measure for the third dimension on the chart, depth. In 3-D charts, the value (*z*) axis usually contains the scale. For a list of the axes Excel uses to plot data, see Table J-1. You can override the Excel default formats for chart axes at any time by using the Format Axis dialog box. ◄▬▬ Because the highest column is so close to the top of the chart, Jim wants to increase the maximum number on the value axis, which in this case is the *y*-axis, and change its number format. To begin, he selects the object he wants to format.

Steps

1. Click the **chart**, click the **Chart Objects list arrow** on the Chart toolbar, then click **Value Axis**
   The vertical axis becomes selected.

2. Click the **Format Object button** 📑 on the Chart toolbar, then click the **Scale tab**
   The Scale tab of the Format Axis dialog box opens. The check marks under Auto indicate the default scale settings. You can override any of these settings by entering a new value.

3. In the Maximum box select **4000**, type **5000**, then click **OK**
   The chart adjusts so that 5000 appears as the maximum value on the value axis. Next, you want the minimum value to appear as a zero (0) and not as a hyphen (-).

4. With the Value Axis still selected, click 📑 on the Chart toolbar, then click the **Number tab**
   The Number tab of the Format Axis dialog box opens. Currently, a custom format is selected under Category, which instructs Excel to use a hyphen instead of 0 as the lowest value.

5. Under Category click **General**, click **OK**, press **[Esc]** twice, then save the workbook
   The chart now shows 0 as the minimum value, as shown in Figure J-7.

FIGURE J-6: **Chart elements in a 3-D chart**

Tick marks

Maximum value

Value (*z*) axis
with scale

Minimum value

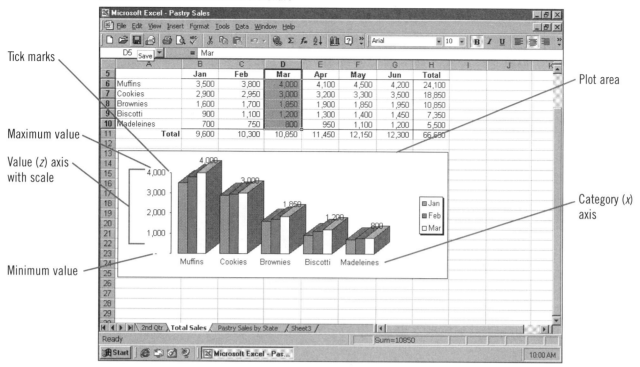

Plot area

Category (*x*)
axis

FIGURE J-7: **Chart with formatted axis**

New maximum
value

New minimum
value

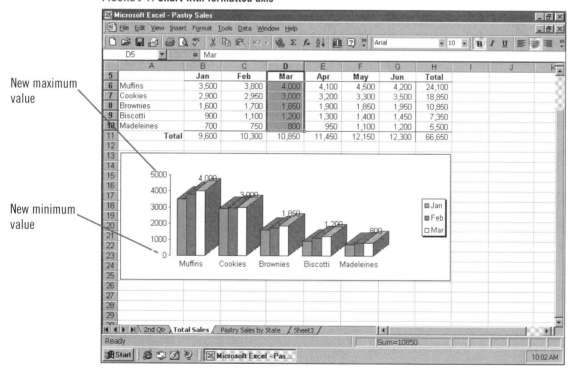

TABLE J-1: **Axes used by Excel for chart formatting**

axes in a two-dimensional chart	axes in a three-dimensional chart
Category (*x*) axis (horizontal)	Category (*x*) axis (horizontal)
Value (*y*) axis (vertical)	Series (*y*) axis (depth)
	Value (*z*) axis (vertical)

Adding a Data Table to a Chart

A **data table**, attached to the bottom of a chart, is a grid containing the chart data. Data tables are useful because they highlight the data used to generate a chart, which might otherwise be difficult to find. Data tables can be displayed in line, area, column, and bar charts, and print automatically along with a chart. It's good practice to add data tables to charts stored separately from worksheet data. ◀━━ Jim wants to emphasize the first-quarter data used to generate his chart. He decides to add a data table.

Steps

1. Click the **chart** to select it, click **Chart** on the menu bar, click **Chart Options**, then click the **Data Table tab**

The Data Table tab in the Chart Options dialog box opens, as shown in Figure J-8. The preview window displays the selected chart.

QuickTip

You also do this when creating a chart in the Step 3 Chart Wizard dialog box.

2. Click the **Show data table check box** to select it

The chart in the preview window changes to show what the chart will look like with a data table added to the bottom. See Figure J-9. The data table crowds the chart labels, making them hard to read. (Your chart may look slightly different.) You'll fix this problem after you close the Chart Options dialog box.

QuickTip

To hide a data table, open the Data Table tab in the Chart Options dialog box, then clear the Show data table check box.

3. Click **OK**, then, if necessary, scroll down to display the chart

The chart and the newly added data table look too crowded inside the current chart area. If you were to drag the chart borders to enlarge the chart, you wouldn't be able to see the entire chart displayed on the screen. It's more convenient to move the chart to its own sheet.

4. If necessary, click the **chart** to select it, click **Chart** on the menu bar, click **Location**, click the **As new sheet option button** under Place chart, click **OK**

The chart is now located on a new sheet, where it is fully displayed in the worksheet window. See Figure J-10.

5. Put your name in the sheet footer, save the workbook, then print the chart sheet

FIGURE J-8: Data Table tab settings

Data Table tab

Click to add a data table

Preview window

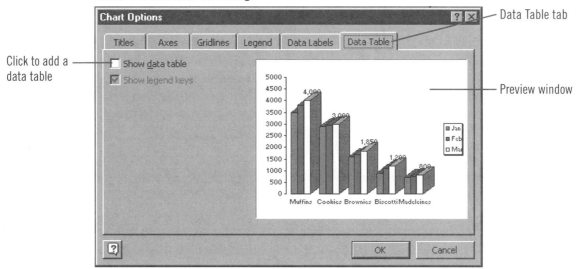

FIGURE J-9: Show Data Table box selected

Chart labels are hard to read

Data table

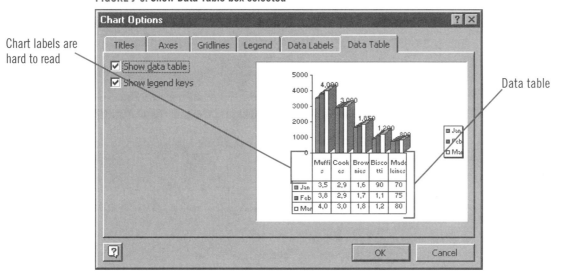

FIGURE J-10: Chart moved to chart sheet

Labels fully displayed

Entire chart visible in window

Data table

New sheet tab

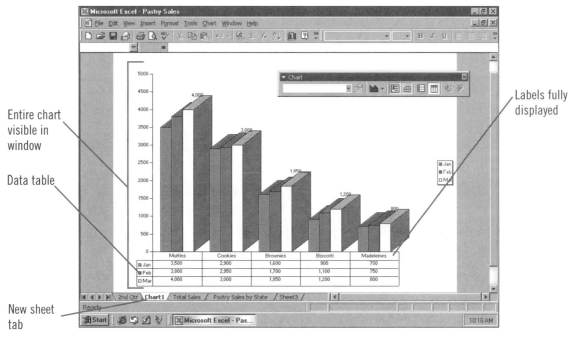

Excel 2000

Rotating a Chart

Three-dimensional (3-D) charts do not always display data in the most effective way. In many cases, data in these charts can be obscured by one or more of the chart's data markers. By rotating and/or elevating the axes, you can improve the visibility of the chart's data. With Excel, you can adjust the rotation and elevation of a 3-D chart by dragging it with the mouse or using the 3-D View command on the Chart menu. ✎ Jim's workbook already contains a 3-D chart illustrating the sales data for the second quarter. He will display that chart, then rotate it so that the June columns are easier to see.

Steps

1. Click the **2nd Qtr sheet tab**, click the **Chart Objects list arrow** on the Chart toolbar, then click **Corners**
   Selection handles appear on the corners of the chart, as shown in Figure J-11.

2. Click the **lower-right corner handle** of the chart, press and hold the left mouse button, then drag the chart left approximately 2" until it looks like the object shown in Figure J-12, then release the mouse button
   The June columns are still not clearly visible. When using the dragging method to rotate a three-dimensional chart, you might need to make several attempts before you're satisfied with the view. It's usually more efficient to use the 3-D View option on the Chart menu.

> **Trouble?**
>
> Don't worry if your 3-D View dialog box settings are different from the ones shown in Figure J-13.

3. Click **Chart** on the menu bar, click **3-D View**, then drag the **3-D View dialog box** to the upper-right corner of the screen
   See Figure J-13. The preview box in the 3-D View dialog box allows you to preview changes to the chart's orientation in the worksheet.

4. Click **Default**
   The chart returns to its original position. Next, Jim decreases the chart's elevation, the height from which the chart is viewed.

> **Trouble?**
>
> If you have difficulty locating the Decrease Elevation button, refer to Figure J-13.

5. To the left of the preview box, click the **Decrease Elevation button**
   Notice how the preview image of the chart changes when you change the elevation.

6. Click **Apply**
   As the number in the Elevation box decreases, the viewpoint shifts downward. Note that the chart gains some vertical tick marks. Next, you'll change the rotation and **perspective**, or depth, of the chart.

7. In the Rotation box, select the current value, then type **55**; in the Perspective box, select the current value, type **0**, then click **Apply**
   The chart is reformatted. You notice, however, that the columns appear crowded. To correct this problem, you change the height as a percent of the chart base.

8. In the Height box, select the current value, type **70**, click **Apply**, then click **OK**
   The 3-D View dialog box closes. The chart columns now appear less crowded, making the chart easier to read.

9. Save your work

FIGURE J-11: **Chart corners selected**

Selection handles

Lower-right corner handle

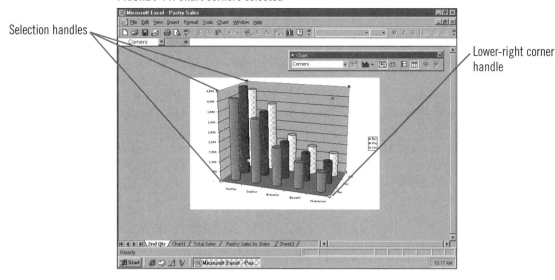

FIGURE J-12: **Chart rotation in progress**

Chart rotation pointer

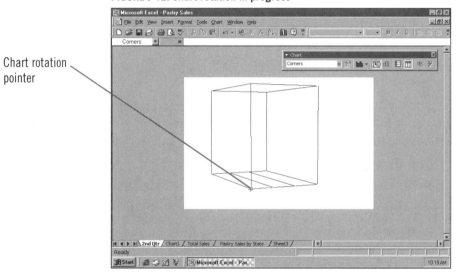

FIGURE J-13: **Screen with chart and 3-D View dialog box**

Increase Elevation button

Decrease Elevation button

Your settings may vary

Increase Rotation button

Preview box

Increase Perspective button

Decrease Perspective button

Your settings may be different

Decrease Rotation button

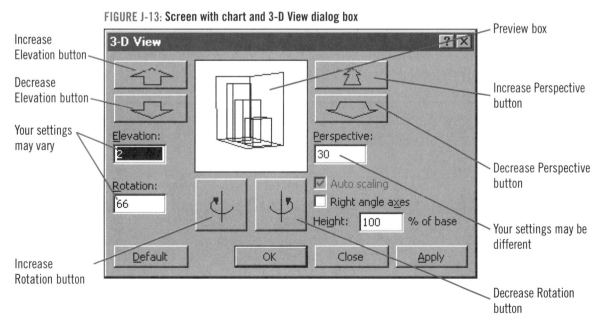

Enhancing a Chart with WordArt

You can enhance your chart or worksheet by adding specially formatted text using the WordArt tool on the Drawing toolbar. Once you've added a piece of WordArt to your workbook, you can edit or format it using the tools on the WordArt toolbar. Text formatted as WordArt is considered a drawing object rather than text. This means that WordArt objects cannot be treated as if they were labels entered in a cell; that is, you cannot sort, spell check, or use their cell references in formulas. ✐▬▬▬ Jim decides to add a WordArt title to the second-quarter chart. He begins by displaying the Drawing toolbar.

Steps

1. Click the **Drawing button** 🎨 on the Standard toolbar

   The Drawing toolbar appears at the bottom of the Excel window. The WordArt text will be your chart title.

2. Click the **Insert WordArt button** 🔷 on the Drawing toolbar

   The WordArt Gallery dialog box opens. This is where you select the style for your text.

3. In the second row, click the **second style from the left**, as shown in Figure J-14; then click **OK**

   The Edit WordArt Text dialog box opens, as shown in Figure J-15. This is where you enter the text you want to format as WordArt. You also can adjust the point size or font of the text or select bold or italic styles.

   > **QuickTip**
   >
   > To delete a piece of WordArt, click it to make sure it is selected, then press [Delete].

4. Type **2nd Quarter Sales**, click the **Bold button** **B**, if necessary select **Times New Roman** in the Font list box and **36** in the Size list box, then click **OK**

   The Edit WordArt Text dialog box closes, and the chart reappears with the new title in the middle of the chart.

5. Place the pointer over 2nd Quarter Sales (the WordArt title) until the pointer changes to ⟐, then drag **2nd Quarter Sales** up until it appears in the upper-right corner of the chart

   The title is repositioned as shown in Figure J-16. Next, you decide to edit the WordArt to change "2nd" to the word "Second."

6. Click **Edit Text** on the WordArt toolbar, double-click **2nd** in the Edit WordArt Text box, type **Second**, then click **OK**

   The Edit WordArt Text dialog box closes, and the edited title appears over the chart.

   > **QuickTip**
   >
   > To change the style of a piece of WordArt, click the WordArt Gallery button 🖼 on the WordArt toolbar and select a new style.

7. Press **[Esc]** to deselect the WordArt, click 🎨, put your name in the chart sheet footer, save the workbook, then print the sheet

FIGURE J-14: **Selecting a WordArt style**

New style to
apply to text

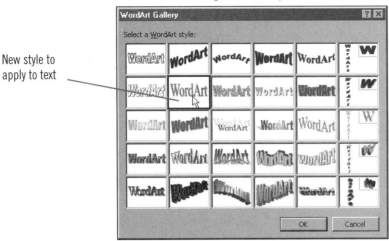

FIGURE J-15: **Entering the WordArt text**

Default font for
this style

Replace with
your text

Default point
size for this
style

Italic button

Bold button

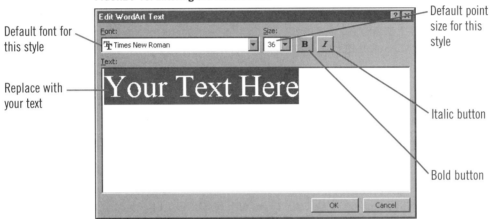

FIGURE J-16: **Positioning the WordArt**

New title
location

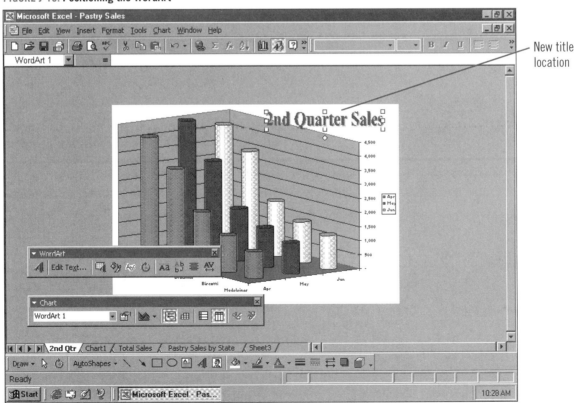

Rotating Text

By rotating text within a worksheet cell, you can draw attention to column labels or titles without turning the text into a drawing object (as in WordArt). Unlike WordArt, rotated text retains its usefulness as a worksheet entry, which means you can still sort it, spell check it, and use its cell reference in formulas. ◄══ Now that he's finished enhancing the two charts in his workbook, Jim wants to improve the worksheet's appearance. He decides to rotate the column labels in cells B5 through G5.

Steps

1. Click the **Total Sales sheet tab**, make sure row 5 is the top row in the worksheet area, then select cells **B5:G5**

2. Click **Format** on the menu bar, click **Cells**, then click the **Alignment tab**
   The Alignment tab of the Format Cells dialog box opens. See Figure J-17. The settings under Orientation enable you to change the rotation of cell entries. Clicking the Vertical Text box on the left (the narrow one) allows you to display text vertically in the cell. To rotate the text to another angle, drag the rotation indicator in the Right Text box to the angle you want, or type the degree of angle you want in the Degrees box. You'll use the Degrees box to rotate the text entries.

3. Double-click the **Degrees box**, type **45**, then click **OK**
   The Format Cells dialog box closes.

4. If necessary, scroll up until row 1 is the top row in the worksheet area, then click cell **A1**
   The column labels for January through June now appear at a 45-degree angle in their cells, as shown in Figure J-18. The worksheet is now finished.

5. Put your name in the sheet footer, then save and print the worksheet

FIGURE J-17: **Alignment tab settings**

Vertical text box ———

Rotation settings ———

Rotation indicator ———

Degrees box ———

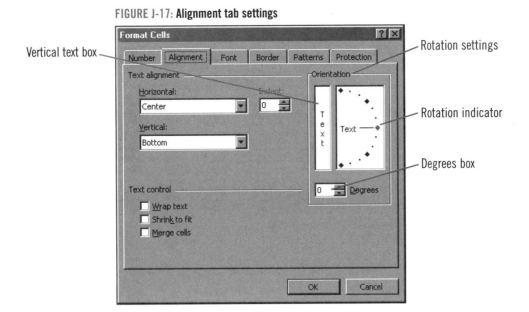

FIGURE J-18: **Rotated column labels**

Column labels rotated at 45-degree angle ———

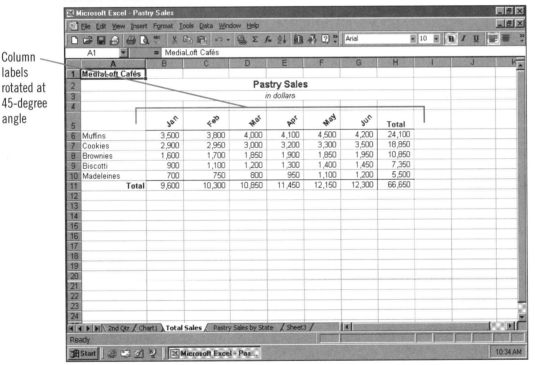

Rotating chart labels

You can easily rotate the category labels on a chart by using the buttons on the Chart toolbar. First, you select the Category Axis in the Chart Objects list box. Then you click either the Angle Text Downward button or the Angle Text Upward button on the Chart toolbar.

Mapping Data

A **data map** shows geographic features and their associated data. To create a simple data map, arrange your worksheet data in two columns—with the first containing geographic data, such as the names of countries or states, and the second column containing the related data. ◆ Jim has compiled detailed sales figures for pastry by state. Now, he wants to create a map that clearly illustrates which states have the highest sales. He begins by selecting the data he wants to map.

Steps

1. Click the **Pastry Sales by State sheet tab**, then select the range **A4:B11**
   The first column of data contains the state names and the second contains the sales figures for each state. The column labels in row 4 (which you also selected) will be used in the legend title.

Trouble?

If you don't see the Map button, click Tools on the menu bar, click Command, and click Insert. Then under Commands, scroll to the Map icon and drag it to the Standard toolbar.

2. Click the **Map button** 🌐 on the Standard toolbar, drag the **crosshair pointer** from the middle of cell C4 to the lower-right corner of cell H23, then release the mouse button
   The map range is outlined on the worksheet, and the Multiple Maps Available dialog box opens on top.

3. Click **United States (AK & HI Inset) if necessary**, then click **OK**
   The map and the Microsoft Map Control dialog boxes appear.

4. Drag the **Microsoft Map Control dialog box** to the lower-left corner of the screen, then scroll up until most of the map is visible on your screen
   See Figure J-19. Excel automatically divides the sales data into intervals and assigns a different shade of gray to each interval, as the map legend indicates. The rectangular border indicates that the map is in Edit mode.

QuickTip

Click the Map Refresh button 🔄 to incorporate any changes to the data range into an existing map.

5. Double-click the **United States (AK & HI Inset) map title**, select the **default text** in the Edit Text Object dialog box, type **MediaLoft Pastry Sales**, then click **OK**
   The new title replaces the default map title. Next, to highlight the sales data more dramatically, you'll change the way values are represented using the Microsoft Map Control dialog box, shown in Figure J-20. You adjust the way data is represented on the map by dragging format buttons into the Format box. You want to change the format from shading to dots of varying density.

6. Click the **Dot Density button** in the Microsoft Map Control dialog box 🔲, then drag it over the top of the Value Shading button in the Format box
   When you release the mouse button, the map display changes from shading to dots, with one dot equal to $6,000 in pastry sales.

7. Click **Map** on the Menu bar, click **Features**, under Fill Color click the **Custom option button**, click the **Custom list arrow**, click the **turquoise square**, then click **OK**
   The map's background color changes to turquoise, as shown in Figure J-21. The legend could be more descriptive.

8. Double-click the **map legend**; click the **Legend Options tab** in the Format Properties dialog box if necessary; select the **default text** in the Title box, type **1st and 2nd Quarter**, then click **OK**

Trouble?

If your map doesn't print, your printer may not have enough memory. Try using another printer.

9. Press **[Esc]** three times to deselect the map, put your name in the sheet footer, save the workbook, print the worksheet, and exit Excel

FIGURE J-19: Newly created map

Section border

Default map title

Microsoft Map Control dialog box

Highest sales

Second highest sales

Map legend

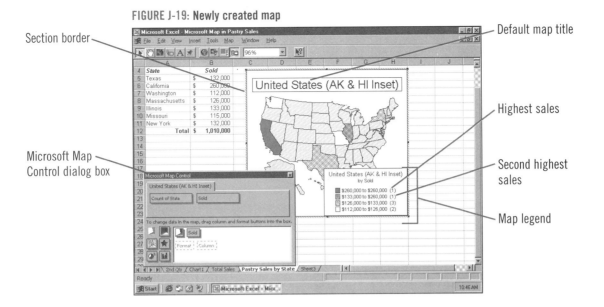

FIGURE J-20: Microsoft Map Control dialog box

Value Shading button

Dot Density button

Format buttons

Columns in data range

Format box

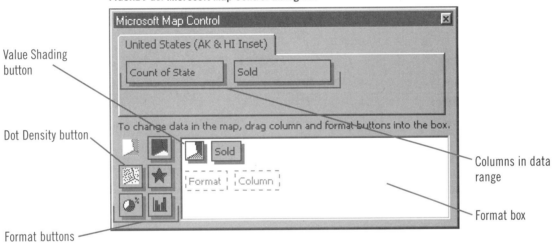

FIGURE J-21: Values formatted as dots

Dots

Turquoise backround

Dot Density button replaces Value Shading button

Updated legend

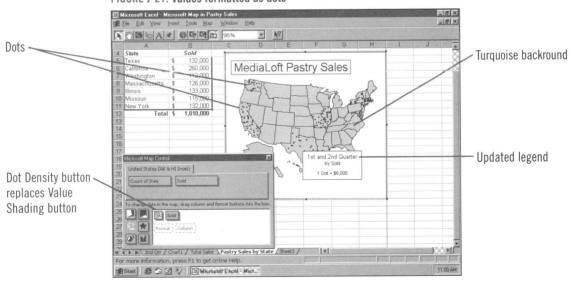

Excel 2000

Practice

▶ Concepts Review

Label each element of the Excel screen shown in Figure J-22.

FIGURE J-22

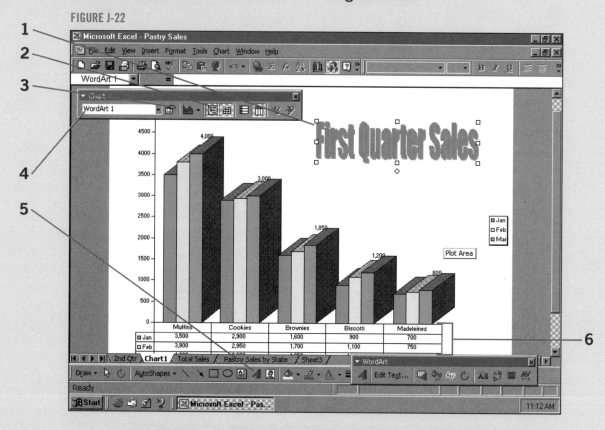

Match each button with the statement that describes it.

7.
8.
9.
10.
11.

a. Opens the WordArt dialog boxes
b. Use to format the selected chart object
c. Use to create a data map
d. Use to change the style of a piece of WordArt
e. Use to display the Drawing toolbar

Select the best answer from the list of choices.

12. A chart's scale
   a. Appears on the category (x) axis.
   b. Displays values on the value (y) axis or the value (z) axis.
   c. Always appears on the value (y) axis.
   d. Cannot be modified.

13. What is the most efficient method of rotating a 3-D chart?
   a. Click Edit on the menu bar, then click Default.
   b. Adjust settings in the 3-D View dialog box.
   c. Select the chart corners, then drag a corner.
   d. Delete the chart, and start over with a new one.

14. How can you change the way data is represented on a map?
   a. Drag format buttons in the Microsoft Data Control dialog box.
   b. Click Map, then click Data Representation.
   c. Click the Map Refresh button.
   d. None of the above.

15. Which statement best describes the difference between two- and three-dimensional column charts?
   a. Two-dimensional charts have category (x) and value (y) axes; three-dimensional charts have category (x), series (y), and value (z) axes.
   b. Two-dimensional charts show the data in three dimensions.
   c. Three-dimensional charts show the data in four dimensions.
   d. Two-dimensional charts have a value scale on the x-axis, and three-dimensional charts have a value scale on the z-axis.

16. What is a data table?
   a. A three-dimensional arrangement of data on the y-axis.
   b. Worksheet data arranged geographically.
   c. A customized data series.
   d. The data used to create a chart displayed in a grid.

17. A custom chart type
   a. Is supplied only by Excel.
   b. Can be supplied by Excel or the user.
   c. Cannot be saved.
   d. All of the above.

18. To rotate text in a worksheet cell,
   a. Adjust settings on the Alignment tab of the Format cells dialog box.
   b. Click the Rotate button on the Standard toolbar.
   c. Select the text, then drag to rotate it the desired number of degrees.
   d. Format the text as WordArt, then drag the WordArt.

▶ Skills Review

1. **Select a custom chart type.**
   a. Open the workbook titled EX J-2, then save it as "MediaLoft Coffee Sales".
   b. On the 1st Quarter sheet, select the range A4:B7.
   c. Open the Chart Wizard, and on the Custom Types tab in the Chart Wizard dialog box, make sure the Built-in option button is selected.
   d. Select Blue Pie in the Chart type box.
   e. Go to the Step 2 Chart Wizard dialog box.
   f. Make sure the data range is correct, then go to the Step 3 Chart Wizard dialog box, read the contents, then go to the Step 4 Chart Wizard dialog box.
   g. Make sure the As Object In button is selected, then finish the Wizard.
   h. Drag the chart to a better location in the worksheet.
   i. Put your name in the sheet footer, then save, preview, and print the worksheet data and chart.

2. **Customize a data series.**
   a. On the 2nd Quarter sheet, move the June data in D4:D7 into the chart area.
   b. Select the April data series and display its data labels.
   c. Use the Format Data Series dialog box to change the color of the May data series to the green color of your choice.
   d. Save the workbook.

3. **Format a chart axis.**
   a. Select the value axis.
   b. Set its maximum to 10000 and its minimum to 0.
   c. On the Number tab in the Format Axis dialog box under Category, use the Currency format to add a dollar sign and two decimal places to the values, then close the dialog box.
   d. Save the workbook.

4. **Add a data table to a chart.**
   a. Show the data table.
   b. Use the Location command on the Chart menu to move the chart to its own sheet.
   c. Display the 3rd Quarter sheet tab.
   d. Use the Data Table tab in the Chart Options dialog box to hide the data table.
   e. Remove the chart legend.
   f. Save the workbook.

5. **Rotate a chart.**
   a. On the Chart1 sheet, use the Chart Objects list arrow to select the chart corners.
   b. Drag a chart corner to rotate the chart.
   c. Return the chart to its default rotation using the 3-D View command on the Chart menu.
   d. Change the rotation to 315.
   e. Change the elevation to 13.
   f. Deselect the chart corners.
   g. Save the workbook.

6. **Enhance a chart with WordArt.**
   a. Display the Drawing toolbar.
   b. Open WordArt and select the second style from the right in the second row.
   c. In the Edit WordArt Text dialog box, enter the text "Second Quarter Sales" and format it in italic.
   d. Position the new title above the chart.
   e. Make sure the WordArt is still selected, then use the WordArt Gallery button on the WordArt toolbar to select a new style for the title.
   f. Save the workbook.
   g. Close the Drawing toolbar.

7. **Rotate text.**
   a. On the 1st Quarter sheet tab, select cells B4:D4.
   b. Change the alignment to 45 degrees.
   c. On the 2nd Quarter sheet tab, select the range B4:D4.
   d. Use the rotation indicator on the Alignment tab in the Format Cells dialog box to change the rotation to 45 degrees.
   e. On the 3rd Quarter sheet tab, rotate the Category Axis labels downward.
   f. Save the workbook.

8. **Map worksheet data.**
   a. Make the Mail Order Contacts sheet active.
   b. Select the range A4:B16.
   c. Start Microsoft Map.
   d. Position the map in the range C4:H23, and use the United States (AK & HI Inset) map.
   e. Change the map title to "Western Region Contacts".
   f. Change the map's background color to bright pink.
   g. Change the data formatting to dot density.
   h. Change the legend title to "Mail Order".
   i. In cell B9, change the data for California to 25.
   j. Double-click the map to put it in Edit mode, then click the Map Refresh button on the Map toolbar to update the map.
   k. Put your name in the sheet footer, save the workbook, then select, preview, and print each sheet in the workbook.

▶ Independent Challenges

1. You are the owner of Sandwich Express, a metropolitan delicatessen. Each week, you order several pounds of cheese: Cheddar, Monterey Jack, Swiss, Provolone, and American. Last month was especially busy, and you ordered an increasing amount of cheese each week in every category except American, which is declining in popularity. Recently, your spouse has joined you in the business and wants to develop a more efficient forecast of the amount of cheese to order each week. To help your spouse analyze last month's cheese orders, you developed a worksheet with a three-dimensional stacked bar chart. Now, you want to enhance the chart by adding data labels, reformatting the value (z) axis, increasing the elevation, and adding several titles.

To complete this independent challenge:

a. Open the workbook titled EX J-3, then save it as "Cheese Order Tracking".
b. Customize the data series. Add the data for 8/22 and 8/29 to the chart. Then add data labels to all data markers.
c. Reformat the value (z) axis to show values every 40 pounds instead of every 50 pounds.

d. Increase the chart's elevation.

e. Add a WordArt title that reads "Cheese Ordered in August".

f. Move the chart to a chart sheet and add a data table.

g. Put your name in the footer of each sheet, preview and print the worksheet and chart together, then save the workbook.

2. As the owner of Sandwich Express, you meet quarterly with your dairy product salesman, James Snyder, to discuss trends in dairy product usage at your delicatessen. These quarterly meetings seem to take longer than necessary, and you are not always sure he has retained all the information discussed. You decide to use charts to communicate during these meetings. As part of your presentation at the end of the third quarter, you decide to generate an additional chart showing what percentage of the total cheese orders for each month each cheese type represents, starting with August. Because this chart will compare parts of a whole, you create a three-dimensional pie chart. Also, to ensure the intended messages are communicated effectively, you add a few enhancements to the chart and worksheet. First, you need to add totals to the worksheet.

To complete this independent challenge:

a. Open the workbook titled EX J-3, then save it as "Cheese Order Pie".

b. Select and delete the current 3-D bar chart from the worksheet.

c. Add monthly totals in column G that total each cheese type across all five weeks. Then calculate a grand total for the month. (*Hint*: To double-check your monthly total, add totals for each week in row 10. Then insert totals for each week, select the totals in B10:F10, and note the sum in the AutoCalculate box in the Status bar.)

d. Use the Chart Wizard to create a custom chart showing what percentage of the total cheese ordered in August (1,745 pounds) each type of cheese represents. (*Hint*: Use the Control key to select nonadjacent ranges of cheese types and totals to be charted before you open the Chart Wizard.) Place the chart on its own sheet.

e. Add the WordArt title "Sandwich Express—August Cheese Orders".

f. Add an italicized WordArt subtitle that reads "(% of total pounds ordered)".

g. In the August worksheet, rotate the dates in row 4 to a 45-degree angle.

h. Put your name in the footer of each sheet, review and save the workbook, then print the worksheet and the chart.

3. You are a real estate agent for Galaxy Properties, which specializes in residential real estate. In September, you were voted salesperson of the month. Your sales manager has asked you to assemble a brief presentation on your sales activity during September to show to the new agents in the office. You decide to include a chart showing how many properties you closed and their respective dollar amounts in each of three areas: single-family homes, condominiums, and townhouses. Using your own data, create a worksheet and accompanying chart to present the data. Enhance the chart as outlined in the following.

To complete this independent challenge:

a. Create a new workbook, then save it as "September Sales, Galaxy Properties".

b. Enter your own worksheet labels, data, and formulas.

c. Create a custom bar chart showing your September sales activity.

d. Include data labels on the condominium data series.

e. Add a WordArt title.

f. Add new data to the worksheet for rental properties, then add the data series to the chart.

g. Move the chart to a chart sheet and add a data table.

h. Rotate the column labels in the worksheet.

i. Put your name in the sheet footers, preview and print the worksheet and chart, then save the workbook.

4. Maria Abbott of the MediaLoft Sales department has asked you to chart some information from a recent survey of MediaLoft book customers.

To complete this independent challenge:

a. Connect to the Internet, and go to the MediaLoft intranet site at http://www.course.com/Illustrated/MediaLoft. Click the Marketing link, then click the Book Survey Results link. Print the results of the survey. Disconnect from the Internet.

b. Open a new Excel worksheet and save it as "Book Survey". Enter the occupation information in question 5 of the survey, and chart it using a pie chart of your choice on the same sheet. Enlarge the chart to be as large as possible while still fitting on the screen.

c. Move the chart to a separate sheet; name the sheet "Occupation".

d. Reformat one of the pie slices by single-clicking the chart, then single-clicking a slice. Format the area with a new color.

e. Chart the # of children data in question 9 as a horizontal bar chart. Do not add a legend or a title. Place it on a sheet named "Children".

f. Add a WordArt Title to each chart.

g. Rotate the category axis labels on the Children sheet so they point downward and to the right.

h. Put your name in the sheet footers, save the workbook, print all three sheets, then exit Excel.

▶ Visual Workshop

Create the worksheet and accompanying custom chart shown in Figure J-23. Save the workbook as "The Dutch Garden". Study the chart and worksheet carefully to make sure you start with the most appropriate chart type, and then make all the modifications shown. Put your name in the sheet footer, preview, and then print the worksheet and chart together in landscape orientation.

FIGURE J-23

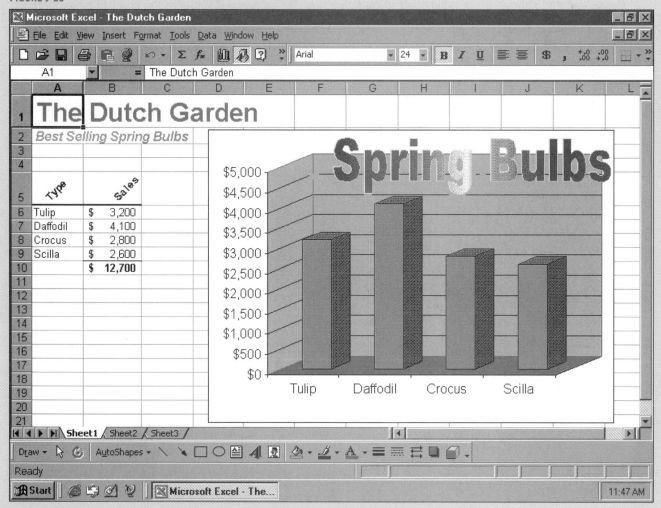

Unit
K

Using a
What-If Analysis

Objectives

- ▶ **Define a what-if analysis**
- ⌐MOUS⌐ ▶ **Track a what-if analysis with Scenario Manager**
- ⌐MOUS⌐ ▶ **Generate a scenario summary**
- ▶ **Project figures using a data table**
- ▶ **Create a two-input data table**
- ⌐MOUS⌐ ▶ **Use Goal Seek**
- ⌐MOUS⌐ ▶ **Set up a complex what-if analysis with Solver**
- ⌐MOUS⌐ ▶ **Run Solver and generate an Answer Report**

Each time you use a worksheet to answer the question "what if?" you are performing a **what-if analysis**. For example, what would happen to a firm's overall expense budget if company travel expenses decreased by 30%? Using Excel, you can perform a what-if analysis in many ways. In this unit, you will learn to track what-if scenarios and generate summary reports using the Excel Scenario Manager. You will design and manipulate one-input and two-input data tables to project multiple outcomes. Also, you will use the Excel Goal Seek feature to solve a what-if analysis. Finally, you will use Solver to perform a complex what-if analysis involving multiple variables. ✐ The MediaLoft corporate office is considering the purchase of several pieces of capital equipment, as well as several vehicles.

Defining a What-If Analysis

By performing a what-if analysis in a worksheet, you can get immediate answers to questions such as "What happens if we sell 30% more of a certain product?" or "What happens if interest rates rise 2 points?" A worksheet used to produce a what-if analysis is often referred to as a **model** because it acts as the basis for multiple outcomes. To perform a what-if analysis in a worksheet, you change the value in one or more **input cells** (cells that contain data rather than formulas) and then observe the effects on dependent cells. A **dependent cell** is a cell—usually containing a formula— whose value changes depending on the values in the input cells. A dependent cell can be located either in the same worksheet as the changing value or in another worksheet.  Jim has created a worksheet model to perform an initial what-if analysis of equipment loan payments. See Figure K-1. Jim follows the guidelines below to perform a what-if analysis.

 Understand and state the purpose of the worksheet model

The worksheet model is designed to calculate a fixed-rate, monthly equipment loan payment.

 Determine the data input value(s) that, if changed, affect the dependent cell results

The model contains three data input values (labeled Loan Amount, Annual Interest Rate, and Term in months), in cells B4, B5, and B6, respectively.

 Identify the dependent cell(s), usually containing formulas, that will contain adjusted results once different data values are entered

There are three dependent cell formulas (labeled Monthly Payment, Total Payments, and Total Interest). The results appear in cells B9, B10, and B11, respectively.

 Formulate questions you want the what-if analysis to answer

Jim wants to answer the following questions with his model: (1) What happens to the monthly payments if the interest rate is 10%? (2) What happens to the monthly payments if the loan term is 60 months (5 years) instead of 48 months (4 years)? (3) What happens to the monthly payments if a less-expensive car with a lower loan amount is purchased?

 Perform the what-if analysis and explore the exact relationships between the input values and the dependent cell formulas, which depend on the input values

Jim wants to see what effect a 10% interest rate has on the dependent cell formulas. Because the interest rate is located in cell B5, any formula that references cell B5 will be directly affected by a change in interest rate—in this case, the Monthly Payment formula in cell B9. Because the formula in cell B10 references cell B9 and the formula in cell B11 references cell B10, however, a change in the interest rate in cell B5 affects these other two formulas as well. Figure K-2 shows the result of the what-if analysis described in this example.

FIGURE K-1: Worksheet model for a what-if analysis

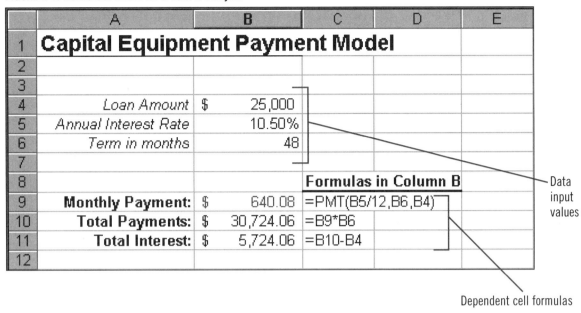

FIGURE K-2: What-if analysis with changed input value and dependent formula results

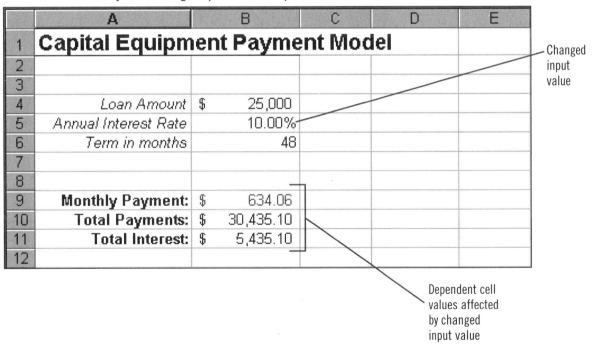

Excel 2000

Tracking a What-If Analysis with Scenario Manager

A **scenario** is a set of values you use to forecast worksheet results. The Excel Scenario Manager simplifies the process of what-if analysis by allowing you to name and save different scenarios with the worksheet. Scenarios are particularly useful when you work with uncertain or changing variables. If you plan to create a budget, for example, but are uncertain of your revenue, you can assign several different values to the revenue and then switch between the scenarios to perform a what-if analysis. ✎ Jim uses Scenario Manager to consider three equipment loan scenarios: (1) the original loan quote, (2) a longer-term loan, and (3) a reduced loan amount.

Steps 1 2 3 4

QuickTip

To return personalized tool-bars and menus to their default state, click Tools on the menu bar, click Customize, click the Options tab in the Customize dialog box, click Reset my usage data to restore the default settings, click Yes, click Close, then close the Drawing toolbar if it is displayed.

1. Open the workbook titled **EX K-1**, then save it as **Capital Equipment Payment Model**
   The first step in defining a scenario is choosing the cells that will vary in the different scenarios; these are known as **changing cells**.

2. Select range **B4:B6**, click **Tools** on the menu bar, then click **Scenarios**
   The Scenario Manager dialog box opens with the following message: "No Scenarios defined. Choose Add to add scenarios."

3. Click **Add** if necessary, drag the Add Scenario dialog box to the right until columns **A** and **B** are visible, then type **Original loan quote** in the Scenario name box
   The range in the Changing cells box reflects your initial selection, as shown in Figure K-3.

4. Click **OK** to confirm the Add Scenario settings
   The Scenario Values dialog box opens, as shown in Figure K-4. Notice that the existing values appear in the changing cell boxes. Because this first scenario reflects the original loan quote input values ($25,000 at 10.5% for 48 months), these values are correct.

5. Click **OK**
   The Scenario Manager dialog box reappears with the new scenario listed in the Scenarios box. Jim wants to examine a second scenario, this one with a loan term of 60 months.

6. Click **Add**; in the Scenario name box type **Longer term loan**, click **OK**; in the Scenario Values dialog box, select **48** in the third changing cell box, type **60**, then click **Add**
   Jim also wants to examine a scenario that uses $21,000 as the loan amount.

7. In the Scenario name box type **Reduced loan amount**, click **OK**; in the Scenario Values dialog box, change the **25000** in the first changing cell box to **21000**, then click **OK**
   The Scenario Manager dialog box reappears. See Figure K-5. All three scenarios are listed, with the most recent—Reduced loan amount—selected. Now that you have defined the three scenarios, you can apply them and see what effect they will have on the monthly payment.

8. Make sure Reduced loan amount is still selected, click **Show**, notice that the monthly payment in the worksheet changes from $640.08 to $537.67; click **Longer term loan**, click **Show**, notice that the monthly payment is now $537.35; click **Original loan quote**, click **Show** to return to the original values, then click **Close**

9. Save the workbook

CLUES TO USE

Merging scenarios

To bring scenarios from another workbook into the current workbook, click the Merge button in the Scenario Manager dialog box. The Merge Scenarios dialog box opens, letting you select scenarios from other workbooks.

FIGURE K-3: Add Scenario dialog box

Cell range to be changed

Your user name and date will be different

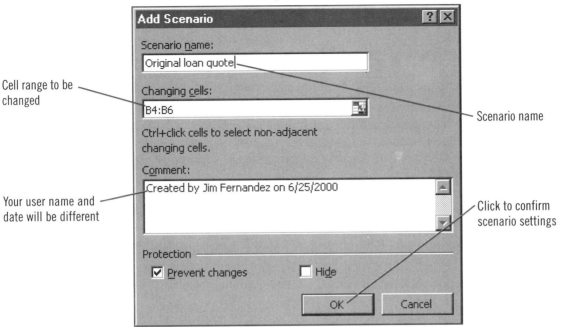

Scenario name

Click to confirm scenario settings

FIGURE K-4: Scenario Values dialog box

Changing cell boxes

Current cell values in B4, B5, B6

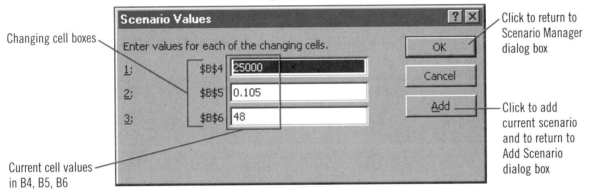

Click to return to Scenario Manager dialog box

Click to add current scenario and to return to Add Scenario dialog box

FIGURE K-5: Scenario Manager dialog box with three scenarios listed

Three scenarios

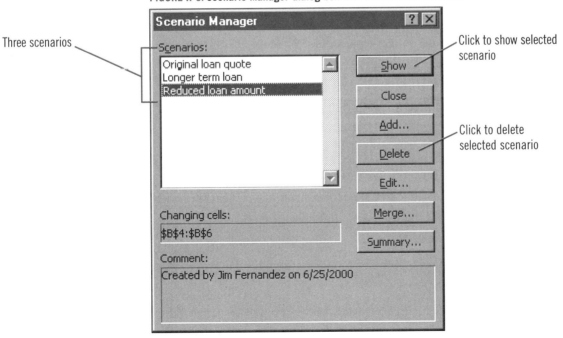

Click to show selected scenario

Click to delete selected scenario

Generating a Scenario Summary

Although it may be useful to switch between different scenarios when analyzing data, in most cases you will want to refer to a single report summarizing the results of the scenarios in a worksheet. A **scenario summary** is an Excel table that compiles data from the changing cells and corresponding result cells for each scenario. You can use a scenario summary to illustrate the best, worst, and most likely scenarios for a particular set of circumstances. ◀▬▬ Now that he's defined his scenarios, Jim needs to generate and print a scenario summary report. Naming the cells makes the summary easier to read because the names, not the cell references, are listed in the report. Jim begins by creating cell names in column B based on the labels in column A (the left column).

Steps

To delete a range, click Insert on the menu bar, click Define, click the range name, then click Delete.

1. **Select range A4:B11, click Insert on the menu bar, point to Name, click Create, click the Left column check box to select it if necessary, then click OK**
   Excel creates the names based on the cell contents.

2. **Click cell B4 to make sure Loan_Amount appears in the name box, then click the name box list arrow**
   All six labels appear in the name box list, confirming that they were created. See Figure K-6. Now you are ready to generate the scenario summary report.

3. **Press [Esc], click Tools on the menu bar, click Scenarios, then click Summary in the Scenario Manager dialog box**
   The Scenario Summary dialog box opens. Notice that Scenario summary is selected, indicating that it is the default report type.

4. **Double-click the Result cells box to select it if necessary, then select range B9:B11 in the worksheet**
   The references in the Result cells box adjust to reflect those cells affected by the changing cells (that is, the references now refer to the result cells). See Figure K-7. With the report type and result cells specified, you are now ready to generate the report.

Scroll right to see all three scenarios included in the report. The scenario summary is not linked to the worksheet. If you change cells in the worksheet, you must generate a new scenario summary.

5. **Click OK**
   The summary of the worksheet's scenarios appears on a new sheet. The report appears in outline format so that you can hide or show report details. Because the Current Values column shows the same values as the Original loan quote column, Jim wants to delete column D.

6. **Press [Ctrl][Home], click the Current Values column header for column D, click the right mouse button, then click Delete in the pop-up menu**
   The column containing the current values is deleted and the Original loan quote column data shifts left to fill column D. Next, Jim wants to delete the notes at the bottom of the report because they refer to the column that no longer exists. He also wants to make the report title more descriptive.

7. **Select range B13:B15, press [Delete], select cell B2, edit its contents to read Scenario Summary for Equipment Loan, then click cell A1**
   The completed scenario summary is shown in Figure K-8.

8. **Add your name to the report footer, save your work, then print the report in landscape orientation**

FIGURE K-6: List box containing newly created names

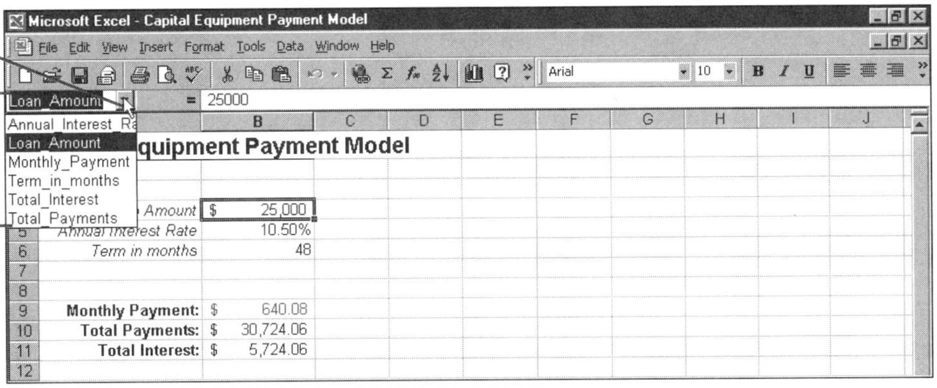

Name box
list arrow

Names
match
labels in
column A

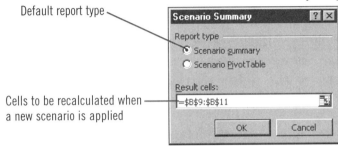

FIGURE K-7: Scenario Summary dialog box

Default report type

Cells to be recalculated when
a new scenario is applied

FIGURE K-8: Completed Scenario Summary report

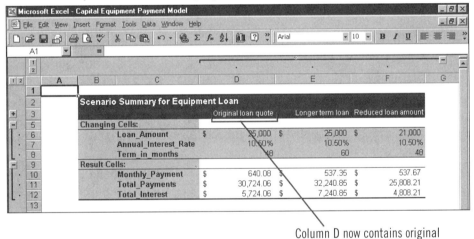

Column D now contains original
loan quote

Using Report Manager

You can create customized, printed reports using the Excel Report Manager, an extra Excel program called an "add-in." A report can contain worksheets, views, or scenarios that you want to print repeatedly in a given order. To create a report, click View on the menu bar, click Report Manager, then click Add. In the Add Report dialog box, type a report name, select the sheets, views, or scenarios you want to include, then click Add. Repeat until you've added all the sections you need, click OK, select the report name, then click Print. The sections of the report print in the order in which you've listed them.

Projecting Figures Using a Data Table

Another way to answer what-if questions in a worksheet is by using a data table. A **data table**, sometimes referred to as a **one-input data table**, is a range of cells that shows the resulting values when one input value is varied in a formula. For example, you could use a data table to calculate your monthly mortgage payment based on several different interest rates. ━━━ Now that he's completed his analysis, Jim wants to find out how the monthly equipment payments would change as interest rates increase by increments of 0.25%. He estimates that the lowest interest rate would be about 9.75% and the highest 11.25%. To project these figures, Jim will generate a one-input data table. First, he creates a table structure, with the varying interest rates listed in the left column.

Steps

1. Click the **Single Loan sheet tab**, select cell **D4**, type **Interest**, select cell **D5**, type **9.75%**, select cell **D6**, type **10.00%**; select range **D5:D6**, drag the fill handle to select range **D7:D11**, then release the mouse button

   With the varying interest rates (that is, the input values) listed in column D, you need to enter a formula reference to cell B9. This tells Excel to use the formula in cell B9 to calculate multiple results in column E, based on the changing interest rates in column D.

2. Click cell **E4**, type **=B9**, then click the **Enter button** ☑ on the formula bar

   Notice that the value in cell B9, $640.08, now appears in cell E4, and the formula reference (=B9) appears in the formula bar. See Figure K-9. Because the value in cell E4 isn't a part of the data table (Excel uses it only to calculate the values in the table), Jim wants to hide the contents of cell E4 from view using a custom number format.

3. With cell E4 selected, click **Format** on the menu bar, click **Cells**, click the **Number tab** in the Format Cells dialog box if necessary; click **Custom** under Category, select the contents of the Type box, type **;;**, then click **OK**

   Because custom number formats usually specify the formats for positive and then negative numbers, with semicolons in between, the two semicolons actually specify no format, so the cell will remain blank. With the table structure in place, you can now generate monthly payment values for the varying interest rates.

4. Select range **D4:E11**, click **Data** on the menu bar, then click **Table**

   You have highlighted the range that makes up the table structure. The Table dialog box opens, as shown in Figure K-10. This is where you indicate in which worksheet cell you want the varying input values (the interest rates in column D) to be substituted. Because the monthly payments formula in cell B9 (which you just referenced in cell E4) uses the annual interest rate in cell B5, you'll enter a reference to cell B5. You'll place this reference in the Column input cell box, rather than the Row input cell box, because the varying input values are arranged in a column.

5. Click the **Column input cell box**, click cell **B5**, then click **OK**

   Excel generates monthly payments for each interest rate. The monthly payment values are displayed next to the interest rates in column E. The new data and the heading in cell D4 need formatting.

6. Click cell **D4**, click the **Bold button** 🅱, then click the **Align Right button** ▤ (both on the Formatting toolbar)

7. Select range **E5:E11**, click the **Currency Style button** 💲 on the Formatting toolbar, deselect the range, add your name to the footer, then save and print the worksheet

   The completed data table appears as shown in Figure K-11. Notice that the monthly payment amount for a 10.50% interest rate is the same as the original loan quote in cell B9 and the reference to it in cell E4. You can use this information to cross-check the values Excel generates in data tables.

Trouble?
If you receive the message "Selection not valid", repeat Step 4, taking care to select the entire range D4:E11.

QuickTip
You cannot delete individual values in a data table; you must clear all values.

Trouble?
If the Bold button does not appear on your Formatting toolbar, click the More Buttons button » to view it.

FIGURE K-9: One-input data table structure

Reference to formula in cell B9

Value displayed in cell B9

Varying interest rates

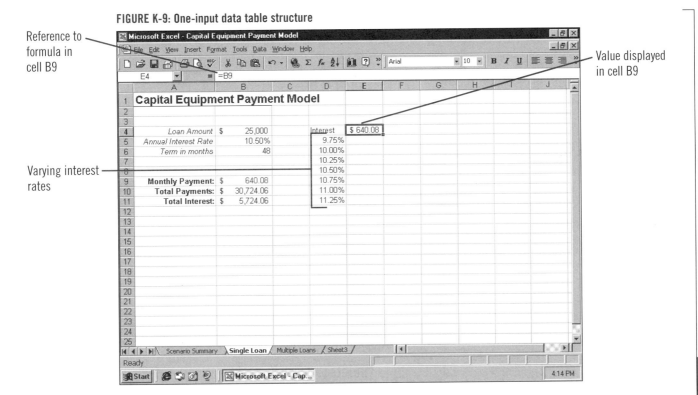

FIGURE K-10: Table dialog box

Enter reference to interest rate input cell here

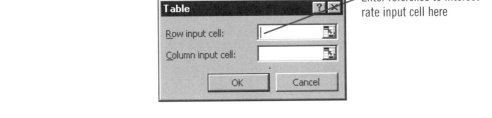

FIGURE K-11: Completed data table with resulting values

Formatted heading

Monthly payments

Completed data table

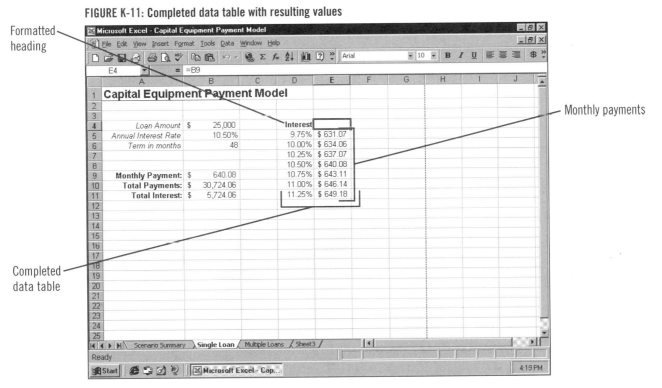

Excel 2000

Creating a Two-Input Data Table

A **two-input data table** shows the resulting values when two different input values are varied in a formula. You could, for example, use a two-input data table to calculate your monthly mortgage payment based on varying interest rates and varying loan terms. In a two-input data table, different values of one input cell appear across the top row of the table, while different values of the second input cell are listed down the left column of the table. ◢ Jim wants to use a two-input data table to see what happens if the various interest rates are applied across several different loan terms, such as 3, 4, and 5 years. He begins by changing the structure of the one-input data table to accommodate a two-input data table.

Steps

1. Move the contents of cell **D4** to cell **C7**; click cell **C8**, type **Rates**, click the **Enter button** ☑ on the formula bar, then click the **Align Right button** ▤ and the **Bold button** **B** (both on the Formatting toolbar)

   The left table heading is in place. You don't need the old data table values, but you will need a heading for the values along the top row of the table.

2. Select range **E4:E11**, press **[Delete]**, click cell **F3**, type **Months**, click ☑, then click **B**

3. Click cell **E4**, type **36**, click ☑, click the **Comma Style button** , on the Formatting toolbar, click the **Decrease decimal button** ☷ twice on the Formatting toolbar, press **[→]**, in cell F4 type **48**, press **[→]**, in cell G4 type **60**, then click ☑

   With both top row and left column values and headings in place, you are ready to reference the monthly payment formula in the upper-left cell of the table. Again, this is the formula Excel will use to calculate the values in the table. Because it is not part of the table (Excel uses it only to calculate the values in the table), it is best to hide the cell contents from view.

4. Click cell **D4**, type **=B9**, click ☑, click **Format** on the menu bar, click **Cells**, in the Format Cells dialog box click the **Number tab** if necessary, click **Custom**, select the contents of the Type box, type **;;**, then click **OK**

   The two-input data table structure is complete, as shown in Figure K-12. You are ready to enter the table values.

5. Select range **D4:G11**, click **Data** on the menu bar, then click **Table**

   The Table dialog box opens. The loan terms are arranged in a row, so you'll enter a reference to the loan term input cell (B6) in the Row input cell box. The interest rates are arranged in a column, so you'll enter a reference to the interest rate input cell (B5) in the Column input cell box.

6. With the insertion point positioned in the Row input cell box, click cell **B6** in the worksheet, click the **Column input cell box**, then click cell **B5**

   See Figure K-13. The row input cell (B6) references the loan term, and the column input cell (B5) references the interest rate. Now, you can generate the data table values.

7. Click **OK**, select range **F5:G11**, click the **Currency Style button** ⑤ on the Formatting toolbar, then click cell **F8**

   The resulting values appear, as shown in Figure K-14. The value in cell F8 matches the original quote: a monthly payment of $640.08 for a 48-month loan term at a 10.50% interest rate.

8. Preview and print the worksheet, then save the workbook

Formula reference

Table headings

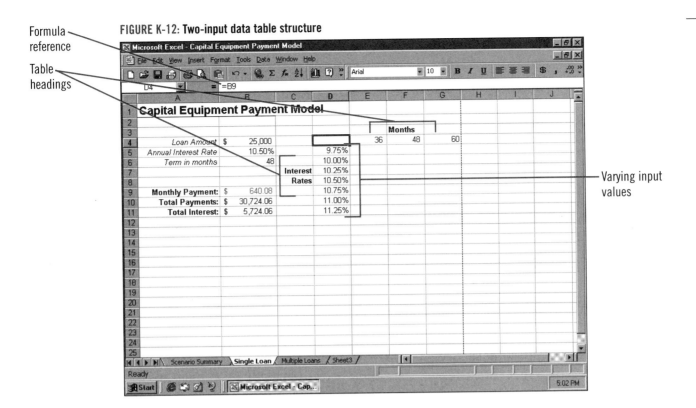

FIGURE K-12: Two-input data table structure

Varying input values

Loan term input cell

Interest rate input cell

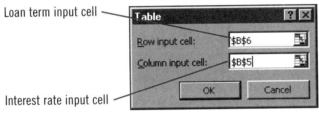

FIGURE K-13: Table dialog box

Hidden reference to cell B9

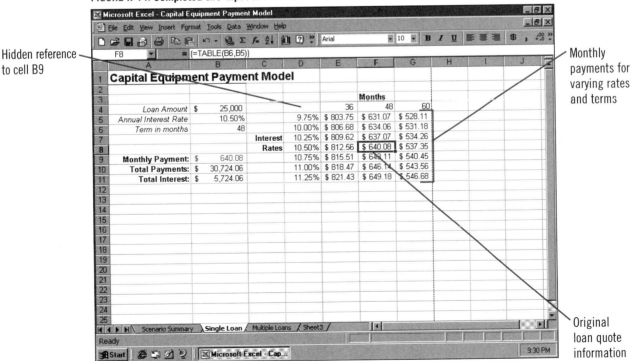

FIGURE K-14: Completed two-input data table

Monthly payments for varying rates and terms

Original loan quote information

Excel 2000

Using Goal Seek

You can think of goal seeking as a what-if analysis in reverse. In goal seeking, you specify a solution and then find the input value that produces the answer you want. Backing into a solution in this way, sometimes referred to as **backsolving**, can save a significant amount of time. For example, you can use Goal Seek to determine how many units must be sold to reach a particular sales goal or to determine the expenses that must be cut to meet a budget. After reviewing his data table, Jim has a follow-up question: How much money could MediaLoft borrow if the company wanted to keep the total payment amount of all the equipment to $28,000? Jim uses Goal Seek to answer this question.

Steps 1 2 3 4

1. Click cell B10

The first step in using Goal Seek is to select a goal cell. A **goal cell** contains a formula in which you can substitute values to find a specific value, or goal. You use cell B10 as the goal cell because it contains the formula for total payments.

2. Click Tools on the menu bar, then click Goal Seek

The Goal Seek dialog box opens. Notice that the Set cell box contains a reference to cell B10, the Total Payments cell you selected in Step 1. You need to indicate that the figure in cell B10 should not exceed 28000.

3. Click the To value box, then type 28000

The 28000 figure represents the desired solution that will be reached by substituting different values in the goal cell.

4. Click the By changing cell box, then click cell B4

You have specified that cell B4 will be changed to reach the 28000 solution. See Figure K-15. With the target value in the target cell specified, you can begin the Goal Seek.

QuickTip

Before you select another command, you can return the worksheet to its status prior to the Goal Seek by pressing [Ctrl][Z].

5. Click OK, then move the dialog box as needed so that column B is visible

The Goal Seek Status dialog box opens with the following message: "Goal Seeking with Cell B10 found a solution". Notice that by changing the Loan Amount figure in cell B4 from $25,000 to $22,783, Goal Seek achieves a Total Payments result of $28,000.

6. Click OK

Changing the loan amount value in cell B4 affects the entire worksheet. See Figure K-16.

7. Save, then print the workbook

FIGURE K-15: Completed Goal Seek dialog box

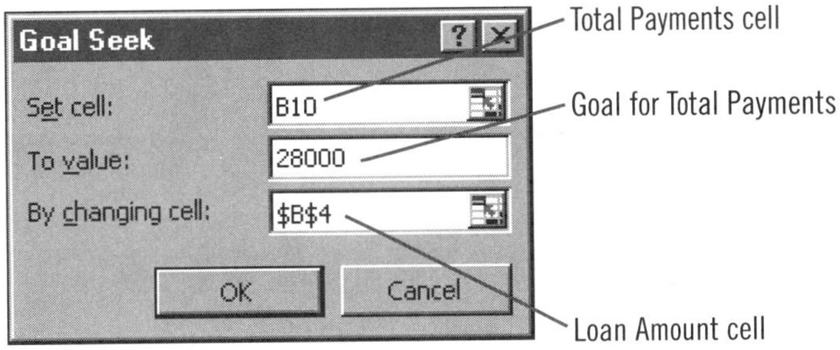

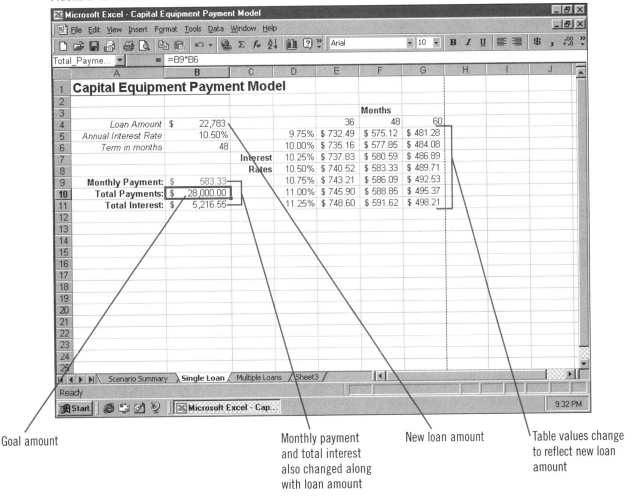

Total Payments cell

Goal for Total Payments

Loan Amount cell

FIGURE K-16: Worksheet with new values

Goal amount

Monthly payment and total interest also changed along with loan amount

New loan amount

Table values change to reflect new loan amount

Setting Up a Complex What-If Analysis with Solver

The Excel Solver finds the most appropriate value for a formula by changing the input values in the worksheet. The cell containing the formula is called the **target cell**. Cells containing the values that change are called **changing cells**. Solver is helpful when you need to perform a complex what-if analysis involving multiple input values or when the input values must conform to specific constraints. ◄━━ After seeing his analysis of interest rates and payments, Jim now addresses the vehicle purchase for the MediaLoft shuttle service. He decides that the best plan is to purchase a combination of vans, sedans, and compact cars that will accommodate a total of 44 passengers, the number of people Jim has estimated the company will need to transport to and from the stores for special events. In addition, the total monthly payments for the vehicles should not exceed $3,700. Jim uses Solver to find the best possible combination of vehicles.

Steps 1 2 3 4

Trouble?

If Solver is not an option on your Tools menu, you need to install the Solver add-in. See your instructor or technical support person for assistance.

1. Click the Multiple Loans sheet tab

See Figure K-17. This worksheet is designed to calculate total loans, payments, and passengers for a combination of vans, sedans, and compact cars. It assumes an annual interest rate of 10% and a loan term of 48 months. You will use Solver to change the purchase quantities in cells B7:D7 (the changing cells) to achieve your target of 44 passengers in cell B15 (the target cell). Your solution will include a constraint on cell C14, specifying that the total monthly payments must be less than or equal to $3,700.

Trouble?

If your Solver Parameters dialog box has entries in the By Changing Cells box or in the Subject to the Constraints box, click Reset All, then click OK, and continue with Step 3.

2. Click Tools, then click Solver

The Solver Parameters dialog box opens. This is where you indicate the target cell, the changing cells, and the constraints under which you want Solver to work. You begin by changing the value in the target cell.

3. With the Set Target Cell box selected in the Solver Parameters dialog box, click cell B15 in the worksheet, click the Value of option button, double-click the Value of box, then type 44

$B$15 appears in the Set Target Cell box, and 44 appears in the Value of box.

4. Click the By Changing Cells box, then select cells B7:D7 in the worksheet

$B$7:$D$7 appears in the By Changing Cells box. You need to specify the constraints on the worksheet values, the values you don't want them to exceed.

5. Click Add

The Add Constraint dialog box opens. This is where you specify the total monthly payment amount—in this case, no higher than $3,700.

6. Click the Cell Reference box, click cell B14 in the worksheet, click the list arrow in the Add Constraint dialog box, select <=, click the Constraint text box, then type 3700

See Figure K-18. The Change Constraint dialog box specifies that cell B14 should contain a value that is less than or equal to 3700. Next, you need to specify that the purchase quantities should be as close as possible to integers. They should also be greater than or equal to zero.

7. Click Add, click the Cell Reference box, select range B7:D7, click the list arrow in the Add constraint dialog box, then select int

8. Make sure "integer" appears in the Constraint box, click Add, click the Cell Reference box, select cells B7:D7 in the worksheet, in the Add Constraint dialog box select >=, click the Constraint box, type 0, then click OK

The Solver Parameters dialog box reappears, with the constraints listed as shown in Figure K-19. In the next lesson, you will run Solver and generate an answer report.

FIGURE K-17: Worksheet setup for complex what-if analysis

Interest rate

Loan term

Amount must be less than $3,700

Target cell

Adjustable cells

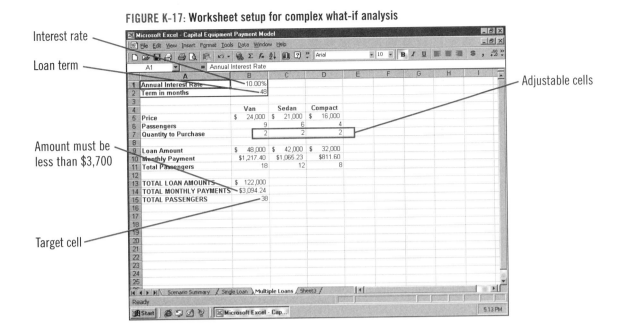

FIGURE K-18: Adding constraints

Constraints will affect this cell

Cell containing total monthly payments

Less than or equal to symbol

Highest possible monthly payment

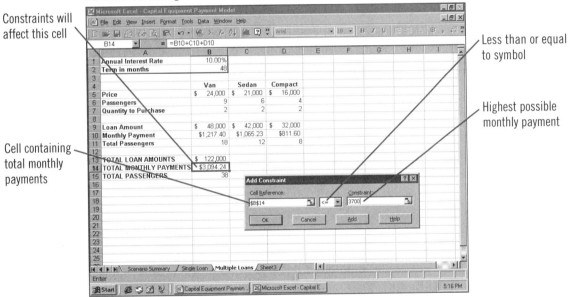

FIGURE K-19: Completed Solver Parameters dialog box

Target cell

Changing cells

Constraints on worksheet values

Target value

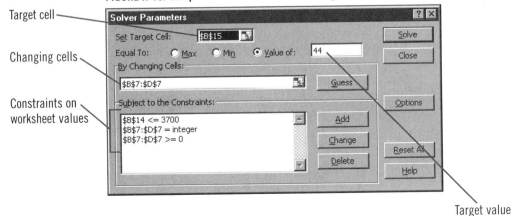

Running Solver and Generating an Answer Report

After entering all the parameters in the Solver Parameters dialog box, you can run Solver to find an answer. In some cases, Solver may not be able to find a solution that meets all of your constraints; then you would need to enter new constraints and try again. Once Solver finds a solution, you can choose to create a special report explaining the solution. Jim has finished entering his parameters in the Solver Parameters dialog box. Now he's ready to run Solver and create an answer report.

Steps 1234

1. Make sure your Solver Parameter dialog box matches Figure K-19 in the previous lesson

2. Click **Solve**

   After a moment, the Solver Results dialog box opens, indicating that Solver has found a solution. See Figure K-20. The solution values appear in the worksheet, but you decide to move them to a special Answer Report and display the original values in the worksheet.

3. Click **Restore Original Values**, click **Answer** in the Reports list box, then click **OK**

   The Solver Results dialog box closes, and the original values are displayed in the worksheet. The Answer Report appears on a separate sheet.

4. Click the **Answer Report 1 sheet tab**

   The Answer Report displays the solution to the vehicle-purchase problem, as shown in Figure K-21. To accommodate 44 passengers and keep the monthly payments to less than $3,700, you need to purchase two vans, three sedans, and two compact cars. Notice that Solver's solution includes two long decimals that are so small as to be insignificant. You'll now format the worksheet cells to display only integers. Also, because the Original Value column doesn't contain any useful information, you'll delete it.

5. Press **[Ctrl]**, click cell **E8** and cell **E14**, click the **Decrease Decimal button** on the Standard toolbar until the cells display no decimal places

6. Right-click the **column D column header**, click **Delete** in the pop-up menu, press **[Ctrl][Home]**, then put your name in the worksheet footer, save the workbook, and print the worksheet

   You've successfully found the best combination of vehicles using Solver. The settings you specified in the Solver Parameters for the Multiple Loans worksheet are saved along with the workbook.

7. Close the workbook and exit Excel

FIGURE K-20: Solver Results dialog box

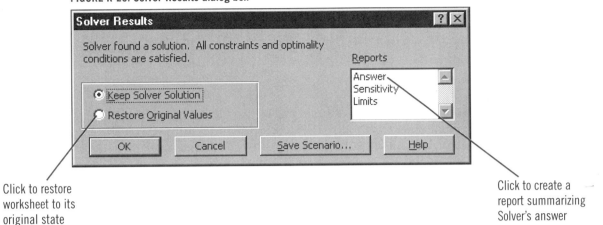

Click to restore
worksheet to its
original state

Click to create a
report summarizing
Solver's answer

FIGURE K-21: Answer Report

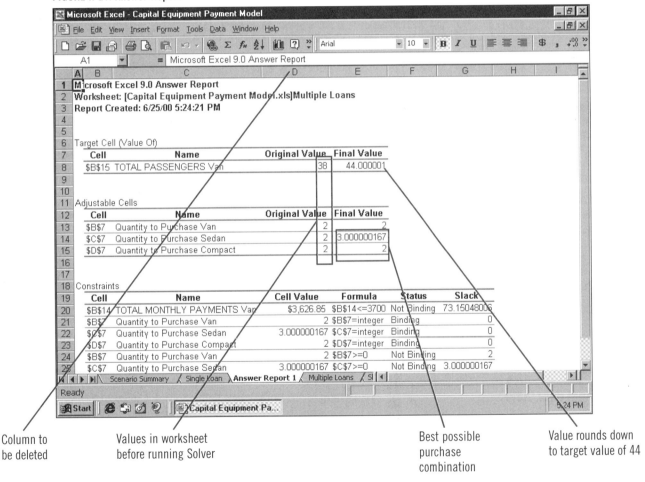

Column to
be deleted

Values in worksheet
before running Solver

Best possible
purchase
combination

Value rounds down
to target value of 44

Practice

► Concepts Review

Label each element of the Excel screen shown in Figure K-22.

FIGURE K-22

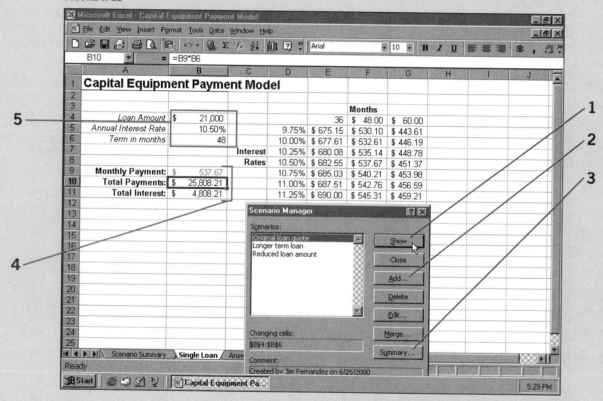

Match each term with the statement that describes it.

6. Two-input data table

7. Scenario summary

8. Goal Seek

9. One-input data table

10. Solver

a. Add-in that helps you solve complex what-if scenarios

b. Separate sheet with results from the worksheet's scenarios

c. Generates values resulting from a formula and input values variations across the top row and left column

d. Helps you backsolve what-if scenarios

e. Generates values resulting from a formula and input values variations across the top row or left column

Select the best answer from the list of choices.

11. A scenario is
   a. A worksheet model.
   b. A set of values used to forecast worksheet results.
   c. The same as a changing cell.
   d. The same as a dependent cell.

12. What are changing cells?
   a. Input cells that change, depending on their formulas.
   b. Formulas that change, depending on their input cells.
   c. Input cells whose values can be changed in a scenario.
   d. Cells that change positions during a what-if analysis.

13. Dependent cells are usually
   a. Formula cells that depend on input from other cells.
   b. Data cells that depend on their formulas.
   c. Input cells that depend on the results of a data table.
   d. Formula cells that depend on the results of a scenario.

14. In Solver, the cell containing the formula is called the
   a. Changing cell.
   b. Input cell.
   c. Output cell.
   d. Target cell.

▶ Skills Review

1. Define a what-if analysis.
   a. Open the workbook titled EX K-2, then save it as "Capital Equipment Repair Models" and make sure the Cappuccino Machine Repair sheet is active.
   b. State the purpose of the worksheet model.
   c. Locate the data input cells.
   d. Locate any dependent cells.
   e. Write three questions this what-if analysis model could answer.

2. Track a what-if analysis with Scenario Manager.
   a. Set up the most likely scenario with the current data input values. Select range B3:B5, then create a scenario called Most Likely.
   b. Add a scenario called Best Case using the same changing cells, but change the $B$3 value to 50, change $B$4 value to 45, then change the $B$5 value to .75. Add the scenario to the list.
   c. Add a scenario called Worst Case. Change the $B$3 value to 75, change the $B$4 value to 70, then change the $B$5 value to 2.
   d. If necessary, drag the Scenario Manager dialog box to the right until columns A and B are visible.
   e. Show the Worst Case scenario results.
   f. Show the Best Case scenario results. Finally, display the Most Likely scenario results.
   g. Close the Scenario Manager dialog box.
   h. Save your work.

3. Generate a scenario summary.

a. Create names for the input value cells and the dependent cell in the range A3:B7 (based on the left column).

b. Verify that the names were created.

c. Create a Scenario Summary report in the result cell B7.

d. Edit cell B2 to read "Scenario Summary for Cappuccino Machine Repair".

e. Delete the Current Values column.

f. Delete the notes beginning in cell B11.

g. Return to cell A1, add your name to the sheet footer, then print the Scenario Summary report in landscape orientation and save your work.

4. Project figures using a data table.

a. Click the Cappuccino Machine Repair sheet tab.

b. Enter the label "Labor $" in cell D3.

c. Adjust the formatting of the label so that it is boldfaced and right-aligned.

d. In cell D4, enter 50; then in cell D5, enter 55.

e. Select range D4:D5, then use the fill handle to extend the series to cell D9.

f. Reference the job cost formula in the upper-right corner of the table structure: In cell E3, enter =B7.

g. Format the contents of cell E3 as hidden, using the ;; Custom formatting type on the Number tab of the Format Cells dialog box.

h. Generate the new job costs based on the varying labor costs: Select range D3:E9 and create a data table. In the Table dialog box, make cell B3 the Column Input Cell.

i. Format range E3:E9 as currency.

j. Add your name to the footer, save the workbook, then preview and print the worksheet.

5. Create a two-input data table.

a. Move the contents of cell D3 to cell C6.

b. Delete the contents of range E4:E9.

c. Format cell E3 using the Currency Style button, then move the contents of cell E3 to cell D3.

d. Format the contents of cell D3 as hidden, using the ;; Custom formatting type on the Number tab of the Format Cells dialog box.

e. Enter "Hrs. per job" in cell F2, and format it so it is boldfaced.

f. Enter "1" in cell E3, enter 1.5 in cell F3, then enter 2 in cell G3.

g. Select range D3:G9 and make it a data table, making cell B5 the row input cell and cell B3 the column input cell.

h. Format range F4:G9 as currency.

i. Save the workbook, preview, then print the worksheet.

6. Use Goal Seek.

a. Determine what the parts would have to cost so that the cost to complete the job is $125: Click cell B7, and open the Goal Seek dialog box.

b. Enter 125 as the To value, and B4 as the By changing cell.

c. Return to the worksheet and note the cost of the parts.

d. Save the workbook.

e. Determine what the labor would have to cost so that the cost to complete the job is $100. Note the result.

f. Save the workbook.

g. Determine what the number of hours would have to be for the cost to complete the job to equal $90. Note the result.

h. On a blank area of the worksheet, enter the results you obtained when the job cost equaled $125, the labor costs when the job cost equaled $100, and the hours when the job cost equaled $90.

i. Save the workbook, then preview and print the worksheet.

7. Perform a complex what-if analysis with Solver and generate an Answer Report.
   a. Click the Vehicle Repair sheet tab to make it active, then open the Solver dialog box.
   b. Make B16 the target cell, with a target value of 146.
   c. Use cells B6:D6 as the changing cells.
   d. Specify that cell B14 must be greater than or equal to 4000.
   e. Specify that cell B15 must be greater than or equal to 6000.
   f. Use Solver to find a solution.
   g. Generate an Answer Report and restore the original values to the worksheet.
   h. Edit the Answer Report to delete the original values column.
   i. Add your name to the footer, save the workbook, preview and print the Answer Report, then close the workbook.

► Independent Challenges

1. You are an independent mortgage broker and have been working on your own for several years. One of your clients is a couple who wants to buy their first home and has qualified for a $150,000 loan. You have created a preliminary worksheet model to determine their monthly payment based on several different interest rates and loan terms. Although they are still saving for a down payment, the couple predicts they will be ready to buy in about six months. Interest rates are on the rise, and you want to show your clients a few different mortgage payment scenarios. The couple wants to secure either a 15-year or a 30-year fixed loan. Using Scenario Manager, create the following three scenarios: the original quote, a 30-year loan at 8%; a 30-year loan at 10%; and a 15-year loan at 7.75%. Then create a Scenario Summary report showing the details.

To complete this independent challenge:

a. Open the workbook titled EX K-3, then save it as "Fixed-Rate Mortgage Loan Payment Model".
b. Using Scenario Manager and assuming a constant loan amount of $150,000, create the following three scenarios: one with the current input values called 30-year loan at 8%; a 30-year loan at 10%; and a 15-year loan at 7.75%. Use cells B4:B6 as the changing cells for each scenario, and create range names as necessary.
c. Show each scenario to make sure it performs as intended.
d. Generate a scenario summary titled "Scenario Summary for Fixed-Rate Mortgage Loan Payment". Eliminate any references to current values in the report.
e. Add your name to the footer, preview, then print the scenario summary.
f. Save the worksheet, return to Sheet1 and delete the range names, then close the workbook.

2. Your real-estate clients are grateful for the information you provided in the what-if scenarios. The couple asks if you can show them what the monthly payments would be for a $150,000 loan, over 15- and 30-year terms, with interest rates ranging in 0.25% increments. Using the workbook provided, create a two-input data table that shows the results of varying loan term and interest rates.

To complete this independent challenge:

a. If you completed Independent Challenge 1, open and use the workbook titled "Fixed-Rate Mortgage Loan Payment Model". Otherwise, open the workbook titled EX K-3, then save it as "Fixed-Rate Mortgage Loan Payment Model".
b. Create a data table structure with varying interest rates for 15- and 30-year terms. Use 7% as the lowest possible rate. Make the highest possible interest rate 3% greater than the lowest, and vary the rates in-between by 0.25%.
c. Reference the appropriate cell in the table.
d. Generate the two-input data table.
e. Add your name to the footer, then preview and print the scenario summary.
f. Save the worksheet, then close the workbook.

3. As the owner of Micros Unlimited, a small personal computer (PC) store, you assemble your own PCs to sell to the home and business markets. You have created a PC production financial model to determine the costs and profits associated with your three models: PC-1, PC-2, and PC-3. You want to show how the hourly cost affects total profit for each PC model your company produces. To do this, you decide to use a one-input data table. Use the workbook provided to create the table.

In addition to the data table, you need to do a what-if analysis regarding the effect of hours per unit on total profit. Specifically, you want to find out by how much you must reduce hours per unit to increase total profits to a specific target value. You decide to solve the problem by changing the hours only for PC-3, using Goal Seek. If that doesn't work, you'll specify more complicated parameters using Solver.

To complete this independent challenge:

a. Open the workbook titled EX K-4, then save it as "PC Production Model".
b. Create a data table structure with varying hourly costs, in $5 increments, from $15 to $45. Reference multiple profit formulas across the top of the table. (*Hint:* Although this is a one-input data table, you will have multiple columns, one for each model's profit formula.)
c. Generate the one-input data table that shows the effect of varying hourly cost on the profitability of each machine.
d. Boldface the table values that are the same as the total profit figures in the table (the current values).
e. Preview, then print the worksheet.
f. Open the Goal Seek dialog box and set cell H9 to 25000 by changing cell B8. Click OK to find a solution.
g. Save the workbook, then print the worksheet.
h. Open the Solver dialog box. Set cell H8 as the target cell, with a value of 10000. Use cells B6:B8 as the changing cells. Specify that cells B6:B8 must be greater than or equal to 0 (zero) and less than or equal to 4.
i. Generate an Answer Report and restore the original values to the worksheet.
j. Add your name to the footer, save the workbook, preview and print the Answer Report, then close the workbook.

4. Jim Fernandez has asked you to help him explore ways to increase MediaLoft's profitability. He asks you to start with the profitability figures for the New York store's café.
To complete this independent challenge:

a. Connect to the Internet, and go to the MediaLoft intranet site at
http://www.course.com/Illustrated/MediaLoft. Click the Accounting link, then click the Café Budget link. Print the page and disconnect from the Internet.

b. Open a new Excel worksheet and save it as "Cafe Profitability". Enter the sales and expense information for the fourth quarter, then enter formulas that calculate total expenses and net profit.

c. Jim is negotiating a new lease for the New York store and wants to know the effect of a reduced rent on fourth-quarter profitability. Use a data table to calculate profitability for the quarter for varying levels of rent from $2,700 to $3,500 in $100 increments.

d. Jim also wants to find a way to increase profitability for the fourth quarter to $40,000. He feels that marketing could be persuaded to reduce advertising expenses to help accomplish this. To what level would advertising have to be reduced for Jim to achieve his goal?

e. Jim feels he could increase profitability by taking out a loan to buy more inventory and rent more warehouse space. He wants to investigate taking out a $50,000 loan for five years at a variable rate. He feels the rate would vary between 6.5% and 8.5%, at .5% increments. He wants to forecast the amount by which MediaLoft's payments would vary for each possible level of interest rate within this range. Display a blank worksheet and use the appropriate Excel feature to find the answer.

f. Jim now tells you he would also consider varying the term of the loan for 5, 10, or 15 years. Use a blank part of the worksheet to calculate MediaLoft's payments in each of these situations, using the same interest rate assumptions. Format and label the figures appropriately, add your name to the footer, then save and print the worksheet.

Excel 2000

► Visual Workshop

Create the worksheet shown in Figure K-23. Make sure to generate the table on the right as a data table. Save the workbook as "Color Laptop Loan Payment Model". Add your name to the footer, then preview and print the worksheet. Print the worksheet again with the formulas displayed.

FIGURE K-23

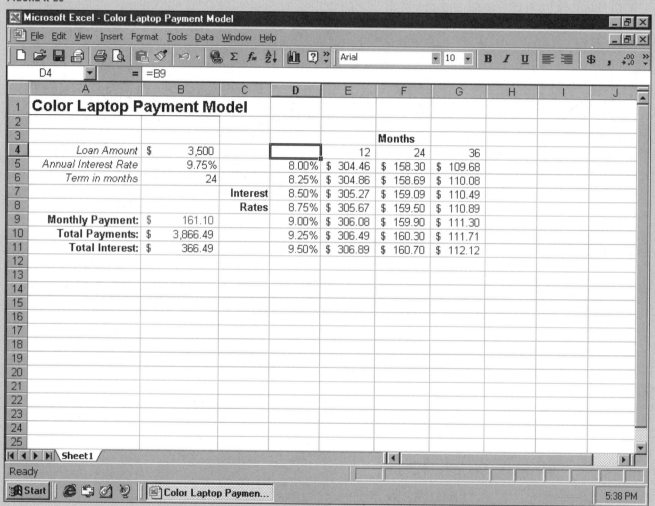

Summarizing
Data with PivotTables

Objectives

- ► **Plan and design a PivotTable report**
- [MOUS] ► **Create a PivotTable report**
- [MOUS] ► **Change the summary function of a PivotTable report**
- [MOUS] ► **Analyze three-dimensional data**
- ► **Update a PivotTable report**
- [MOUS] ► **Change the structure and format of a PivotTable report**
- [MOUS] ► **Create a PivotChart report**
- ► **Use the GETPIVOTDATA function**

With the Excel PivotTable feature, you can summarize selected data in a worksheet, then list and display that data in a table format. The interactive quality of a PivotTable allows you to freely rearrange, or "pivot," parts of the table structure around the data and summarize any data values within the table. You also can designate a PivotTable page field that lets you view list items three-dimensionally, as if they were arranged in a stack of pages. There are two PivotTable features in Excel: PivotTable reports and PivotChart reports. In this unit, you will plan, design, create, update, and change the layout and format of a PivotTable report. You will also add a page field to a PivotTable report, then create a PivotChart report. It's nearing the end of the fiscal year and the Accounting department has asked Jim Fernandez to develop a departmental salary analysis for selected corporate and management positions. Jim uses a PivotTable report to do this.

Excel 2000

Planning and Designing a PivotTable Report

Creating a PivotTable report (often called a PivotTable) involves only a few steps. Before you begin, however, you need to review the data and consider how a PivotTable can best summarize it. Jim plans and designs his PivotTable using the following guidelines:

Details

 Review the list information

Before you can effectively summarize list data in a PivotTable, you need to know what information each field contains and understand the list's scope. Jim is working with a list of corporate and managerial staff that he received from Karen Rosen, MediaLoft's human resource manager. This list is shown in Figure L-1.

 Determine the purpose of the PivotTable, then write down the names of the fields you want to include

The purpose of Jim's PivotTable is to summarize corporate salary information by position across various departments. Jim will include the following fields in the PivotTable: department, position, and annual salary.

 Determine which field contains the data you want summarized and which summary function will be used

Jim intends to summarize salary information by averaging the salary field for each department and position. He'll do this by using the Excel Average function.

 Decide how you want to arrange the data

The layout of a PivotTable is crucial in delivering its intended message. Jim will define department as a column field, position as a row field, and annual salary as a data summary field. See Figure L-2.

 Determine the location of the PivotTable

You can place a PivotTable in any worksheet of any workbook. Placing a PivotTable on a separate worksheet makes it easier to locate, however, and prevents you from accidentally overwriting parts of an existing sheet. Jim decides to create the PivotTable as a new worksheet in the current workbook.

FIGURE L-1: **Management salary worksheet**

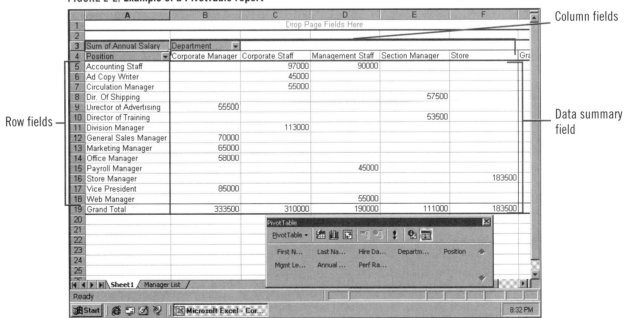

	First Name	Last Name	Hire Date	Department	Position	Mgmt Level	Annual Salary	Perf Rating	I	J
2	Maria	Abbott	10/18/93	Corporate Manager	General Sales Manager	2	70,000	2		
3	Tyler	Amodo	9/5/94	Corporate Staff	Division Manager	3	65,000	3		
4	Michael	Cole	2/6/97	Management Staff	Accounting Staff	2	42,000	3		
5	Katherine	DeNiro	4/29/99	Corporate Staff	Accounting Staff	3	55,000	2		
6	David	Dumont	4/7/86	Section Manager	Director of Training	3	53,500	4		
7	Catherine	Favreau	3/19/99	Corporate Manager	Director of Advertising	2	55,500	3		
8	George	Feake	8/1/94	Store	Store Manager	3	46,000	3		
9	Jim	Fernandez	1/2/96	Corporate Manager	Office Manager	2	58,000	5		
10	Louis	Grazio	5/24/96	Management Staff	Payroll Manager	3	45,000	3		
11	Lois	Greenwood	5/2/94	Store	Store Manager	3	42,000	4		
12	Patrick	Ikutu	3/12/98	Corporate Staff	Division Manager	3	48,000	4		
13	Robert	Jaworski	3/1/98	Corporate Staff	Accounting Staff	2	42,000	4		
14	John	Kim	3/3/99	Section Manager	Dir. Of Shipping	3	57,500	1		
15	Mike	MacDowell	2/8/99	Management Staff	Web Manager	3	55,000	2		
16	Goran	Manchevski	4/5/95	Store	Store Manager	3	47,500	2		
17	Michael	Martin	2/15/98	Store	Store Manager	3	48,000	3		
18	Eileen	Murphy	2/10/94	Corporate Staff	Ad Copy Writer	4	45,000	3		
19	Patricia	Fabel	6/21/96	Management Staff	Accounting Staff	3	48,000	3		
20	Elizabeth	Reed	2/1/96	Corporate Manager	Vice President	1	85,000	5		
21	Evelyn	Storey	1/10/92	Corporate Staff	Circulation Manager	3	55,000	4		
22	Alice	Wegman	1/5/97	Corporate Manager	Marketing Manager	2	65,000	4		
23										
24										

Manager List

Ready

Start   Microsoft Excel - Ex I-1   10:45 PM

FIGURE L-2: **Example of a PivotTable report**

Column fields

	A	B	C	D	E	F	
1			Drop Page Fields Here				
2							
3	Sum of Annual Salary	Department					
4	Position	Corporate Manager	Corporate Staff	Management Staff	Section Manager	Store	Gra
5	Accounting Staff		97000	90000			
6	Ad Copy Writer		45000				
7	Circulation Manager		55000				
8	Dir. Of Shipping				57500		
9	Director of Advertising	55500					
10	Director of Training				53500		
11	Division Manager		113000				
12	General Sales Manager	70000					
13	Marketing Manager	65000					
14	Office Manager	58000					
15	Payroll Manager			45000			
16	Store Manager					183500	
17	Vice President	85000					
18	Web Manager			55000			
19	Grand Total	333500	310000	190000	111000	183500	
20							

Row fields

Data summary field

PivotTable

PivotTable ▾

First N...   Last Na...   Hire Da...   Departm...   Position
Mgmt Le...   Annual ...   Perf Ra...

Sheet1   Manager List

Ready

Start   Microsoft Excel - Cor...   8:32 PM

Excel 2000

Creating a PivotTable Report

Once you've planned and designed your PivotTable, you can create it. The PivotTable Wizard takes you through the process step-by-step. ✏️ With the planning and design stage complete, Jim is ready to create a PivotTable that summarizes corporate salary information. After they add the remaining salary information, the Accounting and Human Resources departments will use this information to budget salaries for the coming year.

Steps

QuickTip

To return personalized tool-bars and menus to their default state, click Tools on the menu bar, click Customize, click the Options tab in the Customize dialog box, click Reset my usage data to restore the default settings, click Yes, click Close, then close the Drawing toolbar if it is displayed.

1. Open the workbook titled **EX L-1**, then save it as **Corporate Salaries**
   This worksheet contains information about some of MediaLoft's corporate employees and managers, including hire date, department, position, management level, salary, and performance rating. Notice that the records are sorted alphabetically by last name.

2. Click cell **A1** if necessary, click **Data** on the menu bar, then click **PivotTable and PivotChart report**
   The first PivotTable and PivotChart Wizard dialog box opens, as shown in Figure L-3. This is where you specify the type of data source you want to use for your PivotTable: an Excel list or database, an external data source (for example, a Microsoft Access file), or multiple consolidation ranges (another term for worksheet ranges). You also have the option of choosing a PivotTable or PivotChart report.

3. Make sure the **Microsoft Excel list or database option button** is selected, make sure **PivotTable** is selected, then click **Next**
   The second PivotTable and PivotChart Wizard dialog box opens. Because the cell pointer was located within the list before you opened the PivotTable Wizard, Excel automatically completes the Range box with the table range that includes the selected cell—in this case, $A$1:$H$22. You can either type a new range in the Range box or confirm that the PivotTable will be created from the existing range.

4. Click **Next**
   The third PivotTable Wizard dialog box opens. You use this dialog box to specify the location of the PivotTable.

Trouble?

If your PivotTable toolbar does not appear, click View on the menu bar, click Toolbars, then click PivotTable to select it. If the PivotTable toolbar blocks your view of the worksheet, drag it to the bottom of the worksheet window.

5. Make sure **New Worksheet** is selected, then click **Finish**
   A worksheet appears with an empty PivotTable, as shown in Figure L-4. The PivotTable toolbar also appears. It contains buttons that allow you to manipulate data as well as field names that you can drag into various "drop areas" of the PivotTable to analyze your data.

6. Drag the **Department field button** from the PivotTable toolbar to the area marked **Drop Column Fields here**, then drag the **Position field button** to the **Drop Row Fields Here** area
   This format will create a PivotTable with the departments as column headers and the management positions as row labels. To display the entire field name in a ToolTip in the PivotTable toolbar, place the pointer over the field button.

QuickTip

You can use more than one summary function in a PivotTable by simply dragging multiple field buttons to the data area.

7. Drag the **Annual Salary field button** to the **Drop Data Items Here** area
   Because SUM is the Excel default function for data fields containing numbers, Excel automatically calculates the sum of the salaries by department and by position. See Figure L-5. Notice that the position titles now appear as row labels in the left column, and the department names are listed across the columns as field names.

FIGURE L-3: First PivotTable Wizard dialog box

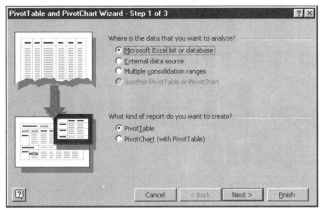

FIGURE L-4: New PivotTable ready to receive field data

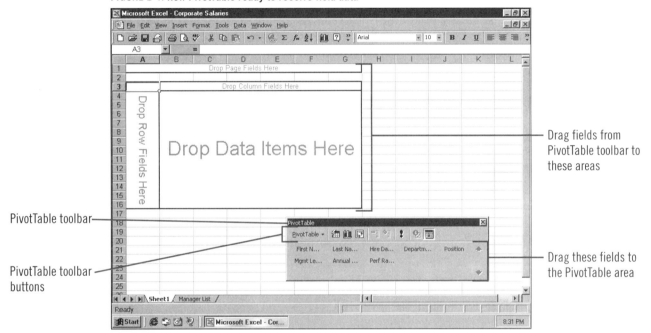

PivotTable toolbar

PivotTable toolbar buttons

Drag fields from PivotTable toolbar to these areas

Drag these fields to the PivotTable area

FIGURE L-5: New PivotTable with fields in place

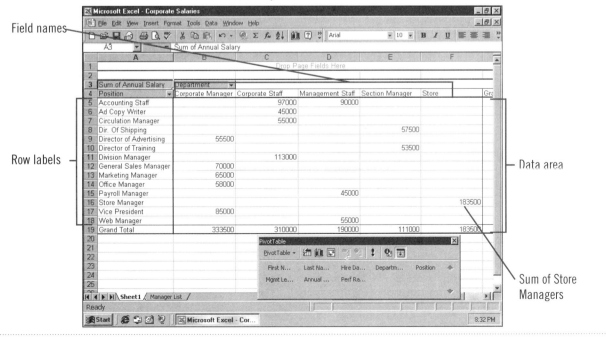

Field names

Row labels

Data area

Sum of Store Managers

Excel 2000

Excel 2000

Changing the Summary Function of a PivotTable Report

A PivotTable's **summary function** controls what type of calculation is applied to the table data. Unless you specify otherwise, Excel applies the SUM function to numeric data and the COUNT function to data fields containing text. However, you can easily change the SUM function in the PivotTable Wizard dialog box to a different function, such as AVERAGE (which calculates the average of all values in the field), PRODUCT (which multiplies all the values in a field), or MAX (which finds the highest value in a field). ◆━━━ Jim wants to calculate the average salary for the managers using the AVERAGE function.

Steps

1. Click any cell in the data area, then click the **Field Settings button** 🔣 on the PivotTable toolbar

   The PivotTable Field dialog box opens. The functions listed in the Summarize by list box designate how the data will be calculated. Other buttons on the PivotTable toolbar are described in Table L-1.

2. In the Summarize by list box, click **Average**, then click **OK**

   The PivotTable Field dialog box closes. The data area of the PivotTable shows the average salary for each position by department. See Figure L-6. The numbers representing sums in the last column and row now represent averages of annual salary. After reviewing the data, you decide that it would be more useful to sum the salary information than to average it.

3. Click the **Field Settings button** 🔣 on the PivotTable toolbar; in the Summarize by list box, click **Sum**, then click **OK**

   The PivotTable Field dialog box closes and Excel recalculates the PivotTable—this time, summing the salary data instead of averaging it.

4. Rename Sheet1 **PivotTable**, add your name to the worksheet footer, save the workbook, then preview and print the worksheet in landscape orientation

FIGURE L-6: PivotTable showing averages

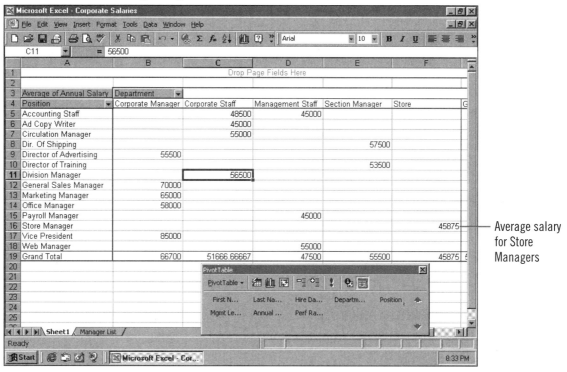

Average salary for Store Managers

TABLE L-1: PivotTable toolbar buttons

button	name	description
PivotTable ▾	**PivotTable Menu**	Displays menu of PivotTable commands
🗟	**Format Report**	Displays a list of PivotTable formats
📊	**Chart Wizard**	Creates a PivotChart report
🗗	**PivotTable Wizard**	Starts PivotTable Wizard
▫☰	**Hide Detail**	Hides detail in table groupings
☰▫	**Show Detail**	Shows detail in table groupings
❗	**Refresh Data**	Updates list changes within the table
🗐	**Field Settings**	Displays a list of field settings
🖼	**Show/Hide Fields**	Displays/hides PivotTable fields on toolbar; in a chart, displays or hides outlines and labels

Analyzing Three-Dimensional Data

When row and column field positions are established in a PivotTable, you are working with two-dimensional data. You can convert a PivotTable to a three-dimensional data analysis tool by adding a **page field**. Page fields make the data appear as if it is stacked in pages, thus adding a third dimension to the analysis. When using a page field, you are in effect filtering data through that field. To add the page field, you simply drag it to the Drop Page Fields Here area. ◄═══ Jim wants to filter the PivotTable so that only one department's data is visible at one time. He uses the PivotTable Wizard to add the Department page field.

Steps

1. Drag the **Department field button** from the column area to the **Drop Page Fields Here** area

   The PivotTable is re-created with a page field showing data for each department. See Figure L-7. You can select and view the data for each department, page by page, by clicking the Department list arrow and selecting the page you want to view.

2. Click the **Department list arrow**

3. Click **Management Staff**, then click **OK**

   The PivotTable displays the salary data for the management staff only, as shown in Figure L-8.

4. Click the **Department list arrow**, click **Corporate Staff**, then click **OK**

   The salaries for the corporate staff appear.

5. Save the workbook, then print the worksheet

QuickTip

To display each page of the page field on a separate worksheet, click PivotTable on the PivotTable toolbar, then click Show Pages, then click OK.

FIGURE L-7: PivotTable with Department as page field

Department now in Page field area →

Data now shows total salaries for each position in all departments

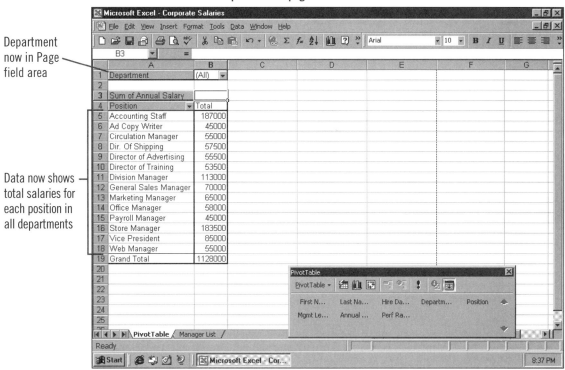

FIGURE L-8: PivotTable filtered to show only salaries for management staff

Department field specifies that only Management Staff should be displayed

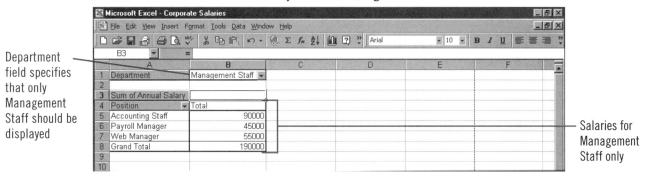

Salaries for Management Staff only →

Updating a PivotTable Report

The data displayed in a PivotTable looks like typical worksheet data. Because the PivotTable data is linked to a source list, however, the values and results in the PivotTable are read-only values. That means you cannot move or modify part of a PivotTable by inserting or deleting rows, editing results, or moving cells. To change PivotTable data, you must edit the items directly in the list you used to create the table, called the **source list**, and then update, or **refresh**, the PivotTable to reflect the changes. ⟍ Jim just learned that the training manager, Howard Freeberg, was never entered into the workbook. Jim needs to add information about this manager to the current list; he starts by inserting a row for Freeberg's information.

Steps

1. Click the **Manager List sheet tab**

   By inserting the new row in the correct position alphabetically, you will not need to sort the list again. Also, by adding the new manager within the named range, Database, the new row data will be included automatically in the named range.

2. Right-click the **row 10 header**; then on the pop-up menu, click **Insert**

   A blank row appears as the new row 10, and the data in the old row 10 moves down to row 11. You'll enter the data on Freeberg in the new row 10.

3. Enter the data for the new manager based on the following information

field name	new data item
First Name	Howard
Last Name	Freeberg
Hire Date	10/29/98
Department	Corporate Staff
Position	Training Manager
Mgmt Level	2
Annual Salary	59,000
Perf Rating	2

   After you add data, you must refresh the PivotTable so that it reflects the additional data.

4. Click the **PivotTable sheet tab**, then make sure the Corporate Staff page is in view

   Notice that the Corporate Staff list does not currently include a training manager and that the grand total is $310,000. Before you select the Refresh Data command to refresh the PivotTable, you need to make sure the cell pointer is located within the current table range.

5. Click anywhere within the table range (A3:B9), then click the **Refresh Data button** ⚡ on the PivotTable toolbar

   A message dialog box opens with the message "The Refresh Data operation changed the PivotTable report" to confirm that the update was successful.

6. Click **OK**

   The PivotTable now includes the training manager in row 9, and the grand total has increased by the amount of his salary (59,000) to $369,000. See Figure L-9.

7. Save the workbook and print the worksheet

FIGURE L-9: Refreshed PivotTable

New record for Training Manager now appears in Corporate Staff salaries

Total reflects new record for Training Manager

	A	B	C	D	E	F	G
1	Department	Corporate Staff ▼					
2							
3	Sum of Annual Salary						
4	Position ▼	Total					
5	Accounting Staff	97000					
6	Ad Copy Writer	45000					
7	Circulation Manager	55000					
8	Division Manager	113000					
9	Training Manager	59000					
10	Grand Total	369000					
11							
12							
13							

Maintaining original table data

Once you select the Refresh Data command, you cannot undo the operation. If you want the PivotTable to display the original source data, you must change the source data list, then re-select the Refresh Data command. If you're concerned about the effect refreshing the PivotTable might have on your work, save a second (working) copy of the workbook so that your original data remains intact.

Excel 2000

Changing the Structure and Format of a PivotTable Report

Although you cannot change the actual data in a PivotTable, you can alter its structure and format at any time. You might, for example, want to rename a PivotTable field button, add another column field, or switch the positions of existing fields. You can quickly change the way data is displayed in a PivotTable by dragging field buttons in the worksheet from a row position to a column position, or vice versa. Alternatively, you may want to enhance the appearance of a PivotTable by changing the way the text or values are formatted. It's a good idea to format a PivotTable using AutoFormat, because once you refresh a PivotTable any formatting that has not been applied to the cells through AutoFormat is removed. ✒ Jim wants to add the performance ratings to the PivotTable in order to supply the Accounting department with additional data needed for salary budgeting. Once the new field is added, Jim will format the PivotTable.

Steps

1. Make sure that the **PivotTable sheet** is active, that the Corporate Staff page is in view, and that the cell pointer is located anywhere inside the PivotTable (range A3:B10)
   When you move fields in a PivotTable, you can drag them as you did when you moved the Department field into the page area. Sometimes, however, you may want to drag fields while looking only at the PivotTable structure, without the data. You can do this by using the PivotTable Wizard Layout dialog box.

2. Click the **PivotTable Wizard button** 🔲 on the PivotTable toolbar

3. Click **Layout**, drag the **Perf Rating button** to the **COLUMN** area and compare your screen with Figure L-10

4. Click **OK**, then click **Finish**
   The PivotTable is re-created, and the new field is added. In addition to displaying the manager's position and annual salary on each department page, each manager's last performance rating on a scale from 1 to 5 appears as a column label. Now you are ready to format the PivotTable.

5. Click cell **B5**, click the **Field Settings button** 🔲 on the PivotTable toolbar, then in the PivotTable Field dialog box, click **Number**

6. Under Category in the Format Cells dialog box, click **Accounting**, edit the Decimal Places box to read **0**, click **OK**, then click **OK** again
   The PivotTable Field dialog box closes, and the annual salaries are formatted with commas and dollar signs.

QuickTip

Report formats 1–10 are indented formats, like a banded database report. Tables 1–10 are not indented. Indented reports contain only row fields, not column fields.

7. Click cell **A3**; click the **Format Report button** 🔲 on the PivotTable toolbar bar; in the AutoFormat dialog box, scroll down and then click **Table 2**, click **OK**, then click outside the range to deselect it
   The PivotTable appears as shown in Figure L-11. The AutoFormat is applied to all pages of the PivotTable.

8. Click the **Department list arrow**, click **Management Staff**, then click **OK**
   The Management Staff page has the same formatting.

9. Save the workbook, then preview and print the active sheet

FIGURE L-10: Revised PivotTable structure

Performance Rating now in COLUMN area ——

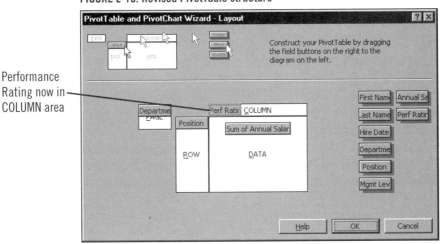

FIGURE L-11: Corporate Staff page with AutoFormat applied

AutoFormat has applied shading as well as blue headings and totals ——

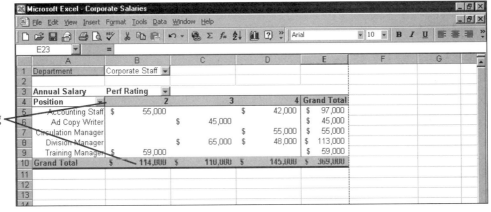

Excel 2000

Creating a PivotChart Report

A PivotChart report is a chart that you create from data or from a PivotTable report. Like a PivotTable report, a PivotChart report has fields that you can drag to explore new data relationships. Table L-2 describes how the elements in a PivotTable report correspond to the elements in a PivotChart report. When you create a PivotChart directly from data, Excel automatically creates a corresponding PivotTable report. When you change a PivotChart report by dragging fields, Excel updates the corresponding PivotTable report to show the new layout. You can create a PivotChart report from any PivotTable report to reflect that view of your data, but if you use an indented PivotTable report format, your chart will not have series fields; indented PivotTable report formats do not include column fields. ◣◣◣◣ Jim wants to chart the annual salary and performance rating information for the Corporate Manager department. He uses the PivotTable and PivotChart Wizard to create a column chart from the PivotTable data.

Steps 1 2 3 4

1. Click the **Manager List tab**, click anywhere in the data range, click **Data**, then click **PivotTable and PivotChart Report**

   The PivotTable and PivotChart Wizard opens.

2. Make sure Excel list or database is selected, then click to select **PivotChart (with PivotTable)** as shown in Figure L-12, click **Next**, then click **Next** again

   A message tells you that your existing PivotTable was created from the same source data and recommends using the same data to save memory.

3. Click **Yes**, click **Next**, then click **Finish**

   A new chart sheet opens, shown in Figure L-13. Jim wants to explore salary levels as they relate to performance ratings and management level.

4. Drag fields to PivotChart areas as follows:

Field	Area
Department	Page Fields
Management Level	Category Fields
Performance Rating	Series Fields
Annual Salary	Data

   The chart representing your data appears in the chart area.

Trouble?

If the Chart toolbar does not appear on your screen, open it: Click View on the menu bar, point to Toolbars, then click Chart.

5. Click **Sum of Annual Salary** on the PivotChart, click the **Field Settings button** 🔲 on the PivotTable toolbar, click **Average** in the PivotTable Field dialog box, then click **OK**

   The PivotChart report is recalculated, as shown in Figure L-14.

6. Click the **Department list arrow**, click **Corporate Manager**, click **OK**, then drag the **Position field** from the PivotTable toolbar to the Series fields area (the legend).

   The positions and ratings appear in the legend. Jim now has more detail on which to base his discussions with Human Resources and upper management.

7. Save the workbook, place your name in the chart sheet footer, then preview and print the PivotChart report

FIGURE L-12: PivotTable and PivotChart Wizard

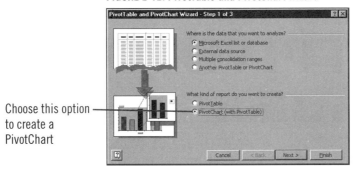

Choose this option to create a PivotChart

FIGURE L-13: New chart sheet, ready to receive fields

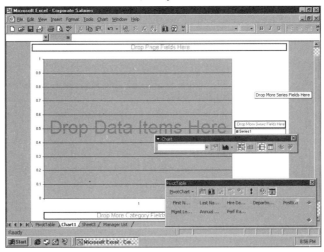

FIGURE L-14: PivotChart report recalculated to show averages

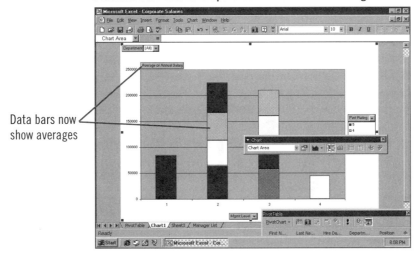

Data bars now show averages

TABLE L-2: PivotTable and PivotChart elements

PivotTable items	become	PivotChart items
row fields		category fields
column fields		series fields
page fields		page fields

Using the GETPIVOTDATA Function

Because a PivotTable is rearranged so easily, you can't use an ordinary cell reference when you want to reference a PivotTable cell in another worksheet. If you change the way data is displayed in a PivotTable (for example, by displaying a different page), the data moves, rendering an ordinary cell reference incorrect. Instead, to retrieve summary data from a PivotTable, you need to use the Excel GETPIVOTDATA function. Its syntax is displayed in Figure L-15. ➤ In creating next year's budget, the Accounting department is allocating money toward the payroll budget for the office manager. The department has asked Jim to include the current total salary for the office manager on the Manager List sheet. Jim uses the GETPIVOTDATA function to retrieve this information from the PivotTable.

Steps

1. Click the **PivotTable sheet tab**

    The Management Staff page is currently visible. You need the salary information for marketing managers in all departments.

2. Click the **Department list arrow**, click **(All)**, then click **OK**

    The PivotTable displays the salary data for all positions. Next, you will reference the total for marketing managers in the Manager List sheet.

Trouble?

If the Align Right button does not appear on your Formatting toolbar, click the More Buttons button 🛠 to view it.

3. Click the **Manager List sheet tab**, click cell **D25**, type **Office Manager Salary:**, click the **Enter button** ✓ on the formula bar, click the **Align Right button** on the Formatting toolbar, then click the **Bold button** on the Formatting toolbar

    The new label appears formatted in cell D25. Now, you'll enter a GETPIVOTDATA function in cell E25 that will retrieve the total salary for marketing managers from the PivotTable.

4. Click cell **E25**, click the **Paste Function button** 𝑓ₓ on the Standard toolbar; under Function category in the Paste Function dialog box, click **Lookup & Reference**; under Function name, click **GETPIVOTDATA**; then click **OK**

    The GETPIVOTDATA formula palette opens. The function's first argument, Pivot_table, can contain a reference to any cell within the PivotTable range. The second argument, Name, can contain the row or column label for the summary information you want (in this case, the column label Grand Total) enclosed in quotation marks.

5. With the pointer in the Pivot_table box, click the **PivotTable sheet tab**; click cell **F14** (or any other cell in the PivotTable range); in the formula palette, click the **Name box**; then type **"Office Manager"**

    Be sure to type the quotation marks. See Figure L-16.

6. Click **OK**, then click the **Currency Style button** 💲 on the Formatting toolbar

    The current total salary for Office Manager is $58,000, as shown in Figure L-17. This is the same value displayed in cell F14 of the PivotTable. The GETPIVOTDATA function will work correctly only when the salary for all departments is displayed in the PivotTable. You can verify this by displaying a different page in the PivotTable and viewing the effect on the Manager List worksheet.

7. Click the **PivotTable sheet tab**, click the **Department list arrow**, click **Corporate Manager**, click **OK**, then click the **Manager List sheet tab**

    The error message in cell E25 will disappear when you redisplay the (All) page.

8. Click the **PivotTable sheet tab**, click the **Department list arrow**, click **(All)**, click **OK**, then click the **Manager List sheet tab**

    Note that the correct value—$58,000.00—is once again displayed in cell E25.

9. Put your name in the footer, save the workbook, print the Manager List worksheet, then close the file and exit Excel

FIGURE L-15: Syntax of GETPIVOTDATA function

GETPIVOTDATA(pivot_table,name)

Reference to any page in the PivotTable that shows the data you want to retrieve.

The row or column label (enclosed in quotation marks) describing the summary value you want to retrieve. For example, "January 2000" for the grand total for January 2000.

FIGURE L-16: Completed GETPIVOTDATA formula palette

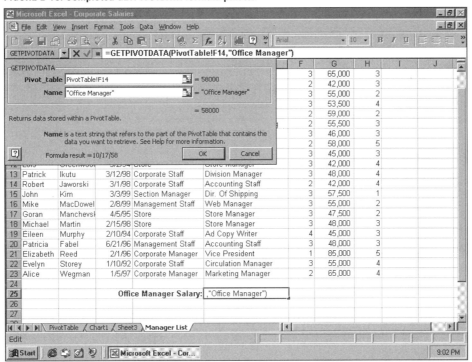

FIGURE L-17: Results of GETPIVOTDATA function

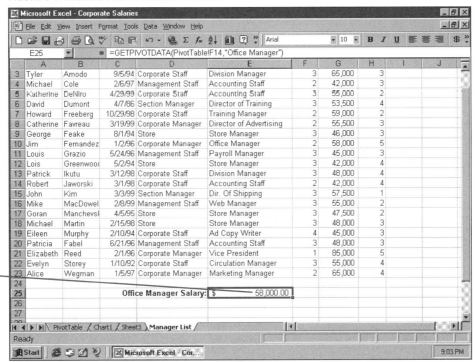

Results of GETPIVOTDATA function

Practice

► Concepts Review

Label each element of the Excel screen shown in Figure L-18.

FIGURE L-18

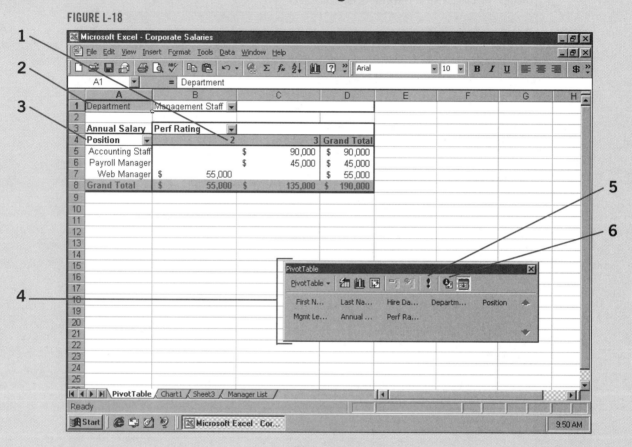

Match each term with the statement that describes it.

7. COLUMN area
8. GETPIVOTDATA function
9. DATA area
10. PivotTable page
11. Summary function

a. Determines how data will be calculated
b. Displays fields as column labels
c. Shows data for one item at a time in a table
d. Displays summarized values
e. Retrieves information from a PivotTable

Select the best answer from the list of choices.

12. **A PivotTable report is best described as an Excel feature that**
    a. Displays columns and rows of data.
    b. "Stacks" pages of data.
    c. Allows you to display, summarize, and analyze list data.
    d. Requires a source list.

13. **Which PivotTable report field allows you to average values?**
    a. Row field
    b. Data field
    c. Page field
    d. Column field

14. **To make changes to PivotTable data, you must**
    a. Create a page field.
    b. Edit cells in the source list and then refresh the PivotTable.
    c. Edit cells in the PivotTable and then refresh the source list.
    d. Drag a column header to the column area.

 # Skills Review

1. **Plan and design a PivotTable.**
    a. Open the workbook titled EX L-2, then save it as "October CDs".
    b. You'll create a PivotTable to show the sum of sales across products and regions. Study the list, then write down the field names you think should be included in the PivotTable. Determine which fields you think should be column fields, row fields, and data fields, then sketch a draft PivotTable.

2. **Create a PivotTable report**
    a. Using the data on the Sales List, generate a PivotTable report on a new worksheet, and arrange the data fields as follows: (*Hint:* In the Row area, place the Store field to the left of the Sales Rep field.):

Field	Area
Store	Row
Sales Rep	Row
Product	Column
Sales $	Data

3. **Change the summary function of a PivotTable report.**
    a. Change the PivotTable summary function to Average, then change it back to Sum.
    b. Rename the new sheet "Oct. 99 PivotTable".
    c. Save your work.

4. Analyze three-dimensional data.
a. Place the Region field in the page area.
b. Display sales for only the East region.
c. Add your name to the worksheet footer, then print the worksheet in landscape orientation.
d. Save your work.

5. Update a PivotTable.
a. On the PivotTable, note the Boston total for The Sunset Trio.
b. Go to the Sales List sheet.
c. Create a new blank row 8 and enter the following data:

field name	new data item
Period	Oct-99
Product	The Sunset Trio
Region	East
Store	Boston
Sales $	4,900
Sales Rep	L. Smith

d. Refresh the PivotTable so it reflects the new data item.
e. Note the Boston total for The Sunset Trio and verify that it increased by $4,900.
f. Add your name to the worksheet footer then print the PivotTable.
g. Save your work.

6. Change the structure and format of a PivotTable.
a. In the PivotTable, redisplay data for all regions and return the summary function to Sum of sales.
b. Drag fields so that the following areas contain the following fields: (*Hint:* To remove fields from an area, drag them back over to the field area in the PivotTable toolbar.)

Field	Area
Product	Row
Sales Rep	Column
Store	Page

c. Change the numbers to Currency format with 0 decimal places.
d. Apply the Report 6 AutoFormat and print the PivotTable.
e. Apply the Table 4 AutoFormat and print the PivotTable in landscape orientation, fitting the information on one page.
f. Save your work.

7. Create a PivotChart report.
a. Go to the Sales List sheet.
b. Create a PivotChart report (with PivotTable), using the existing PivotTable data on a new worksheet.
c. Place fields in the PivotChart report areas as follows:

Field	Area
Product	Series
Region	Category
Store	Category
Sales$	Data

d. Change the Summary function to Average.
e. Add your name to the chart sheet, then preview and print the chart.
f. Save the workbook.

8. Use the GETPIVOTDATA function.

a. In cell E27 of the Sales List, create a function to retrieve the grand total for S. Gupta from the October 99 PivotTable.

b. Format the figure in E27 as currency with no decimal places.

c. Save the workbook, then preview and print the worksheet.

d. Close the workbook and exit Excel.

▶ Independent Challenges

1. You are the bookkeeper for the small accounting firm called Chavez, Long, and Doyle. Until recently, the partners had been tracking their hours manually in a log. Recently, you created an Excel list to track basic information: billing date, partner name, client name, nature of work, and hours spent. You used abbreviated field names to simplify the reports. It is your responsibility to generate a table summarizing this billing information by client. You will create a PivotTable that sums the hours by accountant and date for each project. Once the table is completed, you will print the PivotTable for the partners and the summary page for the managing partner, Maria Chavez, for approval.

To complete this independent challenge:

a. Open the workbook titled EX L-3, then save it as "Partner Billing Report".

b. Create a PivotTable that sums hours by partner and dates according to client. Use Figure L-19 as a guide.

c. Name the new sheet "PivotTable", and format the PivotTable using the AutoFormat of your choice.

d. Add your name to the worksheet footer, then preview and print three copies of the PivotTable, one for each of the three partners. Then preview and print the (All) page.

e. Save the worksheet, then close the workbook.

FIGURE L-19

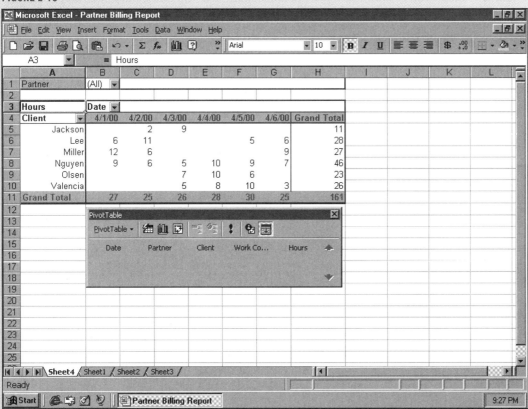

2. You are the owner of three midsized computer stores called PC Assist. One is located downtown, one is in the Plaza Mall, and one is in the Sun Center shopping center. You have been using Excel to maintain a sales summary list for the first-quarter sales in the following three areas: hardware, software, and miscellaneous items. You want to create a PivotTable to analyze and graph the sales in each category by month and store.

To complete this independent challenge:

a. Open the workbook titled EX L-4, then save it as "PC Assist - First Qtr Sales".

b. Create a PivotTable that sums the sales amount for each store across the rows and each category of sales down the columns. Add a page field for month.

c. Change the summary function to Average to show the average sales amount in each category.

d. Format the PivotTable using the Table 6 AutoFormat.

e. Format the amounts as Currency with no decimal places.

f. On a separate sheet, create a PivotChart report for the January sales data in all three stores. (*Hint*: Display the January sales page and click the ChartWizard button on the PivotTable toolbar.) Remember to add a descriptive title to your chart, using the same technique you would on any Excel chart.

g. Add your name to the worksheet footers, then print the PivotTable and the chart.

h. Save, then close the workbook.

3. You manage a group of sales offices in the Western region for a cellular phone company called Digital Ear. Management has asked you to provide a summary table showing information on your sales staff, their locations, and their titles. You will create a PivotTable summarizing this information.

To complete this independent challenge:

a. Open the workbook titled EX L-5, then save it as "Western Sales Employees".

b. Create a PivotTable that lists the number of employees in each city, with the names of the cities listed across the columns and the titles listed down the rows. (*Hint:* Remember that the default summary function for cells containing text is Count.)

c. Name the new sheet "PivotTable".

d. Add and format the label "Total Seattle Staff:" in cell C19 of the Employee List sheet.

e. Create a formula in cell D19 that retrieves the total number of employees located in Seattle.

f. Create a PivotChart that shows the number of employees in each store by position.

g. Drag the State field into the Series area.

h. Add your name to the worksheet footer, then preview and print the PivotTable and the Staff List.

i. Save the worksheet, then close the workbook.

4. Jim Fernandez has asked you to analyze MediaLoft's 1999 Sales and produce a PivotTable report and a PivotChart report that he can manipulate to explore relationships within the data. He gives you an Excel file, but it is missing the data for the Houston store. He asks you to get that information from the company intranet site.

To complete this independent challenge:

a. Connect to the Internet, and go to the MediaLoft intranet site at http://www.course.com/Illustrated/MediaLoft. Click the Sales link, then click the Sales Report link. Print the page and disconnect from the Internet.

b. Open the file EX L-6, save it as "1999 Sales", then insert a blank row just under the headings and enter the data from the Houston store, which is in the West region. Format the data so that it looks like the data in the other rows. Make sure that the totals are updated.

c. Create a PivotTable report from the 1999 Sales data. Experiment with different arrangements of data to determine which layout produces the most useful information. Try filtering by Region and by Store. Name the PivotTable sheet appropriately.

d. Format the sales figures appropriately, apply an AutoFormat, add your name to the worksheet footer, then print the sheet.

e. Create a PivotChart report from your data on a separate sheet. Move at least one field to obtain a different view of the data, format the chart appropriately, add your name to the chart sheet footer, and print the sheet.

f. Use the GETPIVOTDATA function to bring a figure from the PivotTable to the 1999 Sales sheet and label it.

g. Save the file, print your chart, then close the workbook.

Excel 2000

Visual Workshop

Open the workbook titled EX L-7, then save it as "Corner Fruit Stand". Using the data in the workbook provided, create the PivotTable shown in Figure L-20. (*Hint:* There are two data summary fields.) Add your name to the worksheet footer, then preview and print the PivotTable. Save the worksheet, then close the workbook.

FIGURE L-20

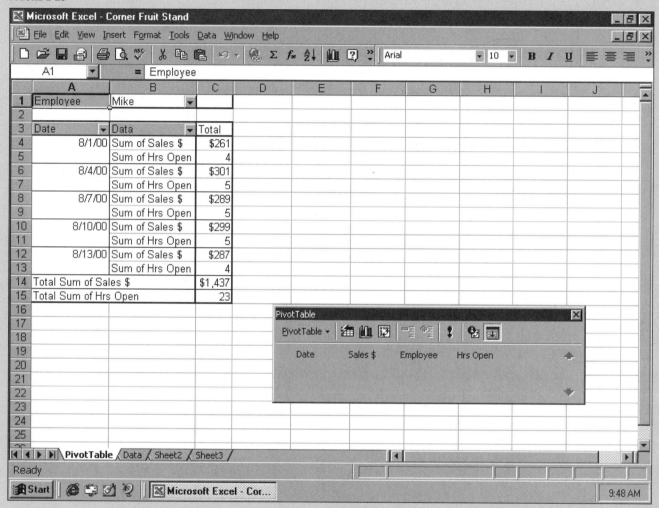

Exchanging
Data with Other Programs

Objectives

- ► **Plan a data exchange**
- [MOUS] ► **Import a text file**
- [MOUS] ► **Import a database table**
- [MOUS] ► **Insert a graphic file in a worksheet**
- [MOUS] ► **Embed a worksheet**
- [MOUS] ► **Link a worksheet to another program**
- [MOUS] ► **Embed an Excel chart into a PowerPoint slide**
- ► **Convert a list to an Access table**

In a Windows environment, you can freely exchange data between Excel and most other Windows programs. In this unit, you will plan a data exchange with Excel. ✎ MediaLoft's upper management has asked MediaLoft office manager Jim Fernandez to research the possible purchase of CafeCorp, a small company that operates cafés in large businesses, hospitals, and, more recently, drug stores. Jim is reviewing the broker's paper documents and electronic files and developing a presentation on the feasibility of acquiring this company. To complete this project, Jim will exchange data between Excel and other programs.

Planning a Data Exchange

Excel 2000

Because the tools available in Windows and Windows-supported programs are so flexible, exchanging data between Excel and other programs is easy. The first step involves planning what you want to accomplish with each data exchange. Jim uses the following guidelines to plan data exchanges between Excel and other programs in order to complete the business analysis project.

Steps

1. Identify the data you want to exchange, its file type, and, if possible, the program used to create it

Whether the data you want to exchange is contained in a graphic file or a worksheet or consists only of text, it is important to identify the data's **source program**, the file type, and the program used to create it. Once the source program has been identified, you can determine options for exchanging that data with Excel. Jim has been asked to analyze a text file containing the CafeCorp product data. Although he does not know the source program, Jim knows that the file contains unformatted text. A file that consists of text but no formatting is sometimes referred to as an **ASCII file**. Because an ASCII file is a universally accepted text file format, Jim can easily import it into Excel.

2. Determine the program with which you want to exchange the specified data

You might want to insert a graphic object into an Excel worksheet or add a spreadsheet to a WordPad document. Data exchange rules vary from program to program. Besides knowing which program created the data to be exchanged, you must also identify which program will receive the data (that is, the **destination program**). Jim received a database table of CafeCorp's corporate customers created with the dBASE IV program. After determining that Excel can import dBASE IV tables, he plans to import that database file into Excel to perform his analysis.

3. Determine the goal of your data exchange

Although it is convenient to use the Clipboard to cut, copy, and paste data within and between programs, you cannot retain a connection with the source program or document using this method. However, there are two ways to transfer data within and between programs that allow you to retain some connection with the source document and/or the source program. These data-transfer options involve using a Windows technology known as object linking and embedding, or **OLE**. The data to be exchanged, called an **object**, may consist of text, a worksheet, or any other type of data. You use **embedding** to insert a copy of the original object in the destination document and, if necessary, to subsequently edit this data separately from the source document. This process is illustrated in Figure M-1. You use **linking** when you want the information you inserted to be updated automatically when the data in the source document changes. This process is illustrated in Figure M-2. Embedding and linking are discussed in more detail later in this unit. Jim has determined that he needs to use both object embedding and object linking for his analysis and presentation project.

4. Set up the data exchange

When you exchange data between two programs, it is best to start both programs prior to initiating the exchange. You might also want to tile the programs on the screen either horizontally or vertically so that you can see both while the data is exchanged. See Table M-1 for a list of file formats that Excel can import. Jim will work with Excel and WordPad when exchanging data for this project.

5. Execute the data exchange

The steps you use will vary, depending on the type of data exchanged. Jim is eager to attempt the data exchanges to complete his business analysis of CafeCorp.

FIGURE M-1: **Embedded object**

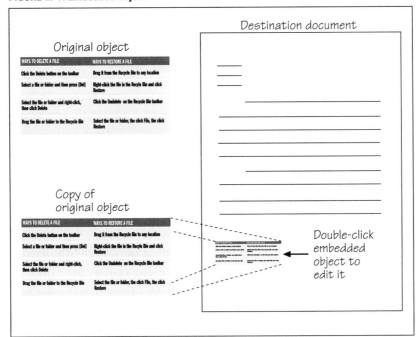

FIGURE M-2: **Linked object**

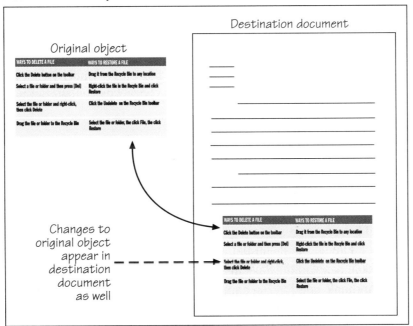

TABLE M-1: **Importable file formats and extensions**

file format	file extension(s)	file format	file extensions
dBASE II, III, IV	DBF	**CSV (Comma Separated Values)**	CSV
Excel 4.0	XLS, XLW, XLC, XLM	**DIF (Data Interchange Format, i.e., VisiCalc)**	DIF
Excel 5.0/7.0	XLS, XLT	**Formatted Text (Space or column delimited)**	TXT, PRN
Lotus 1-2-3	WKS, WK1, WK3, ALL, FMT, WK3, FM3, WK4	**Text (Tab delimited)**	TXT
Quattro/Quattro Pro	WQ1, WBI	**SYLK (Symbolic Link: Multiplan, Microsoft Works)**	SLK

Importing a Text File

You can import data stored in other programs into Excel by simply opening the file, so long as Excel can read the file type. After importing the file, use the Save As command on the File menu to save the data in Excel format. Text files use a tab or space as the **delimiter**, or column separator, to separate columns of data. When you import a text file into Excel, the Text Import Wizard automatically opens and describes how text is separated in the imported file. ◢━━━ Now that he's planned his data exchange, Jim wants to import a tab-delimited text file containing product cost and pricing data from CafeCorp.

Steps

1. In a blank workbook, click the **Open button** 📂 on the Standard toolbar, click the **Look in list arrow**, then click the drive containing your Project Disk

The Open dialog box shows only those files that match the file types listed in the Files of type box—usually Microsoft Excel files. In this case, however, you're importing a text file.

Trouble?

If the Preview window in the Text Import Wizard dialog box contains odd-looking characters, make sure you selected the correct original data type.

2. Click the **Files of type list arrow**, click **Text Files,** click **EX M-1** if necessary, then click **Open**

The first Text Import Wizard dialog box opens. See Figure M-3. Notice that under Original data type, the Delimited option button is selected. In the Preview of file box, line 1 indicates that the file contains three columns of data: Item, Cost, and Price. No changes are necessary in this dialog box.

3. Click **Next**

The second Text Import Wizard dialog box opens. Under Delimiters, the tab character is selected as the delimiter, and the Data preview box contains an image showing where the delimiters divide the data into columns.

4. Click **Next**

The third Text Import Wizard dialog box opens with options for formatting the three columns of data. Notice that under Column data format, the General option button is selected. This is the best formatting option for text mixed with numbers.

5. Click **Finish**

Excel imports the text file into the blank worksheet as three columns of data: Item, Cost, and Price.

6. Click **File** on the menu bar, click **Save As**, make sure the drive containing your Project Disk appears in the Save in box, click the **Save as type list arrow**, click **Microsoft Excel Workbook**, edit the File name box to read **CafeCorp - Product Info**, then click **Save**

The file is saved as a workbook, and the new name appears in the title bar. The worksheet is automatically named after the imported file, EX M-1. The worksheet information would be easier to read if it were formatted and if it showed the profit for each item.

QuickTip

To format numbers with dollar signs, use the Currency or Accounting format on the Numbers tab of the Format Cells dialog box.

7. Double-click the border between the headers in **Columns A** and **B**, click cell **D1**, type **Profit**, click cell **D2**, type **=C2-B2**, click the **Enter button** ✓ on the Formula bar, copy the contents of cell D2 to range **D3:D18**, then center the column labels, apply bold formatting to them, and format the data in columns B, C, and D with two decimal places using the Number style

The completed worksheet, which analyzes the text file imported into Excel, is shown in Figure M-4.

8. Add your name to the worksheet footer, preview and print the list in portrait orientation, then save and close the workbook

FIGURE M-3: First Text Import Wizard dialog box

Original data type is delimited

Three column headings

Preview of file box

Text appears in three columns

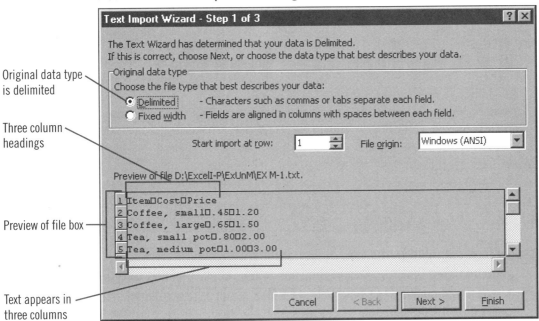

FIGURE M-4: Completed worksheet with imported text file

Columns from text file

Added column with new profit data

Column A widened to longest entry

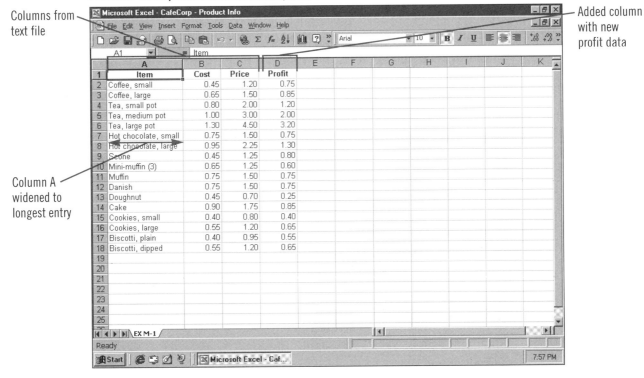

Other ways to import text files

Although the Text Import Wizard gives you the most flexibility, there are other ways to import text files. On the Windows desktop, drag your text file over the Excel program icon. Excel opens your text file. You can also click Insert on the menu bar, click Object, click Create from File, click the Browse button and locate the text file, click Insert, then click OK. The text file is inserted as an icon on your worksheet. Double-click the icon to open the text file in WordPad. You can then copy it into your worksheet.

Importing a Database Table

In addition to importing text files, you can also use Excel to import files from other programs or database tables. To import files that contain supported file formats, simply open the file, then you are ready to work with the data in Excel. ◢═══ Jim received a database table of CafeCorp's corporate customers, which was created with dBASE IV. He will import this table into Excel, then format, sort, and total the data.

Steps

1. Click the **Open button** 🖼 on the Standard toolbar, make sure the drive containing your Project Disk appears in the Look in box, click the **Files of type list arrow**, scroll down and click **dBase Files**, click **EX M-2**, if necessary, then click **Open**
   Excel opens the database table and names the sheet tab EX M-2. See Figure M-5. Before manipulating the data, you should save the table as an Excel workbook.

2. Click **File** on the menu bar; click **Save As**; make sure the drive containing your Project Disk appears in the Save in box; click the **Save as type list arrow**; scroll up, if necessary, and click **Microsoft Excel Workbook**; edit the File name box to read **CafeCorp - Corporate Customer Info**; click **Save**; then rename the sheet tab **Corporate Customer Info**
   The truncated column labels in row 1 are not very readable; they would look better if the text wrapped to two lines.

3. Edit cell A1 to read **COMPANY NAME** (no underscore), click cell **F1**, type **1994**, press **[Alt][Enter]** to force a new line, type **ORDER**, press **Tab**, type **1995**, press **[Alt][Enter]**, type **ORDER**, then press **[Enter]**
   Pressing [Alt][Enter] as you create cell entries forces the text to wrap to the next line. Columns F and G could be wider, and the column labels would look better if they were formatted.

4. Format the numbers in **columns F** and **G** using the Comma style with no decimal places, center and apply bold formatting to all the column labels, then widen the columns as necessary

5. Save the workbook, click cell **G2**, then click the **Sort Descending button** 🔽 on the Standard toolbar
   Columns F and G need totals.

6. Select range **F19:G19**, click the **AutoSum button** Σ on the Standard toolbar, then format the range F19:G19 with the Comma style and no decimal places, add a border around it, then click cell A1
   Your completed worksheet should match Figure M-6.

7. Add your name to the worksheet footer, preview and print the list in landscape orientation, fit the list to one page if necessary, then save the workbook

FIGURE M-5: Imported dBASE table

Excel substitutes
underscores in
place of spaces

Truncated
column label

FIGURE M-6: Completed worksheet containing imported data

Adjusted and
formatted column
labels

Figures for 1995
arranged in
descending order

New totals

Renamed
sheet tab

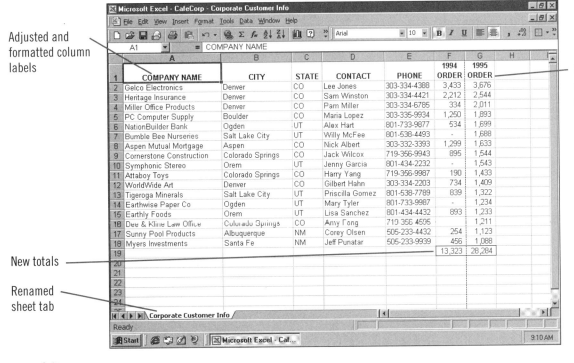

Exporting Excel data

Most of the file types that Excel can import (listed in Table M-1) are also the file types to which Excel can export, or deliver data. Excel can also export Text and CSV formats for Macintosh and OS/2. To export an Excel worksheet, use the Save As command on the File menu, click the Save as type list arrow, then select the desired format. Saving to a non-Excel format might result in the loss of formatting that is unique to Excel.

Excel 2000

Inserting a Graphic File in a Worksheet

A graphic object (such as a drawing, logo, or photograph) can greatly enhance a worksheet's visual impact. The Picture options on the Insert menu make it easy to insert graphics into an Excel worksheet. Once you've inserted a picture, you can edit it using the tools available on the Picture toolbar. ✎▬▬ Jim wants to insert a copy of the MediaLoft logo at the top of his corporate customer database table. He has a copy of the logo, previously created by the company's Marketing department, saved as a graphics file on a disk. He starts by creating a space for it.

Steps

You can insert shapes, clip art, scanned pictures, and special text effects into your worksheet. You can use a graphic as a hyperlink to another file or as a way to start a macro. Search the keyword "text graphics" in Excel help to find "About using graphics in Microsoft Excel."

1. Select **rows 1** through **5**, click **Insert** on the menu bar, then click **Rows**
   Five blank rows appear above the header row. To insert a picture, you start with the Insert menu.

2. Click cell **A1**, click **Insert** on the menu bar, then point to **Picture**
   The Picture menu opens. See Figure M-7. This menu offers several options for inserting graphics. You will insert a picture that you already have in a file.

3. Click **From File**; in the Insert Picture dialog box, make sure the drive containing your Project Disk appears in the Look in box; then click **EX M-3**, if necessary, to select it
   A preview of the selected graphic displays on the right side of the Insert Picture dialog box. See Figure M-8.

4. Click **Insert**
   Excel inserts the graphic and opens the Picture toolbar.

5. Drag the lower-right corner up and to the left so the logo fits within rows 1–5
   See Figure M-9. To improve the look of the graphic, you'll add a border.

You can also use the Line Style button on the Drawing toolbar to add a border for a selected object.

6. With the graphic still selected, click the **Line Style button** ▤ on the Picture toolbar and click the **1½ pt** line style, then press **[Esc]** to deselect the graphic and close the Picture toolbar
   The Drawing toolbar closes and the graphic is displayed with a border.

7. Preview and print the worksheet, save the workbook, then close the workbook and exit Excel

FIGURE M-7: Picture menu

Inserts a ready-made piece of art

Click to insert a graphic saved in a file

Inserts an electronic image captured with a scanner or digital camera

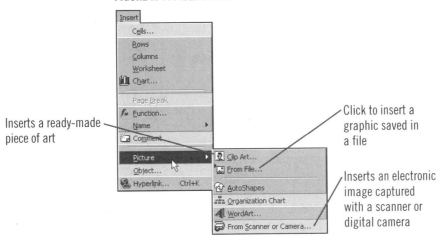

FIGURE M-8: Insert Picture dialog box

File to be inserted

Preview of selected graphic

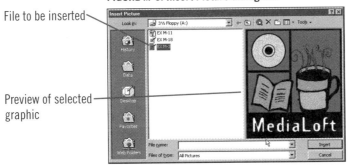

FIGURE M-9: Worksheet with inserted picture

Inserted graphic

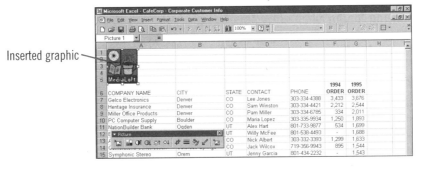

CLUES TO USE

Importing data from HTML files

You can easily import information from HTML files and Web pages into Excel by using drag and drop or the Insert Object command. To use drag and drop, open Internet Explorer, then open the HTML file or Web page that contains the data you want to import. Resize the Explorer window so it covers only half of the screen, then open the Excel file to which you want to import the data and resize the Excel window so it covers the other half of the screen. In the Explorer window, highlight the table or information you want to import, then drag it over to the Excel window. When the pointer changes to a white arrow with a plus sign, release the mouse button. The table will appear in your Excel document, ready for analysis.

You can use this method to update worksheets you have published on the Web. You can also open an HTML file from your intranet or a Web site in Excel and modify it, which is known as HTML round tripping. To use the Object command on the Insert menu to embed an HTML file in an Excel worksheet, click Insert on the menu bar, click Object, click the Create from File tab, click Browse, then navigate to the HTML file you want to Import and click OK. The page appears as an icon in your Excel document. Double-click the icon to view the file. To retrieve data from a particular Web page on a regular basis, use a Web query, which you'll learn about in the next unit.

Embedding a Worksheet

Microsoft Office programs work together to make it easy to copy an object (such as text, data, or a graphic) in a source program and then insert it into a document in a different program (the destination program). If you insert the object using a simple Paste command, however, you retain no connection to the source program. That's why it is often more useful to embed objects rather than simply paste them. **Embedding** allows you to edit an Excel workbook from within a different program using Excel commands and tools. You can embed a worksheet so the data is visible in the destination program or so it appears as an icon in the destination document. To access data embedded as an icon, you simply double-click the icon. ▰▰▰ Jim decides to update Maria on the project status. He uses a WordPad memo, which includes the projected sales revenue worksheet embedded as an icon. First, he starts the WordPad program and opens the memo.

Steps 1 2 3 4

1. Press **[Ctrl][Esc]** to open the Windows Start menu; point to **Programs**; point to **Accessories**; click **WordPad**; then, if necessary, maximize the WordPad window
   The WordPad program opens, with a blank document displayed in the WordPad window.

2. Click **File** on the WordPad menu bar, click **Open**, make sure the drive containing your Project Disk appears in the Look in box, click **EX M-4**, then click **Open**
   The memo opens.

3. Click **File** on the menu bar, click **Save As**, make sure the Save in box contains the drive containing your Project Disk, edit the File name box to read **CafeCorp - Sales Projection Memo**, then click **Save**
   You want to embed the worksheet below the last line of the document.

4. Press **[Ctrl][End]**, click **Insert** on the menu bar, then click **Object**
   After a moment, the Insert Object dialog box opens. You are embedding an existing file.

5. Click the **Create from File option button**

Trouble?
If the entire worksheet appears, not just the icon, you might not have checked the Display As Icon box.

6. Click **Browse**, make sure the drive containing your Project Disk appears in the Look in box, click **EX M-5**, click **Insert**; then in the Insert Object dialog box, select the **Display As Icon check box**
   The Insert Object dialog box now shows the file to be embedded. See Figure M-10. You are now ready to embed the object.

7. Click **OK**, then click outside the object to deselect it
   The memo now contains an embedded copy of the sales projection worksheet, displayed as an icon. See Figure M-11.

QuickTip
To edit an embedded object, double-click the object to open the source program, then make the desired changes. When you save and exit the source program, the embedded object reflects the changes.

8. Double-click the **Microsoft Excel Worksheet icon** 📊
   The Excel program starts and displays the embedded worksheet. See Figure M-12.

9. Click **File** on the Excel menu bar, click **Close & Return to CafeCorp - Sales Projection**, then save the memo

FIGURE M-10: Insert Object dialog box

Click to embed an existing worksheet

Your drive may differ

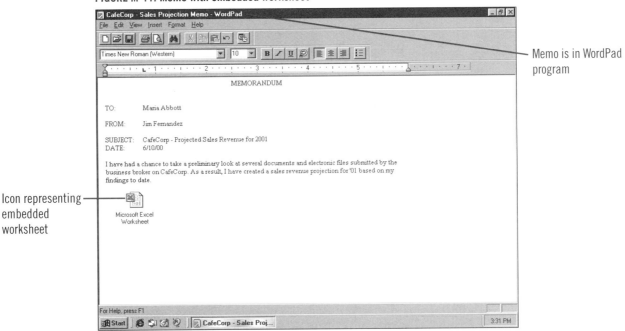

Click to display object as an icon

FIGURE M-11: Memo with embedded worksheet

Memo is in WordPad program

Icon representing embedded worksheet

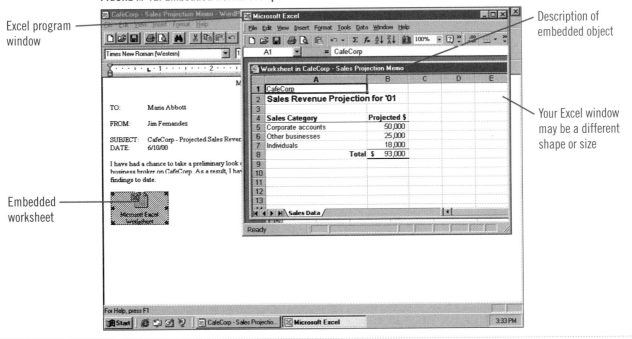

FIGURE M-12: Embedded worksheet opened in Excel

Excel program window

Description of embedded object

Your Excel window may be a different shape or size

Embedded worksheet

Linking a Worksheet to Another Program

You use **linking** when you want to insert a worksheet into another program and retain a connection with the original document as well as the original program. When you link a worksheet to another program, the link contains a pointer to the source document so that, when you double-click it, the source document opens for editing. Once you link a worksheet to another program, any changes you make to the original worksheet document are reflected in the linked object. Jim realizes he may be making some changes to the workbook he embedded in the memo to Maria. To ensure that these changes will be reflected in the memo, he decides to link a copy of the worksheet to the source document rather than simply embed it. First, he deletes the embedded worksheet icon; he then replaces it with a linked version of the same worksheet.

Steps

1. With the WordPad memo still displayed in your window, click the Microsoft Excel Worksheet icon 🔲 to select it if necessary, then press **[Delete]**
   The embedded worksheet is removed. Now, you will link the same worksheet to the memo.

2. Make sure the insertion point is below the last line of the memo, click **Insert** on the WordPad menu bar, click **Object**, then click the **Create from File option button** in the Insert Object dialog box

3. Click **Browse**, make sure the drive containing your Project Disk appears in the Look in box, click **EX M-5**, click **Insert**, then select the **Link check box**
   With the file containing the worksheet object selected, you are ready to link the worksheet object to the memo.

4. Click **OK**; drag the worksheet's **lower-right selection handle** to the right margin to enlarge the window, then click outside the worksheet to deselect it
   The memo now displays a linked copy of the sales projection worksheet. See Figure M-13. In the future, any changes made to the source file (EX M-5) will also be made to the linked copy in the WordPad memo. In the next step, you'll verify this by making a change to the source file and viewing its effect on the WordPad memo.

QuickTip
When you open an Excel workbook containing a linked object, a dialog box will appear asking if you want to update the links.

5. Click the **Save button** 🔲 on the WordPad Standard toolbar, click **File** on the WordPad menu bar, then click **Exit**; start Excel if necessary, then open the file **EX M-5**
   The worksheet appears in the Excel window. You will test the link by changing the sales projection for other businesses to $20,000.

6. Click cell **B6**, type **20,000**, then press **[Enter]**
   Now you will open the WordPad memo to verify that the same change was made automatically to the linked copy of the worksheet.

Trouble?
If you can't read the worksheet clearly, select it, then drag the lower-right selection handle to enlarge it. Continue with Step 8.

7. Press **[Ctrl][Esc]** to open the Windows Start menu, point to **Programs**, point to **Accessories**, click **WordPad**; click **File** on the WordPad menu bar, then click **1 CafeCorp - Sales Projection Memo**
   After a message about updating the link appears briefly, the memo re-displays on your screen with the new amount automatically inserted. See Figure M-14.

8. Click **File** on the WordPad menu bar, click **Exit**, click **No** if you are asked if you want to save changes; click **File** on the Excel menu bar, click **Exit**, then click **No** to close the workbook without saving changes

FIGURE M-13: Memo with linked worksheet

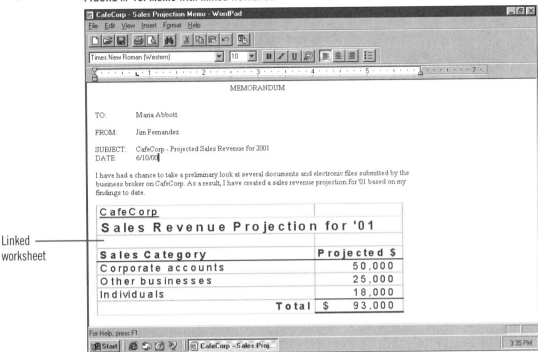

Linked
worksheet

FIGURE M-14: Viewing updated WordPad memo

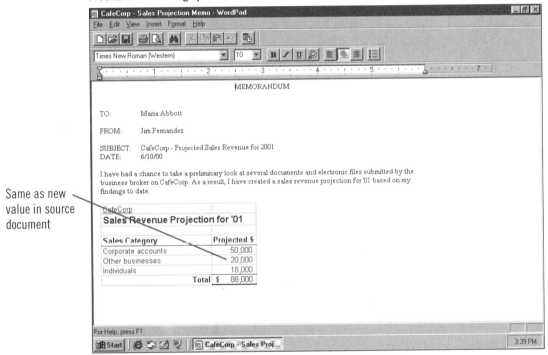

Same as new
value in source
document

Managing links

When you make changes to a source file, the link is updated automatically each time you open the destination document. You can manage linked objects further by choosing Links on the Edit menu. This opens the Links dialog box, which allows you to update a link or to change the source file of a link. You can also **break**, or delete, a link by selecting the linked object in the Links dialog box, then pressing [Delete].

Embedding an Excel Chart into a PowerPoint Slide

Microsoft PowerPoint is a presentation graphics program that you can use to create slide show presentations. For example, you can create a slide show to present a sales plan to management or to inform potential clients about a new service. PowerPoint slides can include a mix of text, data, and graphics. Adding an Excel chart to a slide helps to illustrate complicated data, which gives your presentation more visual appeal. ▰▰▰ Based on his analysis thus far, upper management asks Jim to brief the Marketing department on the possible acquisition of CafeCorp. Jim will make his presentation using PowerPoint slides. He decides to add an Excel chart to one of the presentation slides illustrating the 2001 sales projection data. He begins by starting PowerPoint.

Steps

Trouble?

If you don't see Microsoft PowerPoint on your Programs menu, look for something with a similar name somewhere on the Programs menu or the Start menu. If you still can't find it, Microsoft PowerPoint may not be installed on your computer. See your instructor or technical support person for assistance. If the Office Assistant opens when you start PowerPoint, click close and continue with Step 2.

1. Press **[Ctrl][Esc]** to open the Windows Start menu, point to **Programs**, then click **Microsoft PowerPoint**

The PowerPoint dialog box opens within the Microsoft PowerPoint window. This is where you indicate whether you want to create a new presentation or open a previously created one. You want to open a previously created presentation.

2. Click the **Open an existing presentation option button** if necessary; click **OK**; make sure the drive containing your Project Disk appears in the Look in box; click **EX M-6** if necessary; then click **Open**, then save the presentation as **Marketing Department Presentation**

The presentation appears in Normal view and contains three panes, as shown in Figure M-15. Notice that the outline of the presentation in the outline pane on the left shows the title and text included on each slide. You will add an Excel chart to slide 2, "2001 Sales Projections". To add the chart, you first need to select the slide, then display it in Slide view.

3. Click the **slide 2 icon** ⬚ in the outline pane

The slide appears in the slide pane on the right.

4. Click **Insert** on the PowerPoint menu bar, then click **Object**

The Insert Object dialog box opens. You want to insert an object (the Excel chart) that has already been saved in a file.

QuickTip

The Insert Chart button on the Standard toolbar allows you to create a new chart using a limited spreadsheet program called Microsoft Graph. Experienced Excel users will find it easier to create a chart in Excel.

5. Click the **Create from file option button**, click **Browse**, make sure the drive containing your Project Disk appears in the Look in box, click **EX M-7**, click **OK**; in the Insert Object dialog box click **OK** again, then press **[Esc]** to select the object

After a moment, a pie chart illustrating the 2001 sales projections appears in the slide. The chart is difficult to read in Normal view, so you'll switch to Slide Show view to display the slide on the full screen.

6. Click **View** on the PowerPoint menu bar, then click **Slide Show**

After a pause, the first slide appears on the screen. You need to display slide 2, which contains your graphic.

7. Press **[Enter]**

The finished sales projection slide appears, as shown in Figure M-16. The presentation for the Marketing department is complete.

QuickTip

The Excel worksheet you see in the PowerPoint slide is the one that was active when the workbook was last saved.

8. Press **[Esc]**, click the **Save button** 🖫 on the PowerPoint Standard toolbar, click **File** on the menu bar, then click **Exit**

FIGURE M-15: Presentation in Normal view

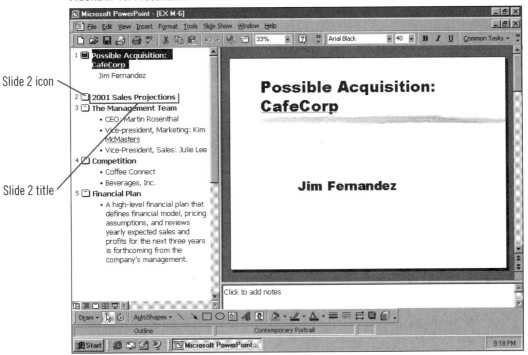

Slide 2 icon

Slide 2 title

FIGURE M-16: Completed Sales Projections slide in Slide Show view

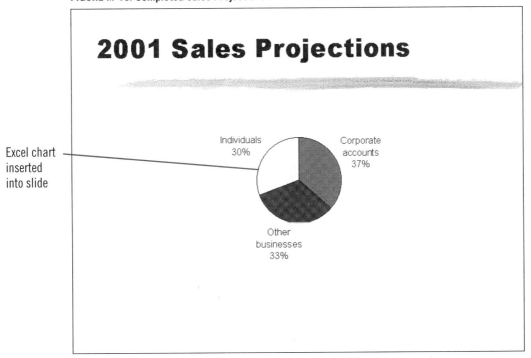

Excel chart inserted into slide

Converting a List to an Access Table

An Excel data list can be easily converted for use in Microsoft Access, a sophisticated database program. You need to make sure, however, that the list's column labels don't contain spaces between words or any of the following special characters: a period (.), an exclamation point (!), an accent mark (`), or brackets ([ ]) so that Access can interpret the labels correctly. Once converted to Access format, a data list is called a **table**. Upper management has just received a workbook containing salary information for the managers at CafeCorp. One of the managers asks Jim to convert the list to a Microsoft Access table so that it can be added to MediaLoft's database of compensation information for all employees. Jim begins by opening the list in Excel.

Steps 1 2 3 4

Trouble?

If you don't see the Convert to MS Access command on the Excel Data menu, you need to install the Microsoft AccessLinks Add-in program. See your instructor or technical support person for assistance.

1. Start Excel, open the workbook **EX M-8**, then save it as **CafeCorp Management**
2. With cell A1 selected, click **Data** on the menu bar, then click **Convert to MS Access**; in the Convert to Microsoft Access dialog box, make sure the **New database option button** is selected, then click **OK**

   The Microsoft Access window opens, followed by the First Import Spreadsheet Wizard dialog box. See Figure M-17. In the next step, you'll indicate that you want to use the column headings in the Excel list as the field names in the Access database.
3. Select the **First Row Contains Column Headings check box** if necessary, then click **Next**

   In the next Import Spreadsheet Wizard dialog box, you specify whether you want to store the Excel data in a new or an existing table. In this case, you want to store it in a new table.
4. Make sure the **In a New Table option button** is selected, then click **Next**

   The next Import Spreadsheet Wizard dialog box opens. This is where you specify information about the fields (the Excel columns) you are converting. Notice that the column headings from the Excel list are used as the field names. You can also indicate which columns from the Excel list you do not want to import. In this case, you do not want to import the Annual Salary column.
5. Scroll right until the **Annual Salary column** is in view; click anywhere in the column to select it, then select the **Do not import field (Skip) check box** under Field Options

   Your completed Import Spreadsheet Wizard dialog box should match Figure M-18.
6. Click **Next**

   The next Import Spreadsheet Wizard dialog box opens. This is where you specify the table's primary key. A **primary key** is the field that contains unique information for each record (or row) of information. Specifying a primary key allows you to retrieve data more quickly in the future. In this case, you use the Social Security field as the primary key because the Social Security number for each person in the list is unique.

QuickTip

If Access chooses your primary key, it will select a field with unique data or create a new field that assigns a unique number.

7. Click the **Choose my own primary key option button**; make sure Social Security appears in the list box next to the selected option button; click **Next**; in the next Import Spreadsheet Wizard dialog box, click **Finish**; click **OK**; then click the **Maximize button** on the Microsoft Access window

   The icon and name representing the new Access table are shown in the new database. See Figure M-19. Next, you'll open the table to make sure it was imported correctly.
8. Make sure **Compensation** is selected, then click **Open**

   The data from the Excel workbook is displayed in the new Access table. When you click the Save button on the Access toolbar, Access automatically saves the database to the same location as the original Excel workbook.
9. Click the **Save button** on the Access toolbar, click **File** on the Access menu bar, then click **Exit**; in the Excel window, save the workbook, then exit Excel

FIGURE M-17: First Import Spreadsheet Wizard dialog box

Column labels will become field names

Preview of Access table

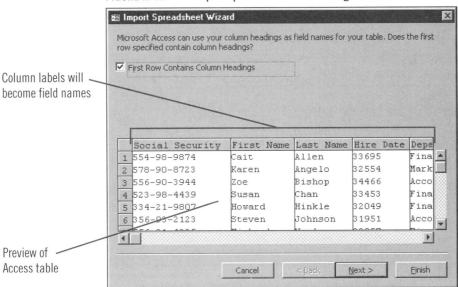

FIGURE M-18: Completed Input Spreadsheet Wizard dialog box

Click to select

Field names

Horizontal scroll bar

Annual Salary column

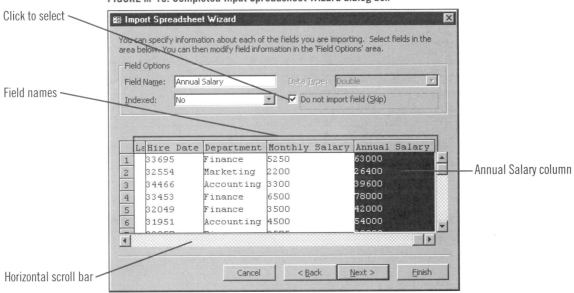

FIGURE M-19: Maximized Microsoft Access window

Database name taken from Excel workbook name

Icon indicates new table

New table name taken from sheet name in Excel workbook

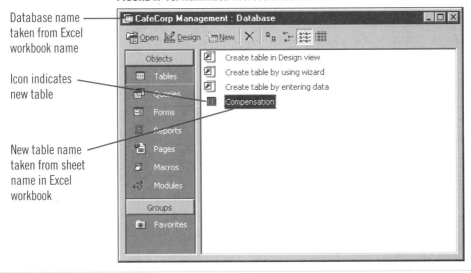

Practice

► Concepts Review

Label each element of the Excel screen shown in Figure M-20.

FIGURE M-20

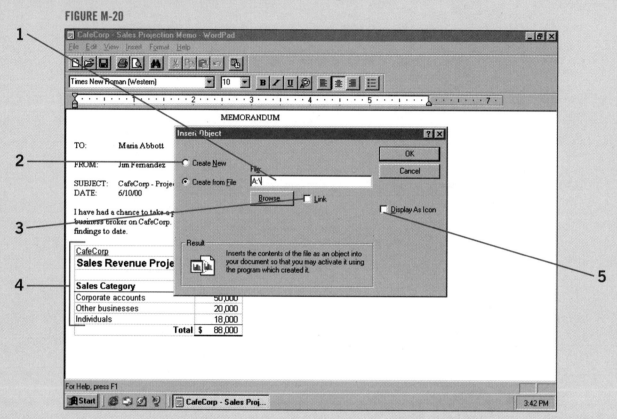

Match each term with the statement that describes it.

6. **Source document**
7. **Linking**
8. **Destination document**
9. **Embedding**
10. **Presentation program**
11. **Table**

a. Used to create slide shows
b. Copies and retains a connection with the source program and source document
c. Document receiving the object to be embedded or linked
d. An Excel list converted to Access format
e. Copies and retains a connection with the source program
f. File from which the object to be embedded or linked originates

Select the best answer from the list of choices.

12. An ASCII file
- **a.** Contains formatting but no text.
- **b.** Contains an unformatted worksheet.
- **c.** Contains text but no formatting.
- **d.** Contains a PowerPoint presentation.

13. An object consists of
- **a.** Text only.
- **b.** Text, a worksheet, or any other type of data.
- **c.** A worksheet only.
- **d.** Database data only.

14. Which of the following is true about converting an Excel list to an Access table?
- **a.** The column labels cannot contain spaces.
- **b.** You must convert all the columns in the list to an Access table.
- **c.** The column headings cannot be used as the table's field names.
- **d.** All of the above.

15. To view a worksheet that has been embedded as an icon in a WordPad document, you need to
- **a.** Click View, then click Worksheet.
- **b.** Drag the icon.
- **c.** Click File, then click Open.
- **d.** Double-click the worksheet icon.

16. To diplay numbers with a dollar sign you can use the following format:
- **a.** Accounting
- **b.** Currency
- **c.** Number
- **d.** a and b

▶ **Skills Review**

1. Import a text file.
- **a.** Start Excel, then open the tab-delimited text file EX M-9.
- **b.** Save the file as an Excel workbook with the name "Sunshine Temporary - Income Summary".
- **c.** Widen the columns so that all the data is visible.
- **d.** Center the column labels and apply bold formatting.
- **e.** Add your name to the worksheet footer, preview and print your work, then save and close the workbook and close Excel.
- **f.** At the Windows desktop, drag the text file EX M-9 over the Excel program icon. When the file opens, save it as an Excel file named "Sunshine Temporary - Income Summary 2", then close the file.
- **g.** Use the Object command on the Insert menu to insert the text file EX M-9 into a blank worksheet as an icon. Double-click the icon to open the file in Notepad, then copy the data into the worksheet below the icon.
- **h.** Save the file as "Sunshine Temporary - Income Summary 3", then close the file.

2. Import a database table.

a. In Excel, open the dBase file EX M-10.

b. Save the file as an Excel workbook with the name "Sunshine Temporary - Company Budget".

c. Rename the sheet tab "Company Budget".

d. Change the column labels so they read as follows: BUDGET CATEGORY, BUDGET ITEM, MONTH, and AMOUNT BUDGETED.

e. Use AutoSum to calculate a total in cell D26, then add a top and bottom border to the cell.

f. Format range D2:D26 using the Accounting style with no decimal places.

g. Add bold formatting to the column labels, then wrap the text on two lines.

h. Center the column labels and manually adjust the column widths as necessary.

i. Save your work.

3. Embed a graphic file in a worksheet.

a. Add four rows above row 1 to create space for the graphic file.

b. Insert the picture file EX M-11 in the space.

c. Make the graphic smaller so it doesn't cover up any column headings.

d. Open the Drawing toolbar, if necessary.

e. Use the Line style button to add a 1-point border around the graphic.

f. Adjust the size and position as necessary, using [Ctrl] with the arrow keys to move it in small increments.

g. Press [Esc] to deselect the graphic, then close the Drawing toolbar, if necessary.

h. Add your name to the worksheet footer, preview and print the worksheet, then save your work.

4. Embed a worksheet in another program.

a. In cell A33, type "For details on Green Hills salaries, click this icon:".

b. In cell D33, embed the worksheet object EX M-12 and display it as an icon.

c. Double-click the icon to verify that the worksheet opens, then close it.

d. Preview, then print the Sunshine Temporary - Company Budget worksheet.

e. Save your work.

5. Link a worksheet.

a. Delete the embedded object icon.

b. Link the spreadsheet object EX M-12 to cell D33, displaying the worksheet, not an icon.

c. Save, then close the Sunshine Temporary - Company Budget worksheet.

d. Open the EX M-12 workbook, change the Manager salary to 5,000, correct the first and last name order of employees Smith and Hargrove, then open the Sunshine Temporary - Company Budget worksheet; click Yes when you are asked if you want to update links, then verify that the manager salary has changed to 5,000 and that the name order is correct in the linked workbook.

e. Preview, then print the worksheet with the linked object on one page.

f. Close both workbooks without saving changes, then exit Excel.

6. Paste an Excel chart into a PowerPoint slide.

a. Open the Microsoft PowerPoint program.

b. Open the PowerPoint presentation file EX M-13.

c. Save the presentation as "Monthly Budget Meeting".

d. Display Slide 2, January Expenditures.

e. Embed the Excel file EX M-14, then drag the chart until it is centered in the blank area of the slide.

f. View the slide with the chart in Slide Show view.

g. Press [Esc] to return to Normal view, save the file, and exit PowerPoint.

7. Converting an Excel list to an Access database.

a. Start Excel, open the workbook EX M-15, then save it as Budget List.

b. Convert the worksheet into a new Access database table, using the first row as column headings. Do not import the month column, and let Access add the primary key.

c. Open the January Budget table in the Budget List in Access and drag the column borders as necessary to fully display the field names.

d. Save the database file and exit Access.

e. In the Excel window, add your name to the worksheet footer, print the worksheet (along with the conversion notice), then save the workbook and exit Excel.

▶ Independent Challenges

1. You are opening a new store, called Bridge Blades, that rents in-line skates. The store is located right outside Golden Gate Park in San Francisco, California. Recently, you heard that Tim Botano, the owner of Gateway In-line, a similar store, is planning to retire. You ask him for a list of his suppliers, and he agrees to sell it to you for a nominal fee. Because you have a personal computer (PC) running Excel, you ask him if he can put the list on a disk. The next day, you stop by his store and he sells you the text file containing the supplier information. You need to import this file and convert it to a workbook so that you can manipulate it in Excel. Then you will convert the file to an Access table, so that you can share it with your partner, who has Access, but not Excel, on her PC.

To complete this independent challenge:

a. Open the file titled EX M-16 (a text file). (*Hint*: The data type of the original file is tab delimited.)

b. Save the file as an Excel workbook titled "In-line Skate Supplier List".

c. Adjust the column labels and widths so that all the data is visible. Add any formatting you feel is appropriate.

d. Sort the list in ascending order, first by item purchased, then by supplier.

e. Add your name to the worksheet footer, preview and print your work on a single page, then save your work.

f. Save the workbook with the new name "Supplier List Converted to Access", then convert the worksheet to an Access table in a new database. Use the column labels as the field names, store the data in a new table, import all columns in the list, then let Access add the primary key.

g. Open the Access table and autofit the columns, then save the table and exit Access.

h. In the Excel window, save the open worksheet, print it (along with the conversion notice) on one page, then close the workbook.

2. You are the newly hired manager at Burger Pit, the local burger joint in your small town. A past employee, Roberta Carlson, has filed a grievance that she was underpaid in January 1996. The files containing the payroll information for early 1996 are in Lotus 1-2-3 (WK1) format. In June 1996, the owner switched the business records to Microsoft Excel. You have located the files containing the payroll information you need. You import the Lotus 1-2-3 file, convert it to an Excel workbook, and correct the formatting in order to verify the values and formulas, especially those for Roberta Carlson, to determine if she was indeed underpaid.

To complete this independent challenge:

a. Open the Lotus 1-2-3 file titled EX M-17.

b. Save the file as an Excel workbook titled "Burger Pit Payroll Info".

c. Click Tools on the menu bar, click Options, click the View tab, then select the Gridlines check box to turn on the worksheet gridlines and click OK.

d. Check all values and formulas for discrepancies. If you find any, open the Drawing toolbar and note the discrepancy: Click AutoShape on the Drawing toolbar, point to callouts, choose one of the callout AutoShapes to draw a line to the discrepancy, then describe the discrepancy by typing in the callout box. Do *not* change any spreadsheet formulas or values.

e. Correct the formatting. Delete any row(s) containing dashes or equal signs and add appropriate borders. Format all dollar values using the Number style with two decimal places. Add or delete any other formatting you feel is appropriate.

f. Add your name to the worksheet footer, preview and then print your work on a single page.

g. Save the worksheet, then close the workbook.

3. You are a loan officer for a local bank. You have been asked to give a talk about the banking industry to a local high school economics class. As part of your talk, you decide to give a presentation explaining the most popular consumer loans. To illustrate your comments, you will add an Excel chart to one of your slides showing the most popular loan types and the number of applications received yearly for each.

To complete this independent challenge:

a. Create a worksheet containing popular loan types, then save it as "Most Popular Consumer Loans". Include the loans and the corresponding number of applications shown in Table M-2.

b. Create a pie chart from the loan data on a new sheet. Add an appropriate title to your chart.

c. Save the workbook, print the chart, then (with the chart sheet the active sheet) close the workbook.

d. Start PowerPoint, click the Blank presentation option button, then click OK.

e. In the New Slide dialog box, click the layout on the far right in the bottom row (Blank), then click OK.

f. Make sure the slide is displayed in Normal view, then insert the Excel chart into the blank slide.

g. Double-click the chart on slide 1 and observe how Excel tools appear in the toolbar, and how the Chart toolbar appears. Use the Chart toolbar to change the title to 28 point bold and the legend to 22-point type.

TABLE M-2

loan type	number of applications
Fixed home loans	1456
New-car loans	5400
Used-car loans	3452
Adjustable home loans	760
Boat loans	250

h. Click outside the chart to return to PowerPoint.

i. View the slide in Slide Show view, then press [Esc] to end the show.

j. Click File on the PowerPoint menu bar, click Save As, then save the presentation as "Banking Industry Presentation".

k. Close the presentation, then exit PowerPoint and Excel.

4. The MediaLoft Product department wants to create a handout listing out-of-stock products that it can give to customers who ask for it. You know that this information exists on the MediaLoft intranet site, but you would like to reformat it, and Mike MacDowell, the MediaLoft Web manager, has the original .xls and .htm files for the intranet site and he is out of town. You decide to e-mail Mike to obtain the files when he returns. In the meantime, you download the data into an Excel worksheet, reformat it, and print it. Several days later, Mike e-mails you the HTML file, which you then decide to embed in a workbook.

To complete this independent challenge:

a. Open a blank Excel workbook and save it as "Out of Stock".

b. Use Internet Explorer to connect to the Internet, and go to the MediaLoft intranet site at http://www.course.com/Illustrated/MediaLoft. Click the Products link, then click the Out of Stock items link.

c. Select the table of out-of-stock items, then use drag and drop to place the information in the Excel worksheet starting in cell A1.

d. Reformat the sheet as follows:

   • Change the blue cells to a light green. (*Hint*: Remember that you can use the F4 function key to repeat your previous action.)
   • Use the Alignment tab in the Format Cells dialog box to unwrap the text within cells.
   • Sort the café items by the "Expected" date. (*Hint*: In the Sort dialog box, sort on column C.)
   • Delete any blank columns if necessary.
   • Add any other formatting you think would make the handout attractive.

e. Place your name in the workbook footer, save your changes, then print the workbook. Republish it in HTML format as "Out of Stock - Web". You have now received the HTML file from Mike MacDowell. Create a new workbook called Out of Stock File, and use the Insert Object command to insert an icon representing the file "Out of Stock - Web".

f. Save the file, then double-click the icon to verify that the HTML file appears.

g. Close Internet Explorer, then close the Excel file and exit Excel.

▶ Visual Workshop

Create the worksheet shown in Figure M-21. Insert the graphic file EX M-18, resizing it as necessary. (*Hint*: Drag the resize handles as necessary to enlarge the art to the proper size.) Save the workbook as "Atlantic Price List". Preview, add your name to the worksheet footer, then print the worksheet.

FIGURE M-21

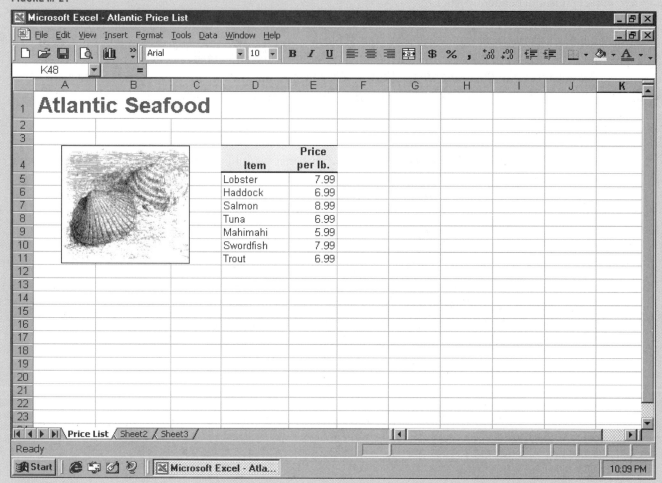

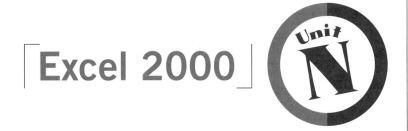

Sharing

Excel Files and Incorporating Web Information

Objectives

► Share Excel Files
► Set up a shared workbook
► Track changes in a shared workbook
► Apply and remove passwords
► Create an interactive worksheet for an intranet or the Web
► Create an interactive PivotTable for an intranet or the Web
► Create hyperlinks between Excel files and the Web
► Run queries to retrieve data on the Web

With the recent growth of networks, company intranets, and the World Wide Web, people are increasingly sharing electronic spreadsheet files with others for review, revision, and feedback. They are also incorporating information from intranets and the World Wide Web into their worksheets. Jim Fernandez has some MediaLoft corporate information he wants to share with corporate office employees and store managers. He also wants to track information on MediaLoft's competitors.

Excel 2000

Sharing Excel Files

Microsoft Excel provides many different ways to share spreadsheets electronically with people in your office, company, or anywhere on the World Wide Web. Users can not only retrieve and review your workbooks and worksheets, but they can modify them electronically and return their revisions to you for incorporation with others' changes. When you share workbooks, you also have to consider how you will protect information that you don't want everyone to see. You can post workbooks, worksheets, or other parts of workbooks for users to interact with on a company intranet or on the World Wide Web. You can also use Excel workbooks to run queries to retrieve data from the Web. Jim considers the best way to share his Excel workbooks with corporate employees and store managers. He also thinks about how to get Web data for use in his workbooks. He considers the following issues:

Details

Allowing others to use a workbook

When you pass on Excel files to others, you could just have them write their comments on a printed copy. But it's easier to set up your workbook so that several users can simultaneously open the workbook from a network server and modify it. Then you can view each user's name and the date the change was made. Jim wants to get feedback on selected store sales and customer information from MediaLoft corporate staff and store managers.

Controlling access to workbooks on a server

When you set up a workbook on a network server, you may want to control who can open and make changes to it. You can do this easily with Excel passwords. Jim assigns a password to his workbook and gives it to the corporate staff and store managers, so only they will be able to open it and make changes.

Distributing workbooks to others

There are several ways of making workbook information available to others. You can send it to recipients simultaneously as an e-mail attachment or as the body of an e-mail message; you can **route** it, or send it sequentially to each user, who then forwards it on to the next user using a **routing slip**, or list of recipients. You can also save the file in HTML format and post it on a company intranet server or on the Web, where people can view it with their Web browsers. Jim decides to make an Excel workbook available to others by putting it on a central company server.

Publishing a worksheet for use on an intranet or the World Wide Web

When you save a workbook in HTML format, you can save the entire workbook or just part of it—a worksheet, a chart, a filtered list, a cell range, or a print area. When you save only part of a workbook, you can specify that you want to make that particular part, or object, **interactive**, meaning that users can make changes to it when they view it in their browsers. They do not have to have the Excel program on their machines. See Figure N-1. The changes remain in effect until users close their browsers. Jim decides to publish part of a worksheet about MediaLoft café pastry sales.

Interactive PivotTables

You can save a PivotTable in HTML format so people can only view it, but the data is much more useful if people can interact with it from their browsers, just as they would in Excel. To make an Excel PivotTable interactive, you need to save it as a PivotTable list. Jim wants corporate staff to explore some sales data using their browsers just as he would with Excel.

Creating hyperlinks to the Web

You can make Web information available to users by creating hyperlinks to any site on the Web. Jim decides to include a hyperlink to a competitor's Web site.

Using an Excel query to retrieve data from the Web

By using Microsoft Query from Excel, you can get data from the Web that you can bring into your workbooks, and then organize and manipulate it with Excel spreadsheet and graphics tools. See Figure N-2. Jim uses a query to get stock information about one of MediaLoft's competitors.

FIGURE N-1: Interactive worksheet in Web browser

Toolbar allows users to manipulate worksheet data and format in browser

Adding a worksheet total in Internet Explorer

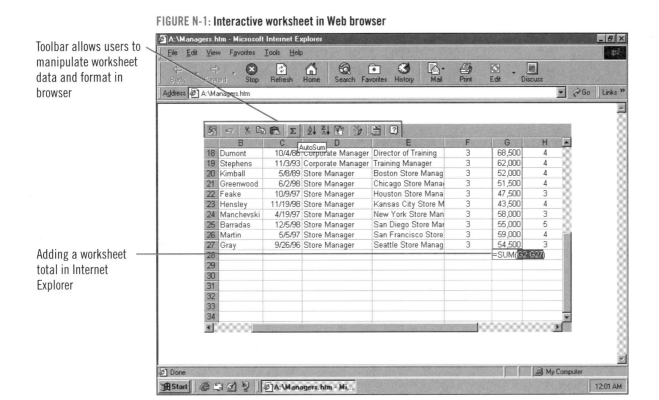

FIGURE N-2: Retrieving data from the World Wide Web using a Web query

Excel workbook contains stock data imported from the World Wide Web

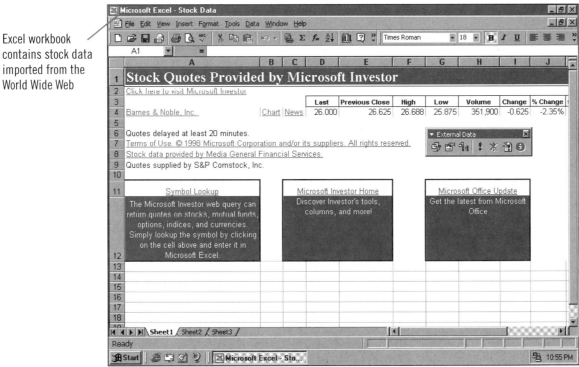

Setting Up a Shared Workbook

You can make an Excel file a **shared workbook** so that several users can open and modify it at the same time. This is very useful for workbooks that you want others to review on a network server. The workbook is equally accessible to all users who have access to that location on the network. When you share a workbook, you can have Excel keep a list of all changes to the workbook, called a **change history**, that you can view and print at any time. Users must have Excel 97 or later to modify the workbook. ◀▬▬ Jim makes his workbook containing customer and sales data a shared workbook. He will later put it on a network server and ask for feedback from selected corporate staff and store managers before using the information in a presentation at the next corporate staff meeting.

Steps

1. **Open the workbook titled EX N-1, then save it as Sales Info**
   The workbook with the sales information opens. It contains three worksheets. The first is the chart of café pastry sales for the first quarter, the second contains the worksheet and map of pastry sales by state, and the third contains a listing of sales for selected stores and sales representatives for the last four quarters.

2. **Click Tools on the menu bar, then click Share Workbook**
   The Share Workbook dialog box opens, similar to Figure N-3.

3. **If necessary, click the Editing tab**
   The lower part of the dialog box lists the names of people who are currently using the workbook. You are the only user, so your name (or the name of the person entered as the machine user) appears, along with the date and time.

4. **Click to select the check box next to Allow changes by more than one user at the same time, then click OK**
   A dialog box appears, asking if you want to save the workbook. This will resave it as a shared workbook.

5. **Click OK**
   Excel saves the file as a shared workbook. The toolbar now reads Sales Info [Shared]. See Figure N-4. This version replaces the unshared version.

FIGURE N-3: Share Workbook dialog box

Select this option to allow more than one person to use the workbook at the same time

If the workbook is already shared, people currently using the workbook are listed here

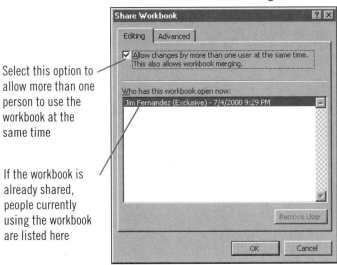

FIGURE N-4: Shared workbook

Title bar indicates workbook is shared

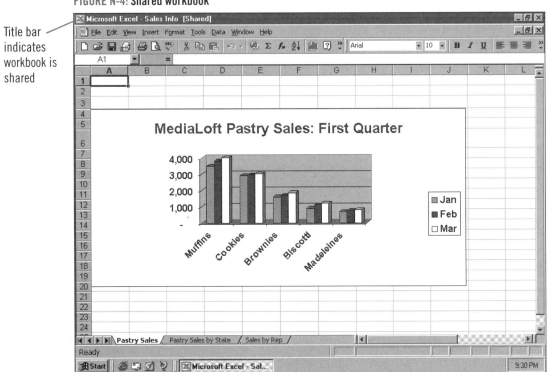

Tracking Changes in a Shared Workbook

When you share workbooks, it is often helpful to **track** modifications, or identify who made which changes. If you disagree with any of the changes, you can reject them. When the Excel change tracking feature is activated, changes are highlighted in a different color for each user. Each change is identified with the user name and date. In addition to highlighting changes, Excel keeps track of all changes in a **change history**, a list of all changes that you can place on a separate worksheet so you can review them all at once. ✍ Jim sets up the shared Sales Info workbook so that all future changes will be tracked. He then opens another workbook that has been on the server and reviews the changes and the change history.

Steps 1234

1. **Click Tools on the menu bar, point to Track Changes, click Highlight Changes**
   The Highlight Changes dialog box opens, allowing you to turn on change tracking, to specify which changes to highlight, and to display changes on the screen or save the change history in a separate worksheet.

2. **Click to select Track changes while editing, remove check marks from all other boxes except for Highlight changes on screen, compare your screen to Figure N-5, click OK, then click OK in the dialog box that informs you that you have yet to make changes**
   To track all changes, you can leave the When, Who, and Where check boxes blank.

3. **Click the Pastry Sales by State tab, then change the sales figure for Texas to 133,000**
   A border with a small triangle in the upper-left corner appears around the figure you changed.

4. **After you enter the change, move the mouse pointer over the cell you just changed, but do not click**
   A screen tip appears with your name, the date, the time, and a phrase describing the change. See Figure N-6. Cells that other users change will appear in different colors.

5. **Save and close the workbook**
   Alice Wegman and Maria Abbott have made changes to a version of this workbook.

6. **Open the workbook EX N-2 and save it as Sales Info Edits**

7. **Click Tools on the menu bar, point to Track Changes, click Highlight Changes, in the Highlight Changes dialog box click the When check box to deselect it, click to select List changes on a new sheet, then click OK**
   The History tab appears, as shown in Figure N-7, with a record of each change in the form of a filtered list. Notice that you could, for example, click the Who list arrow in row 1 and show a list of Maria Abbott's changes only.

8. **Examine the three sheets, holding the pointer over each change, then click the History sheet tab**

9. **Put your name in the History sheet footer, preview and print the History sheet on one page, then save the workbook, which closes the History worksheet, and close the workbook**
   The change history prints, showing who has made which changes to the workbook.

Click here so that all changes will be visible on the worksheet

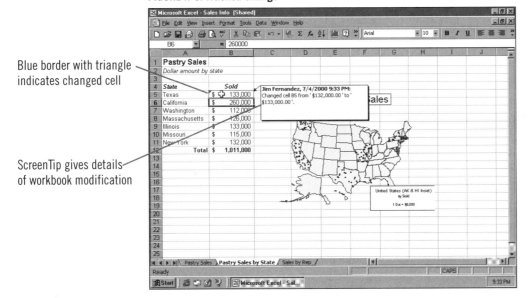

FIGURE N-6: **Tracked change**

Blue border with triangle indicates changed cell

ScreenTip gives details of workbook modification

FIGURE N-7: **History sheet tab with change history**

Details of each change listed here

Two users made changes to this worksheet

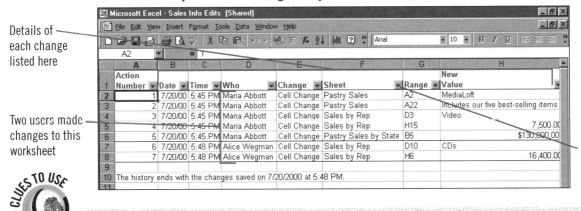

Click any list arrow to filter changes

Merging workbooks

Instead of putting the shared workbook on a server, you may want to distribute copies to your reviewers, perhaps via e-mail. Once everyone has entered their changes, you can merge the changed copies into one workbook that will contain all the changes. Each copy you distribute must be designated as shared, and the Change History feature must be activated. Once you get the changed copies back, open your master copy of the workbook, click Tools on the menu bar, click Merge Workbooks, then save when prompted. The Select Files to Merge Into Current Workbook dialog box opens. Click the name of the workbook you want to merge, then click OK. Repeat for all shared workbooks. It's important that you specify that each copy of the shared workbook keep a change history from the date you copy them to the merge date. In the Advanced tab in the Share Workbooks dialog box, set Keep change history for a large number, such as 1,000 days.

Excel 2000

Excel 2000

Applying and Removing Passwords

When you place a shared workbook on a server, you may want to use a password so that only certain people will be able to open it or make changes to it. If you do assign a password, it's very important that you write it down and keep it in a secure place where you can access it, in case you forget it. *If you lose your password, you will not be able to open or change the workbook.* Remember also that all passwords are case sensitive, so you must type them exactly as you want users to type them, with the same spacing and upper- and lowercase letters. For example, if your password to open a workbook is Stardot, and a user enters stardot, star dot, or StarDot, the workbook will not open. ◢━━ Jim wants to put the Sales Info 2 workbook on a server, so he decides to save a copy with two passwords: one that users will need to open it, and another to make changes to it.

Steps

1. Open the workbook **EX N-1**, click **File** on the menu bar, then click **Save As**

2. In the Save As dialog box, click **Tools**, then click **General Options**
   The Save Options dialog box opens, with two password boxes: one to open the workbook, and one to allow changes to the workbook, similar to Figure N-8.

3. In the Password to open box, type **Saturn**
   Be sure to type the capital S and the rest of the letters lowercase. This is the password users will have to type to open the workbook. Whenever you type passwords, they appear as asterisks (***) so that no one nearby will be able to see them.

4. Press **[Tab]**, then in the Password to modify box type **Atlas**, compare your screen to Figure N-8, then click **OK**
   This is the password users will have to type to make changes to the workbook. A dialog box asks you to verify the password by re-entering it.

5. In the first Confirm Password dialog box, type **Saturn**, then click **OK**; in the second Confirm Password dialog box, type **Atlas**, click **OK**, edit the workbook name so it reads **Sales Info PW**, then click **Save** and close the workbook

6. Reopen the workbook **Sales Info PW**, enter the password **Saturn** when prompted in order to open the workbook as shown in Figure N-9, click **OK**, then type **Atlas** to obtain write access and click **OK**

7. In the Pastry Sales by State worksheet, click cell A-14 and enter **One-year totals**
   You have confirmed that you can make changes to the workbook.

8. Save and close the workbook

FIGURE N-8: Save options dialog box

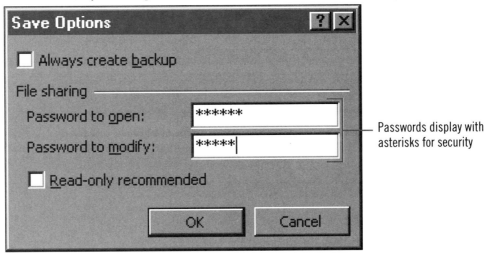

Passwords display with asterisks for security

FIGURE N-9: Password entry prompt

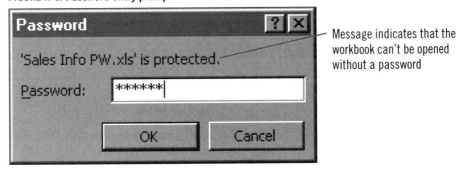

Message indicates that the workbook can't be opened without a password

Removing passwords

You must know a workbook's password in order to change or delete it. Open the workbook, click File on the menu bar, then click Save As. In the Save As dialog box, click Tools, then click General Options. Double-click the symbols for the existing passwords in the Password to open or Password to modify boxes, and press [Delete]. Change the filename if you wish, then click Save.

Creating an Interactive Worksheet for an Intranet or the Web

You can save an entire workbook in HTML format for users to view. But you can also save part of a workbook—a worksheet, chart, or PivotTable—in HTML format and make it interactive. You cannot save an entire workbook in interactive format. To work with interactive data, users must have installed Internet Explorer version 4.01 or later as well as the Office Web Components. Anyone with Office 2000 will have these. Users do not need to have Excel. ▰ Jim decides to save the Pastry Sales by State sheet as an interactive Web page.

Steps 1 2 3 4

QuickTip

Internet Explorer 4.01 or later must be your default browser or you will not be able to use interactive features.

1. Open **EX N-1**, save it as **Sales Info 2**, then click the **Pastry Sales by State sheet**

2. Click **File** on the menu bar, click **Save as Web Page**, then click **Publish**
   The Publish as Web Page dialog box opens.

3. Click the **Choose list arrow** and choose **Items on Pastry Sales by State**, then under Viewing options click to select **Add interactivity with**

4. In the Publish as section, click **Change** and type **Pastry Sales by State**, click **OK**, click **Browse**, make sure your project disk name appears as the Save in location, type the filename **Pastry Sales Web**, then click **OK**

QuickTip

See the Microsoft Excel Help topic "Limitations of putting interactive data on a Web page" for more information about which features might not work or might appear differently on your Web page.

5. If necessary, click to select **Open published Web page in browser** at the bottom of the dialog box, click **Publish**, then maximize your browser window
   After a pause, Internet Explorer opens the HTML version of your data. See Figure N-10. Notice that only the worksheet appears, not the map.

6. Change the Sold number for Washington in cell B7 to **115,000**, press **Enter**, and observe the total update automatically to 1,013,000
   You know the interactive feature is working. Changes you make to the HTML file in your browser remain in effect until you close your browser.

7. Select the range **A5:B11**, click the **Sort Ascending button** ↓ on the toolbar above the worksheet, then click **State**
   The data is sorted in a new order according to state name.

8. Select the range **A4:B11**, click the **AutoFilter button** , click the **State list arrow**, click the **Total check mark** to remove it, click **OK**, then click the **Property Toolbox button**
   The total is no longer visible on the worksheet. The Spreadsheet Property Toolbox opens and should look similar to that shown in Figure N-11.

9. Click the **Fill Color list arrow** after Cell format, click the **light green color** in the bottom row, then click the Spreadsheet **Property Toolbox close button** ✕ and click outside the selected range
   The range fills with the light green color.

10. Enter your name in any worksheet cell, click **File** on the menu bar, click **Print**, click **OK**, then close your browser

FIGURE N-10: Pastry Sales worksheet as Web page in Internet Explorer

Spreadsheet toolbar
shows that work-
sheet is interactive
and allows users to
manipulate data

Map does
not appear
in Web
version

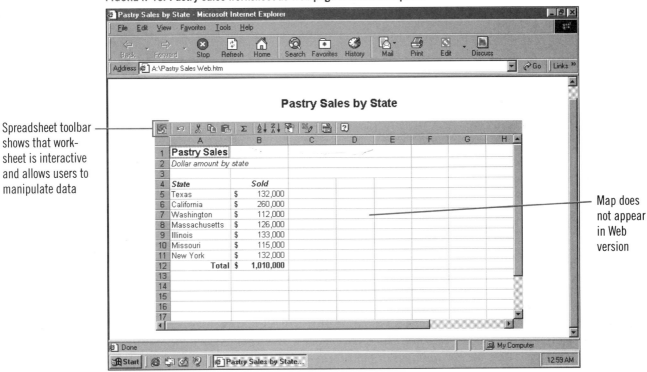

FIGURE N-11: Spreadsheet Property Toolbox

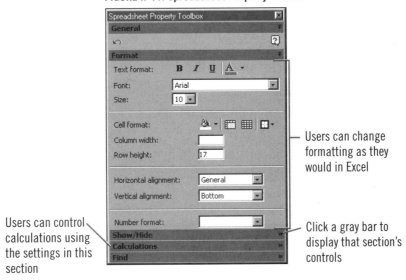

Users can change
formatting as they
would in Excel

Users can control
calculations using
the settings in this
section

Click a gray bar to
display that section's
controls

Managing HTML files on an intranet or Web site

Once you save your Excel file or item in HTML format, determine the best location for saving your file: an HTTP site, an FTP (File Transfer Protocol) site, or a network server. Check with your system administrator or Internet Service Provider (ISP) to see how your files should be organized—whether they should all be in one folder, whether graphics and other supporting files should be in a separate folder, and the like.

Excel 2000

Creating an Interactive PivotTable for an Intranet or the Web

Not only can you create interactive worksheets that users can modify in their Web browsers, but you can also create interactive PivotTables that users can analyze by dragging fields to get different views of the data. An interactive PivotTable for the Web is called a **PivotTable list**. Users cannot enter new values to the list, but they can filter and sort data, add calculations, and rearrange data to get a different perspective on the information. As the PivotTable list creator, you have complete control over what information is included from the source data, which could be an Excel worksheet, a PivotTable, or external data (for example, an Access database). You can include only selected columns of information if you wish. You can also include charts with your PivotTable data. As with spreadsheets you publish in HTML format, users view PivotTable lists in their browsers, and changes they make to them are retained for only that browser session. The HTML file remains in its original form. ✒️ Jim has compiled some sales information about sales representatives at selected stores for the last four quarters. He saves it as a PivotTable list so he and selected corporate staff and store managers can review it using their Web browsers.

Steps 1234

QuickTip
As with saving spreadsheets in interactive format, you need Office Web Tools and Internet Explorer 4.01 or later to create and use PivotTable lists.

1. **In the Sales Info 2 workbook, click the Sales by Rep tab**
   Jim will create the PivotTable list directly from the data rather then creating an Excel PivotTable first.

2. **Click File on the menu bar, click Save as Web Page, then click Publish**

3. **Click the Choose list arrow, click Items on Sales by Rep, then in the Choose list make sure Sheet All contents of Sales by Rep is selected**
   This will select all the items on the selected PivotTable sheet.

4. **Under Viewing options, click Add interactivity with, click the Add interactivity with list arrow, and click PivotTable functionality**
   PivotTable functionality will give users the option to move list items around on the PivotTable list as they would move data items on a PivotTable in Excel.

5. **Click Browse, type Sales Info PT List, make sure your Project Disk is selected, click OK, make sure Open published web page in browser is checked, and compare your screen to Figure N-12**

QuickTip
To retain the PivotTable in its original state, click the Address box containing the URL and press [Return]

6. **Click Publish, then maximize the Internet Explorer window if necessary**
   The new PivotTable list opens in Internet Explorer. Its layout looks similar to a PivotTable report in Excel, with row and column fields and field drop-down arrows. As with an Excel PivotTable, you can change the layout to view the data in different ways. In this case, however, there is no PivotTable toolbar; you simply drag the field headings to the desired drop areas.

7. **Drag the Store field to the Row area, then drag the Department field to the Column area**
   The layout of the PivotTable list changes, and you now see the data rearranged by region, department, and store. See Figure N-13.

8. **Click File on the menu bar, click Print, then close your browser**

FIGURE N-12: Publish as Web Page dialog box

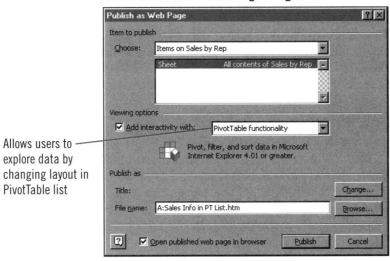

Allows users to explore data by changing layout in PivotTable list

FIGURE N-13: PivotTable list with new layout in Internet Explorer

User drags fields to drop areas to explore data relationships

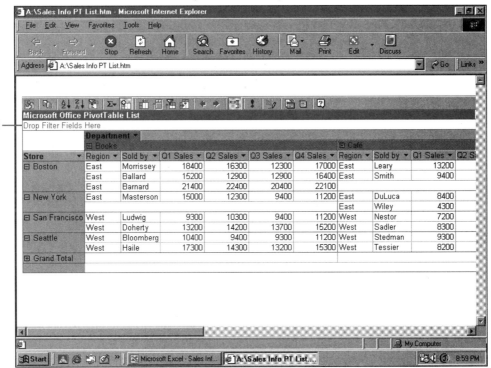

Adding fields to a PivotTable list using the Web browser

You can add filter, data, or detail fields to the PivotTable list to display data. On the toolbar above the PivotTable list, click the Field List button. In the PivotTable Field List dialog box locate the name of the field you want to add. Click the field, and in the lower-right corner of the box, click the area list arrow, then click the section to which you want to add the field: Filter Area, Data Area, or Detail Data. If Add to is not available, the PivotTable creator may have restricted access to it.

Excel 2000

Creating Hyperlinks between Excel Files and the Web

In addition to using hyperlinks to connect related Excel files, you can also create hyperlinks between files created in other Windows programs. You can even use hyperlinks to move between Excel files and information stored on the Web. Every Web page is identified by a unique address called a **Uniform Resource Locator (URL)**. You create a hyperlink to a Web page in the same way you create a hyperlink to another Excel file—by specifying the location of the Web page (its URL) in the Link to File or URL text box in the Insert Hyperlink dialog box. You enter a URL for an intranet site or a site on the World Wide Web using the same method. ◀━━━ Jim decides that users of the Pastry Sales worksheet would find it helpful to view competitive information. He decides to include a hyperlink to the URL of one of MediaLoft's competitors, Barnes and Noble, which is also a café bookstore.

Steps

1. Activate the **Pastry Sales worksheet**, click cell **A2**, type **Barnes and Noble**, then click the **Enter button** on the Formula bar

Trouble?

If this button does not appear on your Standard toolbar, click the More Buttons button to view it.

2. Click the **Insert Hyperlink button** on the Standard toolbar
   The Insert Hyperlink dialog box opens. This is where you specify the target for the hyperlink, the Barnes and Noble Web site, by entering its URL in the Link to file or URL section of the Insert Hyperlink dialog box.

QuickTip

Make sure the URL address appears in the text box exactly as shown in Figure N-14. Every Web page URL begins with "http://". This acronym stands for HyperText Transfer Protocol, the method all intranet and Web page data use to travel over the Internet to your computer.

3. Under Link to, click **Existing File or Web Page**, click in the Type the file or Web page name text box, and type the URL for the Barnes and Noble Web site: **http://www.barnesandnoble.com**
   Your completed Insert Hyperlink dialog box should match Figure N-14. The program will automatically add a slash after the URL, as shown in Figure N-14, if you return to the dialog box and enter a Web address that you've entered previously.

4. Click **OK**
   The Barnes and Noble text is blue and underlined, indicating that it is a hyperlink. You should always test new hyperlinks to make sure they link to the correct destination. To test this hyperlink, you must have a modem, a Web browser installed on your computer, and access to an Internet Service Provider (ISP).

5. Click the **Barnes and Noble** hyperlink in cell A2
   After a moment, the Web browser installed on your computer starts and displays the Barnes and Noble Web page in your browser window.

6. If necessary, click the **Maximize button** on the browser title bar to maximize the browser window

7. Click **File** on the menu bar, click **Print**, click **OK**, then click the **Back button** on the Web toolbar
   Now that you know the hyperlink works correctly, you return to the Sales Info 2 worksheet.

8. Save and close the workbook, then if necessary close your browser, but stay connected to the Internet

▶ EXCEL N-14   **SHARING EXCEL FILES AND INCORPORATING WEB INFORMATION**

FIGURE N-14: Insert Hyperlink dialog box

URL for Barnes and Noble Web site

Previously visited Web sites are listed here

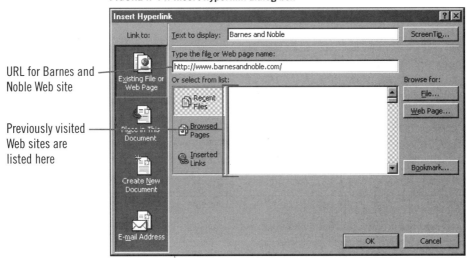

FIGURE N-15: Barnes and Noble Web site in Internet Explorer

URL appears here

Your screen contents may differ because Web pages are revised frequently

CLUES TO USE

Using hyperlinks to navigate large worksheets

Previously, when you needed to locate and view different sections of a particularly large worksheet, you used the scroll bars, or, if there were range names associated with the different worksheet sections, the name box. You can also use hyperlinks to more easily navigate a large worksheet. To insert a hyperlink that targets a cell or a range of cells at another location in the worksheet or another sheet in the workbook, click the cell where you want the hyperlink to appear, then click the Insert Hyperlink button on the Standard toolbar. In the Insert Hyperlink dialog box, click Place in This Document. Enter the cell address or range name of the hyperlink target in the Type the cell reference text box, or select a sheet or a defined name from the list box below it, then click OK.

Running Queries to Retrieve Data on the Web

Often you'll want to access information on the Web or the Internet to incorporate into an Excel worksheet. Using Excel, you can obtain data from a Web, Internet, or intranet site by running a **Web query**. You can then save the information as an Excel workbook and manipulate it in any way you choose. ◄ As part of a special project for Leilani Ho, Jim needs to obtain stock information on MediaLoft's competitors. He will run a Web query to obtain the most current stock information from the World Wide Web.

Steps 1 2 3 4

1. Open a new workbook, then save it as **Stock Data**

2. Click **Data** on the menu bar, point to **Get External Data**, then click **Run Saved Query**

   The Run Query dialog box opens, similar to Figure N-16. This is where you select the Web query you want to run from a list of predefined queries.

3. Click **Microsoft Investor Stock Quotes**, then click **Get Data**

   The Returning External Data to Microsoft Excel dialog box opens. This is where you specify the location to place the incoming data.

4. Make sure the **Existing worksheet option button** is selected, then click **OK**

   The Enter Parameter Value dialog box opens, prompting you to enter a stock symbol. The stock symbol for Barnes and Noble is BKS.

Trouble?

If you don't have a modem and access to the Web through an ISP, check with your instructor or technical support person. If your ISP's connection dialog box opens, follow your standard procedure for getting online, then continue with Step 6.

5. Type **BKS**, then click **OK**

   Your Internet Service Provider connects to the Web. The Microsoft Investor stock quote for Barnes and Noble appears on the screen. The External Data toolbar also appears, as shown in Figure N-17. Now you have the stock information that Jim can use to research one of MediaLoft's competitor's stock values.

6. Click **File** on the menu bar, click **Print**, then click **Chartlink** on the stock quote page

   A chart appears, showing the stock price and company income for the last year, similar to Figure N-18.

7. Print the chart, close your browser, disconnect from the Internet, save and close the workbook, then exit Excel and your browser

Finding stock symbols

If you want to check on a stock but don't know its symbol, click the Symbol Lookup hyperlink on the Stock Data worksheet. You may need to download the Microsoft Investor software, which takes about five minutes.

FIGURE N-16: Run Query dialog box

Predefined queries from Microsoft

Use this query to get up-to-date stock information

FIGURE N-17: Stock quote in Stock Data worksheet

Stock name

Click here to view chart of this stock's performance in the last year

Click here to find stock symbols for other stocks

Stock information for Barnes and Noble (your screen will display updated information)

External Data toolbar

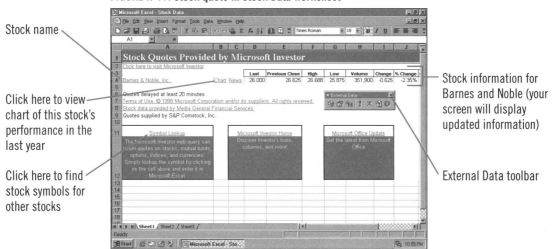

FIGURE N-18: Stock chart for Barnes and Noble

Stock name and time period covered are listed here

Creating a new query to retrieve Web page data

To retrieve data from a particular Web page on a regular basis, it's easiest to create a customized Web query. Click Data on the menu bar, point to Get External Data, then click New Web Query. In the New Web Query dialog box, click Browse Web to start your browser, go to the Web page from which you want to retrieve data, click the Web page, then return to the dialog box; the address of the Web page will appear in the address text box. Specify which part of the Web page you want to retrieve (for example, only the tables) and how much formatting you want to keep. Click Save Query to save the query for future use with the Run Saved Query command. Then click OK. Specify the location in the worksheet where you want the data, then click OK. The data from the Web page appears in the open Excel worksheet.

Practice

▶ Concepts Review

Label each of the elements shown in Figure N-19

FIGURE N-19

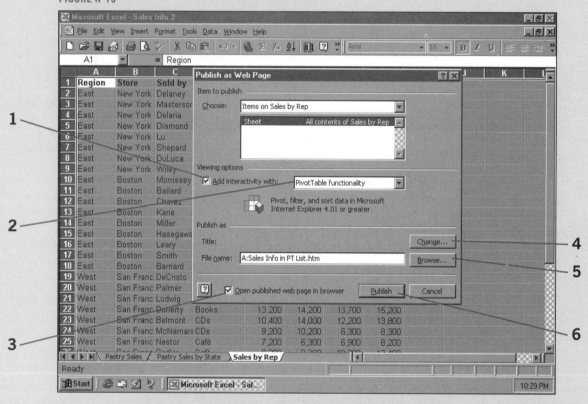

Match each item with the statement that describes it.

7. Web query

8. Change history

9. Shared workbook

10. Interactive worksheet or PivotTable

11. URL

a. A unique address on the World Wide Web

b. Used by many people on a network

c. Can be manipulated using a Web browser

d. Starts the installed Web browser to search the WWW

e. A record of edits others have made to a worksheet

12. A _____ **is a list of recipients to whom you are sending a workbook sequentially.**
   a. PivotTable
   b. Hypertext document
   c. Routing slip
   d. Shared workbook

13. Which of the following can be saved in HTML format, placed on a server, and then manipulated on an intranet or Internet using a Web browser?
   a. A worksheet
   b. A PivotTable
   c. A workbook
   d. a and b only

14. Which of the following allows you to obtain data from a Web or intranet site?
   a. Web Wizard
   b. PivotTable
   c. Data query
   d. Web query

15. A shared workbook is a workbook that
   a. Has hyperlinks to the Web.
   b. Is on the World Wide Web.
   c. Several people can use at the same time.
   d. Requires a password to open.

16. In an interactive worksheet or PivotTable,
   a. You can make changes and they are saved to the HTML file.
   b. You can make changes but they are not saved to the HTML file.
   c. You can change formatting but not perform calculations.
   d. You can perform calculations but not change formatting.

▶ Skills Review

1. Set up a shared workbook
   a. Open the file EX N-3 and save it as Ad Campaigns.
   b. Set up the workbook so that more than one person can use it at one time.
   c. On the Advanced tab, specify that the change history should be maintained for 1,000 days.

2. Track changes in a shared workbook
   a. Specify that all changes should be highlighted. Changes should be both highlighted on the screen and listed in a new sheet.
   b. In the Ads Q1 All Stores worksheet, change the Billboards totals to $600 for each month.
   c. Save the file.
   d. Display and print the History sheet. (If the History worksheet does not appear, reopen the Highlight Changes dialog box and reselect the options for All and List changes on a new sheet.)
   e. Save and close the workbook.

3. Apply and remove passwords

a. Open the file EX N-3, open the Save As dialog box, then open the General Options dialog box.

b. Set the password to open as Marsten and the password to modify as Spring.

c. Resave the password-protected file as Ad Campaigns PW.

d. Close the workbook.

e. Reopen the workbook and verify that you can change it, using passwords where necessary.

4. Create an interactive worksheet for an intranet or the Web.

a. Save the Ads Q1 All Stores worksheet as an interactive Web page, with spreadsheet functionality.

b. Set the title bar to read Ad Campaign Forecast, automatically preview it in Internet Explorer, if that is your Web browser, and save it to your Project Disk using the filename Ad Campaigns. If you use a different Web browser, don't use the automatic preview option.

c. If you can open the HTML file in Internet Explorer, do so.

d. In Internet Explorer, add totals for each month in B11:D11, then add a grand total to cell E11.

e. In F3, enter a formula that calculates the percentage newspaper ads are of the grand total. (*Hint:* You will need to type in the formula instead of clicking cells, and use the Property Toolbox to change the number format to a percent.)

f. Use the Property Toolbox to fill the range B11:E11 with yellow.

g. Sort the list in ascending order by ad type. You might need to reenter the percentage formula.

h. Print the worksheet from Internet Explorer, then close Internet Explorer.

5. Create an interactive PivotTable for an intranet or the Web.

a. In the Ad Campaigns PW workbook, save the worksheet Ad Detail as an interactive PivotTable with PivotTable functionality. Make the title Ad Forecast 4 Stores, and save it as Ads4Stores. Open the file in Internet Explorer.

b. Drag fields to analyze the data by Region, Ad Piece, Store, and Department.

c. Print the page showing changed data.

6. Create Hyperlinks between Excel files and the Web.

a. On the Ads Q1 All Stores worksheet, enter the text "American Ad Foundation" and make it a hyperlink to the American Ad Foundation at http://www.aaf.org in cell A13.

b. Test the hyperlink and print the Web page.

c. Save and close the workbook.

7. Run queries to retrieve data on the Web.

a. Open a new workbook and save it as Stock Quotes.

b. Use the Run Saved Query command to locate Microsoft Investor Major Indices.

c. Specify that you want to return the data to cell A1 of the current worksheet.

d. After the stock quotes appear, click one of the stock indices listed and print the results.

e. Display a chart for one of the indices, then print the chart. (*Hint:* If you are prompted to download MSN Money Central and you are unable to download software at your site, continue with step f.)

f. Preview and print the Stock Quotes sheet, then save and close the workbook.

g. Open a new workbook and save it as MediaLoft Products.

h. Create a new Web query that retrieves the following page from the MediaLoft intranet site: www.course.com/illustrated/MediaLoft/Product.html. Import the entire page with full HTML formatting, and save the query as MediaLoft Products on your project disk.

i. Test the hyperlinks on the imported Web page, use the Back arrow to return to the workbook, then save and close the workbook.

► Independent Challenges

1. Blantyre Consulting helps small businesses attain and maintain profitability by monitoring their sales and expense information. The company makes it a practice to hold a monthly phone conference with clients to discuss strategy. There are 10 consultants in the organization, and they share information via the company intranet. They have adopted a team approach to their accounts, so five consultants work on each account. You are setting up the information for a new client, Boston Touring Company, which specializes in giving trolley and bus tours in Boston, Massachusetts, and the surrounding area. You are preparing the workbook to be placed on the company intranet so that only the consultant group for that account can view the information.

To complete this independent challenge:

a. Open the file EX N-4 and save it as Boston Touring.

b. Format the workbook so it is more attractive and the information is easy to read.

c. Make the workbook shared so that all consultants can access it.

d. Set up the workbook so that all changes will be tracked. Make two changes to the worksheets as a test and print the change history.

e. Password protect the workbook for both opening and editing, and write down the passwords you have chosen.

f. Save and close the workbook, then reopen it, using passwords as necessary.

g. Save the Q1 Sales worksheet as an interactive worksheet with spreadsheet functionality. Make the browser title bar read "Boston Touring Company" using the filename Boston Touring - Web.

h. Open the worksheet in Internet Explorer, then calculate the percentage that half-day tours of Cambridge are of the total.

i. Add the heading Total over the column of totals and format it in a different text color.

j. Print the interactive worksheet, then close the browser.

k. Save and close the Boston Touring worksheet.

2. The First Southern Bank has a Web page containing information about its current rates and procedures for opening an account. The bank would like to expand the site in order to help customers find answers to more of the questions the Customer Service line receives. Customers frequently call in asking for the bank's Mortgage Calculator, a printed table that shows various mortgage amounts and interest rates, and lets customers look up what their monthly payments would be. John Barnes, the Customer Service Manager, has asked you to set up an Excel worksheet for their Web site that will allow customers to enter various mortgage amounts and interest rates, and automatically see what their monthly payments, total payments, and total interest would be. He wants you to make the worksheet both attractive and easy to use.

To complete this independent challenge:

a. Open the file EX N-5 and save it as Mortgage Calculator.

b. Add the bank's name and any other marketing-oriented information that will identify what the worksheet is and how to use it.

c. Format the worksheet with colors, fonts, or other formats to make it attractive for public use.

d. Save the worksheet in HTML format with interactive spreadsheet functionality and an appropriate title in the title bar.

e. Open the HTML file in Internet Explorer, then test the calculator. Enter various mortgage amounts and interest rates and make sure the payment information changes appropriately.

f. Close Internet Explorer, the Mortgage Calculator worksheet, and Excel, saving as necessary.

Excel 2000

3. Tuckerman Teas is a tea import and export firm with offices in Tokyo and London that distributes teas to shops in the United States and Canada. Tuckerman wants the officers in both offices to be able to analyze sales data, but because of incompatible software, they must rely on their Web browsers. They have asked you to help them set up a file that they will all be able to access on their intranet site.

To complete this independent challenge:

a. Open the file EX N-6 and save it as Tuckerman Teas.

b. Format the worksheet using fonts and colors to make it more attractive.

c. Save the file as a Web page with PivotTable functionality. Assign the title bar an appropriate title.

d. Open the file in Internet Explorer and manipulate the data to determine the following:

- How do shipments of the flavored afternoon blends compare to the flavored breakfast blends?
- Considering only blends, flavored, and Japanese teas, what is the total kilos shipped for afternoon and breakfast teas?
- Which category consistently did better than the others during the quarter?

e. Explore any other data relationships you wish.

f. Return to the Tuckerman Teas worksheet, and on a blank sheet, write three or four sentences summarizing your conclusions.

4. Jim Fernandez, MediaLoft's office manager, has been asked by the Accounting department to examine CD sales trends. Assuming that a higher stock price reflects higher sales, he has decided to compare MediaLoft CD sales patterns to the stock price of Amazon.com, which also sells CDs, to see if both display seasonal trends, particularly the higher sales at the end of the calendar year. You will get sales information from the MediaLoft intranet site, retrieve stock data on Amazon.com, then create charts that illustrate trends of each one for easy comparison.

To complete this independent challenge:

a. Connect to the Internet, and go to the MediaLoft intranet site at http://www.course.com/Illustrated/MediaLoft. Click the Accounting link, then click the CD Sales Analysis link. Print the page and disconnect from the Internet.

b. Open a new workbook, then enter the total figures for CD sales for each of the four quarters. Save the workbook as Trend Analysis.

c. Create a line chart of the figures on the same worksheet as the sales figures, assigning the chart an appropriate title.

d. Name the sheet Trends.

e. Run a Microsoft Investor Stock Quote Web query to obtain a stock quote for Amazon.com, stock symbol AMZN, placing the data in a new worksheet.

f. Display the chart of this data by clicking Chart.

g. On the File menu above the chart, select Export Data. The data will appear in Excel in a separate workbook called AMZN.

h. In the new workbook, delete all the rows of data except the row representing the earliest date for each month. Generally, this will be the first of the month, unless that falls on a weekend, in which case it might be the second or third of the month. You should end up with one row of data for each month, showing the High, Low, Close, and Volume. If any line is blank, use the date nearest to it that has data.

i. Delete the columns for High, Low, and Volume, leaving the Date and Close columns.

j. Sort the rows in ascending order by date, then copy the data into the Trends sheet in the Trend Analysis workbook.

k. Create a line chart of the Amazon data, and assign it an appropriate title. Place it on the same sheet as the MediaLoft chart. Use any Excel features to point out similarities or differences you see. Do both rise toward the end of the year?

l. On the chart sheet, create a hyperlink to Amazon.com.

m. Save and close the Trend Analysis workbook, close the AMZN workbook without saving, then close Internet Explorer.

► Visual Workshop

Create the interactive Web page shown in Figure N-20. Use Excel to create the company name, product listing, and the sales figures for each quarter, all in black text. Save and print the worksheet. Save the worksheet in interactive HTML format, using the title bar text shown. Use Internet Explorer to obtain totals for each quarter and to apply formatting to totals, column headings, and the company name. (*Hint:* If you have any trouble with AutoSum, try formatting the figures using the Number format.) Print the HTML worksheet with your modifications applied.

FIGURE N-20

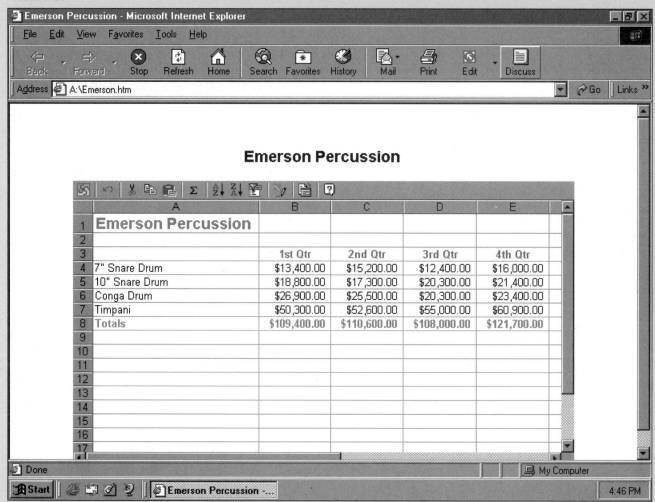

Gaining
Control over Your Work

Objectives

- ► Find files
- `MOUS` ► Audit a worksheet
- ► Outline a worksheet
- ► Control worksheet calculations
- ► Create custom AutoFill lists
- ► Customize Excel
- `MOUS` ► Add a comment to a cell
- `MOUS` ► Save a workbook as a template

Excel includes numerous tools and options designed to help you work as efficiently as possible. In this unit, you will learn how to use some of these elements to find errors and hide unnecessary detail. You'll also find out how to eliminate repetitive typing chores, save calculation time when using a large worksheet, and customize basic Excel features. Finally, you'll learn how to document your workbook and save it in a format that makes it easy to reuse. ✐ MediaLoft's assistant controller, Lisa Wong, routinely asks Jim Fernandez to help with a variety of spreadsheet-related tasks. The numerous options available in Excel help Jim perform his work quickly and efficiently.

Unit O

Excel 2000

Finding Files

The Open dialog box in Excel contains powerful searching tools that make it easy for you to find files. You can search for a file in several ways, such as by name or according to specific text located within a particular file. ▰▰ Recently, Jim created a workbook that tracks the number of overtime hours worked in each MediaLoft store. He can't remember the exact name of the file, so he searches for it by the first few letters of the filename.

Steps 1234

1. **Start Excel, then click the Open button 🗁 on the Standard toolbar**
   At the top of the Open dialog box, there are two menus: the Views menu (represented by the Views icon ▦▾ and the Tools menu. The Views menu controls the amount of information displayed about each file and folder. See Table O-1 for a description of Views menu selections. The amount of detail currently on your screen depends on the view option that you clicked the last time you opened this dialog box. The Tools menu helps you find, delete, and print files, as well as perform other file management tasks. First you'll display files so they match the figures in this lesson.

QuickTip

You can cycle through the four available views by clicking the Views button repeatedly.

2. **Click the Views list arrow ▦▾, click each of the views to observe the results, then click Details**
   Your files display with the filename, size, type, and date modified.

3. **Click Tools, then click Find**
   The Find dialog box opens, similar to Figure O-1. You can find files by specifying one or more criteria, or conditions that must be met, to find your file. For example, you can specify that Excel should find only files that have the word "Inventory" in the filename and that were created after 6/15/2000. The criteria list in the "Find files that match these criteria" list is already set to find only Excel files. You'll specify another criterion. Jim thinks his filename starts with the prefix EX O but he's not sure of the number.

QuickTip

You can also search for text within Excel files. For example, if you know your worksheet contains the text "Overtime hours", you can specify Contents under property, and then specify the appropriate "include" condition and value. To use this feature you may need to install the Find Fast utility from your Office 2000 CD.

4. **In the Define more criteria area, under Property, select File name if necessary, then under Condition select includes if necessary**

5. **Click in the Value box, then type EX O***
   Be sure you type the letter "O" and not a zero. Because you know only the first few letters of the filename, you'll use the wildcard symbol * (an asterisk) to substitute for the remaining unknown characters. Next, you need to specify where you want Excel to search for the file. This saves you time if you have access to several disks and you want to limit the search to one or two of them.

6. **Click the Look in list arrow, click the drive that contains your Project Disk, then click the Search subfolders check box to select it**

Trouble?

If Excel doesn't find the files you're looking for, you may have typed zero instead of the letter "O" or you may not have selected the Search subfolders check box. Repeat the steps from Step 4, being sure to use the letter "O".

7. **Click Find Now, then click Yes to add your search criterion to the criteria list**
   After a moment, Excel displays five files that begin with "EX O", along with detailed information about the files. See Figure O-2. You can check to see if the criterion was added.

8. **Click Tools, then click Find**
   The criterion "Filename **begins with** EX O." appears in the criteria list.

9. **Click Cancel, double-click the file EX O-1 in the Open dialog box, then save the workbook as Overtime Hours**

FIGURE O-1: Find dialog box

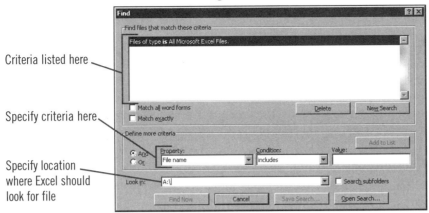

Criteria listed here

Specify criteria here

Specify location where Excel should look for file

FIGURE O-2: Search results

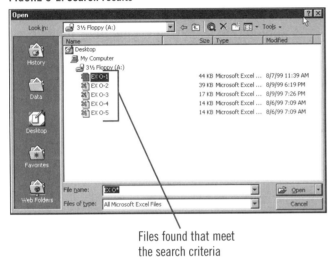

Files found that meet the search criteria

FIGURE O-3: Properties dialog box

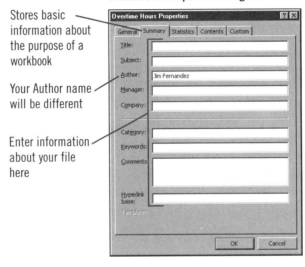

Stores basic information about the purpose of a workbook

Your Author name will be different

Enter information about your file here

TABLE O-1: Views menu selections

button	name	description
	List	Displays file and folder names
	Details	Displays file and folder names, along with the file type and the date last modified
	Properties	Displays information about the highlighted file, such as subject and keywords
	Preview	Displays the upper-left corner of the first sheet in a workbook
Arrange Icons	Arrange icons	Lets you rearrange your file icons by name, type, size, and date

CLUES TO USE

File properties

Excel automatically tracks specific file properties, such as author name, file size, and file type, and displays them when you display file details. You can also enter additional file properties, such as a descriptive title or a subject. Right-click the file in the Open dialog box, click Properties to open the [Filename] Properties dialog box, click the Summary tab, then add any information you want. See Figure O-3. To search for a file by a specific property, in the Open dialog box, click Tools, then click Find. In the Find dialog box select Text or property in the Property list, then enter the property text in the Value box.

Auditing a Worksheet

The Excel auditing feature helps you track errors and determine worksheet logic—that is, how a worksheet is set up. Because errors and faulty logic can be introduced at any stage of worksheet development, it is important to include auditing as part of your workbook-building process. Jim audits the worksheet that tracks the number of overtime hours at each store to verify the accuracy of the year-end totals. Before beginning the auditing process, Jim adds a vertical pane to the window so he can view the first and last columns of the worksheet at the same time.

Steps 1 2 3 4

1. **Drag the vertical split box** (the small box to the right of the horizontal scroll arrow) to the left until the vertical window pane divider is situated between columns A and B, then scroll the worksheet to the right until columns P through S are visible in the right pane
   See Figure O-4.

Trouble?

If the Auditing toolbar blocks your view of the worksheet, drag it to another place on the worksheet.

2. **Click Tools on the menu bar, point to Auditing, then click Show Auditing Toolbar**
   You use the buttons on the Auditing toolbar, shown in Figure O-5, to identify any errors in your worksheet. Notice the #DIV/0! error in cell S6. These symbols indicate a **divide-by-zero error**, which occurs when you divide a value by zero. The Trace Error button on the Auditing toolbar helps locate the source of this problem.

3. **Click cell S6, then click the Trace Error button** ◈ **on the Auditing toolbar**
   The formula bar reads =R6/$R$16, indicating that the value in cell R6 will be divided by the value in cell R16. Tracer arrows, or **tracers**, point from cells that might have caused the error to the active cell containing the error, as shown in Figure O-5. The tracers extend from cells R6 and R16 to cell S6. Note that cell R6 contains a value, whereas cell R16 is blank. In Excel formulas, blank cells have a value of zero. That means the value in cell R6 cannot be divided by the value in cell R16 (zero) because division by zero is impossible. To correct the error, you must edit the formula so that it references cell R15, the grand total of overtime hours, not R16.

4. **Press [F2] to switch to Edit mode, edit the formula to read =R6/$R$15, then click the Enter button** ☑ **on the formula bar**
   The error message and trace arrows disappear, and the formula produces the correct result, 9%, in cell S6. Next, notice that the total for the Boston store in cell R5 is unusually high compared with the totals of the other stores. You can investigate this value by tracing the cell's precedents—the cells on which cell R5 depends.

QuickTip

To find cells with formulas that refer to a specific cell, click the cell, then click the Trace Dependents button ⬇ on the Auditing toolbar.

5. **Click cell R5, click the Trace Precedents button** ⬈ **on the Auditing toolbar, then scroll left until you identify the tracer's starting point**
   The tracer arrow runs between cells B5 and R5, indicating that the formula in cell R5 reflects the quarterly *and* monthly totals of overtime hours. Because both the quarterly totals and monthly totals are summed in this formula, the resulting figure is twice what it should be. Only the quarterly totals should be reflected in cell R5.

Trouble?

If the AutoSum button does not appear on your Standard toolbar, click the More Buttons button ⯈ to view it.

6. **If necessary, click cell R5, click the AutoSum button** Σ **on the Standard toolbar, then press [Enter]**
   The tracer arrow disappears, the formula changes to include only the quarterly totals, and the correct result, 490, appears in cell R5. Correcting the formula in cell R5 also adjusts the Grand Total percentage in cell S5 to 13%. Now that all the errors in the worksheet have been identified and corrected, you are finished auditing.

QuickTip

You can also double-click the split to remove it.

7. **Click Window on the menu bar, click Remove Split, then close the Auditing toolbar and save the workbook**

FIGURE O-4: Worksheet ready for auditing

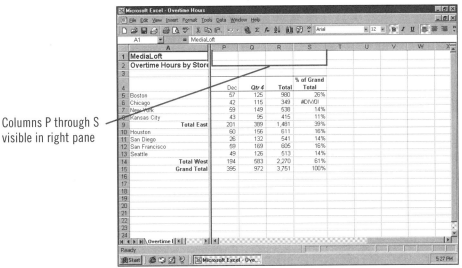

Columns P through S
visible in right pane

FIGURE O-5: Worksheet with traced error

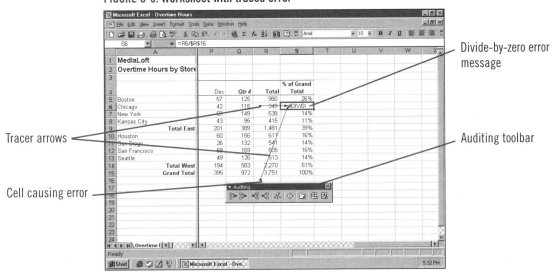

Divide-by-zero error
message

Tracer arrows

Auditing toolbar

Cell causing error

Circular references

A cell with a **circular reference** contains a formula that refers to its own cell location. If you accidentally enter a formula with a circular reference, a warning box will open, alerting you to the problem, and the Circular Reference toolbar appears. Click OK to open a Help window explaining how to find the circular reference using the Circular Reference toolbar. In simple formulas, a circular reference is easy to spot. To correct it, simply edit the formula to remove any reference to the cell where the formula is located.

Hiding and displaying toolbars

You display the Auditing toolbar using the Tools menu, however, to display other toolbars, right-click the Standard or Formatting toolbar, then click the name of the toolbar you want to display. To hide the toolbar, right-click it and select its name from the pop-up menu.

Outlining a Worksheet

The Excel Outline command displays a worksheet with buttons that allow you to adjust the display of the worksheet to show only the critical rows and columns. For outlining to function properly, worksheet formulas must point consistently in the same direction: Summary rows, such as subtotal rows, must be located below related data, whereas summary columns, such as grand total columns, must be located to the right of related data. (If you're not sure which way your formulas point, click the Trace Precedents button on the Auditing toolbar.) ◄— Jim needs to give Lisa Wong, the MediaLoft assistant controller, the updated year-end totals. To emphasize the subtotals for both East and West regions, as well as the grand total of overtime hours, he decides to outline the worksheet first.

Steps 1 2 3 4

1. **If necessary, press [Ctrl][Home] to display the upper-left corner of the worksheet**

2. **Click Data on the menu bar, point to Group and Outline, then click Auto Outline**
   The worksheet is displayed in Outline view, as shown in Figure O-6. There are several ways to change the amount of detail in an outlined worksheet, but the easiest is by using the Column Level and Row Level buttons, which hide a varying amount of detail. The Row Level 1 button hides everything in the worksheet except the most important row or rows—in this case, the Grand Total row.

3. **Click the Row Level 1 button** ▣
   This selection doesn't display enough information, so you'll try the Row Level 2 button, which hides everything except the second most important rows—in this case, the subtotal rows and the Grand Total row.

4. **Click the Row Level 2 button** ▣
   Now you can see the rows you want. Next, you'll display only the columns you choose—in this case, the Qtr 1–Qtr 4 columns, the Total column, and the % of Grand Total column. Like the Row Level 2 button, the Column Level 2 button displays the Grand Total column, along with its corresponding subtotals.

5. **Click the Column Level 2 button** ▣
   The quarterly totals appear and the monthly figures are no longer visible. Jim needs to give a printed copy of the worksheet outline to Lisa.

6. **Place your name in the worksheet footer, then print the worksheet**
   Your printed worksheet should look like the one shown in Figure O-7. You're finished using the outlining feature.

7. **Click the Row Level 3 button** ▣, **then click the Column Level 3 button** ▣
   The monthly figures for each store reappear.

8. **Click Data on the menu bar, point to Group and Outline, then click Clear Outline**

FIGURE O-6: Worksheet in Outline view

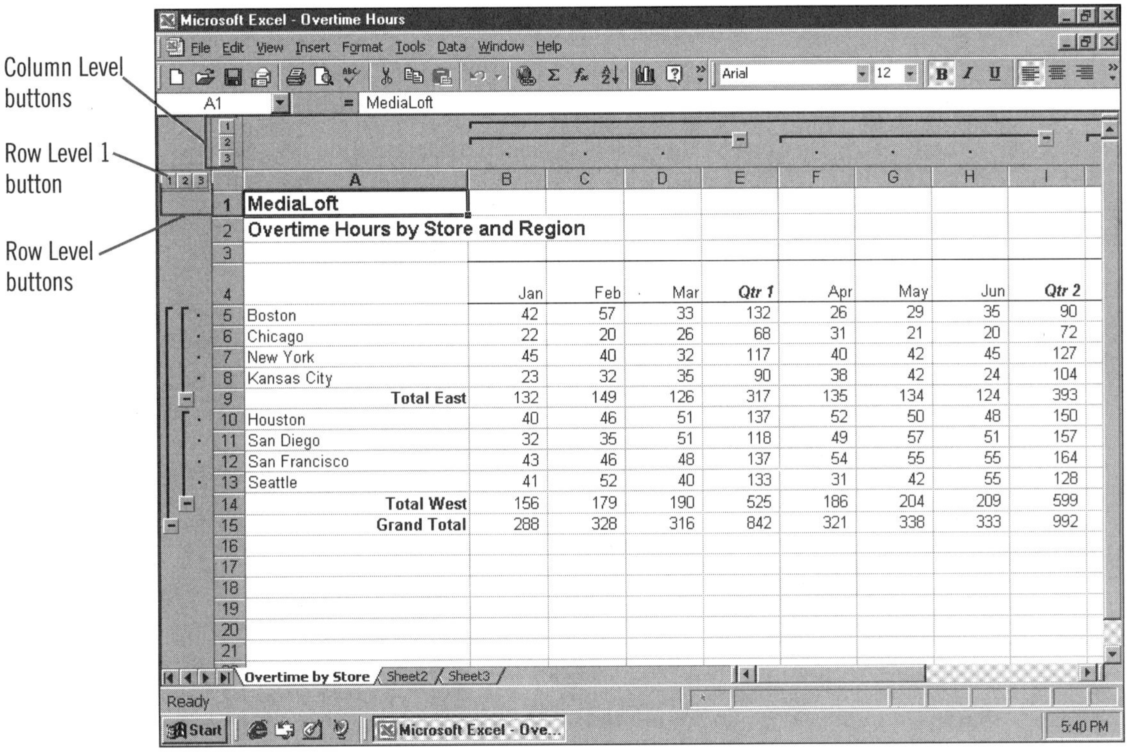

Column Level buttons

Row Level 1 button

Row Level buttons

	A	B	C	D	E	F	G	H	I
1	MediaLoft								
2	Overtime Hours by Store and Region								
3									
4		Jan	Feb	Mar	Qtr 1	Apr	May	Jun	Qtr 2
5	Boston	42	57	33	132	26	29	35	90
6	Chicago	22	20	26	68	31	21	20	72
7	New York	45	40	32	117	40	42	45	127
8	Kansas City	23	32	35	90	38	42	24	104
9	Total East	132	149	126	317	135	134	124	393
10	Houston	40	46	51	137	52	50	48	150
11	San Diego	32	35	51	118	49	57	51	157
12	San Francisco	43	46	48	137	54	55	55	164
13	Seattle	41	52	40	133	31	42	55	128
14	Total West	156	179	190	525	186	204	209	599
15	Grand Total	288	328	316	842	321	338	333	992

FIGURE O-7: Printed worksheet outline

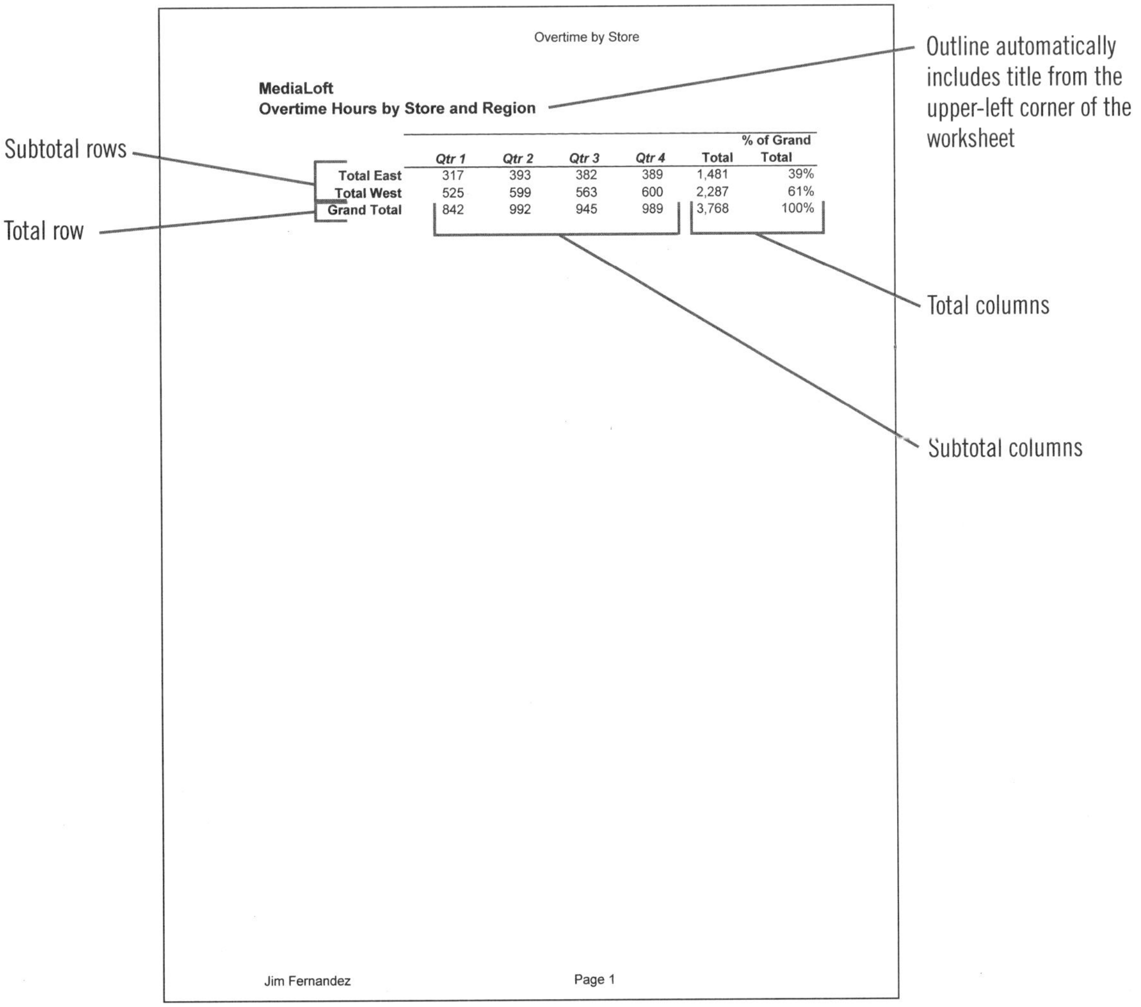

Subtotal rows

Total row

Outline automatically includes title from the upper-left corner of the worksheet

Total columns

Subtotal columns

Overtime by Store

MediaLoft
Overtime Hours by Store and Region

	Qtr 1	Qtr 2	Qtr 3	Qtr 4	Total	% of Grand Total
Total East	317	393	382	389	1,481	39%
Total West	525	599	563	600	2,287	61%
Grand Total	842	992	945	989	3,768	100%

Jim Fernandez   Page 1

GAINING CONTROL OVER YOUR WORK EXCEL O-7 ◀

Excel 2000

Controlling Worksheet Calculations

Whenever you change a value in a cell, Excel automatically recalculates all the formulas in the worksheet based on that cell. This automatic calculation is efficient until you create a worksheet so large that the recalculation process slows down data entry and screen updating. Worksheets with many formulas, data tables, or functions may also recalculate slowly. In these cases, you might want to selectively determine if and when you want Excel to perform calculations automatically. You do this by applying the manual calculation option. Once you change the calculation mode to manual, the manual mode is applied to all open worksheets. ◄──── Because Jim knows that using specific Excel calculation options can help make worksheet building more efficient, he decides to change from automatic to manual calculation.

Steps 1 2 3 4

1. **Click Tools on the menu bar, click Options, then click the Calculation tab**
   The Calculation tab of the Options dialog box opens, as shown in Figure O-8.

2. **Under Calculation, click the Manual option button**
   The Recalculate before save box automatically becomes active and contains a checkmark when you select the Manual option. Because the workbook will not recalculate until you save or close and reopen the workbook, make sure to recalculate your worksheet before you print and after you make changes.

> **QuickTip**
>
> To automatically recalculate all worksheet formulas except one- and two-input data tables, under Calculation, click Automatic except tables.

3. **Click OK**
   Jim just received word that the December total for the San Francisco store is incorrect. You'll adjust the entry in cell P12 accordingly.

4. **Click cell B5, click Window on the menu bar, click Freeze Panes, then scroll right to bring columns P through S into view**

5. **Click cell P12, type 76, then click the Enter button ☑ on the formula bar**
   See Figure O-9. Notice that the formula results in the worksheet are *not* updated. (For example, the percentage in cell S12 is still 16%.) The word "Calculate" appears in the status bar to indicate that a specific value in the worksheet did indeed change and must be recalculated. You can press [F9] at any time to calculate all the open worksheets manually or [Shift][F9] to calculate just the active worksheet.

> **QuickTip**
>
> If a worksheet formula is linked to a worksheet that you have not recalculated and you update that link, you will see a message informing you of the situation. To update the link using the current value, click OK. To use the previous value, click Cancel.

6. **Press [Shift][F9], then save the workbook**
   See Figure O-10. The percentage in cell S12 is now 17% instead of 16%. The other formulas in the worksheet affected by the value in cell P12 changed as well. Because this is a relatively small worksheet that recalculates quickly, you will return to automatic calculation.

7. **Click Tools on the menu bar, click Options if necessary, click the Calculation tab if necessary, under Calculation click the Automatic option button, then click OK**
   Now any additional changes you make to the worksheet will again be recalculated automatically.

FIGURE O-8: Calculation tab of the Options dialog box

Calculation tab ——————

Manual option button ——————

Some of your settings ——————
may differ

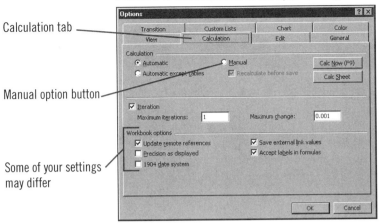

FIGURE O-9: Worksheet in manual calculation mode

Value still needs
to be updated

Changed value

Indicates that work-
sheet needs to be
recalculated

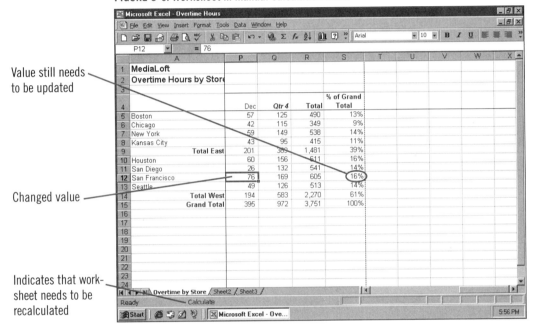

FIGURE O-10: Worksheet with updated values

Updated values

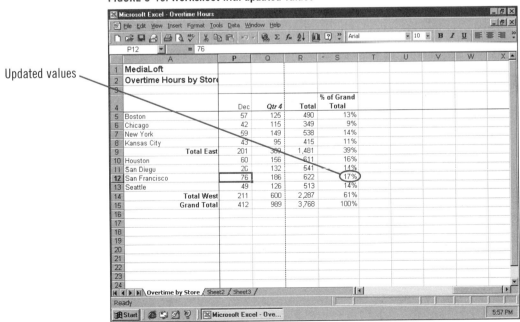

Creating Custom AutoFill Lists

Whenever you need to type a list of words regularly, you can save time by creating a custom AutoFill list. Then you need only to enter the first value in a blank cell and drag the AutoFill handle. Excel will enter the rest of the information for you automatically. Figure O-11 shows some examples of AutoFill lists. ✎ Jim often has to repeatedly enter MediaLoft store names and regional total labels in various worksheets. He decides to create an AutoFill list to save time in performing this task. He begins by selecting the names and total labels in the worksheet.

Steps

1. Select the range **A5:A15**

Trouble?

If a list of store names already appears in the Custom lists box, the person using the computer before you forgot to delete it. Click the list, click [Delete], and proceed with Step 3. You cannot delete the four default lists for days and months.

2. Click **Tools** on the menu bar, click **Options**, then click the **Custom Lists** tab
   See Figure O-12. The Custom Lists tab shows the existing AutoFill lists. The Import list from cells box contains the range you selected in Step 1.

3. Click **Import**
   The list of names is highlighted in the Custom lists box and displays in the List entries box. Jim wants to test the custom AutoFill list by placing it in a blank worksheet.

4. Click **OK**, click the **Sheet2 tab**, then type **Boston** in cell A1

5. Position the pointer over the AutoFill handle in the lower-right corner of cell A1
   Notice that the pointer changes to ┼, as shown in Figure O-13.

QuickTip

You also can drag the AutoFill handle down or to the right to repeat the AutoFill in other rows or columns.

6. Click and drag the pointer down to cell **A11**, then release the mouse button
   The highlighted range now contains the custom list of store names and total rows you created. Now that you've finished creating and applying your custom AutoFill list, you need to delete it from the Options dialog box in case others will be using your computer to complete the lesson. If no one else will be using the computer, skip Step 7 and proceed to the next lesson.

7. Click **Tools** on the menu bar, click **Options** if necessary, click the **Custom Lists tab**, click the list of store and region names in the Custom lists box, click **Delete**, click **OK** to confirm the deletion, then click **OK** again

8. Save the workbook

FIGURE O-11: Sample AutoFill list

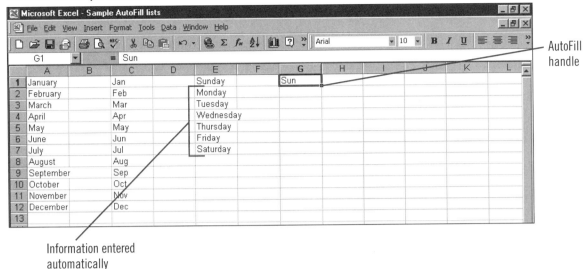

AutoFill handle

Information entered automatically

FIGURE O-12: Custom Lists tab

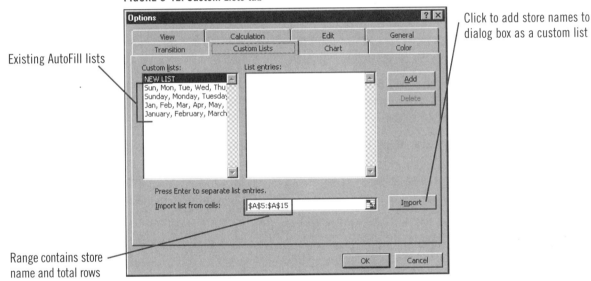

Click to add store names to dialog box as a custom list

Existing AutoFill lists

Range contains store name and total rows

FIGURE O-13: Applying a custom AutoFill list

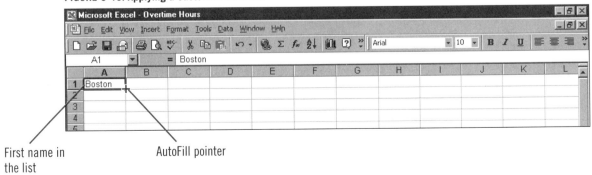

First name in the list

AutoFill pointer

Customizing Excel

Excel 2000

The Excel default settings for editing and viewing the worksheet are designed with user convenience in mind. You may find, however, that a particular setting doesn't always fit your needs (for example, where the cell selector moves after you press [Enter]). The eight tabs of the Options dialog box allow you to customize Excel to suit your work habits and needs. You've already used the Calculation tab to switch to manual calculation and the Custom Lists tab to create your own AutoFill list. The most commonly used functions of the Options dialog box tabs are explained in more detail in Table O-2. It's especially important not to permanently change any other General tab settings if you're sharing a computer. ✒ Jim is curious about how he can customize Excel to allow him to work more efficiently. He decides to use a blank workbook to explore some of the features of Excel accessed through the Options dialog box.

Steps

QuickTip

Do not change any settings in the Options dialog box other than those covered in this lesson.

1. **Click the New button on the Standard toolbar, click Tools on the menu bar, click Options, then click the Edit tab**
   In some worksheets, it's more convenient to have the cell selector automatically move right one cell, rather than down one cell, after you press [Enter].

2. **Click the Direction list arrow, then click Right**
   See Figure O-14. Now when you press [Enter] the selector will move to the right. You can enter detailed information (or properties) to document your workbook in the Properties dialog box. This documentation may be useful to co-workers because it allows them to read a summary of your workbook without actually having to open it; they can right-click the file in the Open dialog box, then click Properties.

3. **Click the General tab, then click the Prompt for workbook properties check box**
   Now, when you save a workbook, Excel will open a dialog box asking you to enter file properties. Finally, Jim thinks the workbook would look better without gridlines.

4. **Click the View tab, then under Window options click the Gridlines check box to deselect it**
   This setting, as well as the others under "Window options", affects only the active worksheet. Next you'll check the results of your new workbook settings.

5. **Click OK, type Accounts Receivable in cell A1, then press [Enter]**
   The information in your new worksheet is displayed without any gridlines. In addition, the cell selector moved to the right of cell A1 when you pressed [Enter]. Next, as you save the workbook, you'll enter some information in the Properties dialog box.

QuickTip

For more information about file properties, see the Clues to Use in the "Finding Files" lesson earlier in this unit.

6. **Save the workbook as Accounts to your Project Disk, in the Accounts Properties dialog box click the Summary tab if necessary, then in the Comments text box type Sample workbook used to practice customizing Excel**
   See Figure O-15.

7. **Click OK**
   Now that you're finished exploring the Options dialog box, you need to reestablish the original Excel settings. You don't need to adjust the Gridlines setting because that change applied only to the active worksheet.

8. **Click Tools on the menu bar, click Options, click the Edit tab, click the Direction list arrow, click Down, click the General tab, click the Prompt for workbook properties check box to deselect it, click OK, then close the workbook**
   The Overtime Hours workbook reappears.

FIGURE O-14: Edit tab in the Options dialog box

Some of your settings may differ

Updated setting moves cell selector right after you press [Enter]

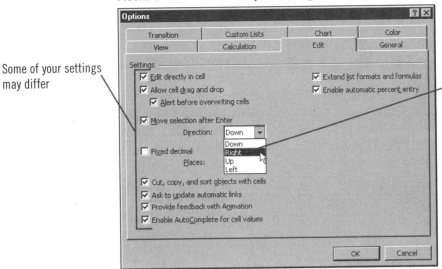

FIGURE O-15: Properties dialog box

Your information will differ

Description of the workbook

Click to enable workbook preview in Open dialog box

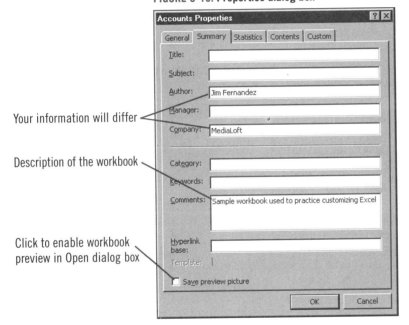

TABLE O-2: Options dialog box tabs

tab	description
Calculation	Controls how the worksheet is calculated; choices include automatic versus manual
Chart	Controls how empty cells are treated in a chart and whether chart tips are displayed
Color	Allows you to copy a customized color palette from one workbook to another
Custom Lists	Allows you to add or delete custom AutoFill lists
Edit	Controls the direction in which the cell selector moves after you press [Enter] and the ability to edit directly in cells
General	Controls the option to display the Properties dialog box after saving a workbook, the number of sheets in a new workbook, and the drive and folder used in the Save dialog box by default; User name is also listed here
Transition	Provides options useful for users familiar with Lotus 1-2-3
View	Controls the visibility of the formula bar, status bar, gridlines, row and column headers, and scroll bars; also controls the option to display formulas in a worksheet

Adding a Comment to a Cell

Whenever you'll be sharing a workbook with others, it's a good idea to **document**, or make notes about, basic assumptions, complicated formulas, or questionable data. By reading your documentation, a co-worker can quickly become familiar with your workbook. The easiest way to document a workbook is to use **cell comments**, which are notes you've written about your workbook that appear when you place the pointer over a cell. When you sort or copy and paste cells, any comments in them will move to the new location. In PivotTable reports, however, the comments stay in the original cell locations. ➤ Jim thinks one of the figures in the worksheet may be incorrect. He decides to add a comment for Lisa, pointing out the possible error.

Steps

1. Click the **Overtime by Store sheet tab**, then right-click cell **P11**

QuickTip

You can also insert a comment by clicking the New Comment button on the Auditing or Reviewing toolbar.

2. Click **Insert Comment** on the pop-up menu
   The Comment box opens, as shown in Figure O-16. Notice that Excel automatically includes the user name at the beginning of the comment. The user name data was collected from information previously entered in the General tab of the Options dialog box. Notice the white sizing handles on the border of the Comment box. You use these handles to change the size of the box by dragging.

3. Type **Is this figure correct? It looks low to me.**
   Notice how the text automatically wraps to the next line as necessary.

4. Click outside the Comment box
   A red triangle appears in the upper-right corner of cell P11, indicating that a comment is attached to the cell. People who use your worksheet can easily display comments.

QuickTip

To edit an existing comment, select the cell to which the comment is attached, click Insert on the menu bar, then click Edit Comment. To copy only comments, copy the cell contents, right-click the destination cell, select Paste Special, then click Comments.

5. Place the pointer over cell P11
   The comment appears next to the cell. When you move the pointer outside of cell P11, the comment disappears. The worksheet is now finished and ready for printing. You'll print the worksheet in landscape orientation on one page. On a second printed page, you print only the cell comment along with its associated cell reference.

6. Click **File** on the menu bar, click **Page Setup**, click the **Page tab** if necessary, under Orientation click the **Landscape option button**, under Scaling click the **Fit to option button**, click the **Sheet tab**, under Print click the **Comments list arrow**, click **At end of sheet**, click the **Row and column headings check box** to select it, click **Print**, then click **OK**
   Excel prints two pages.

7. Save the workbook

FIGURE O-16: Comment box

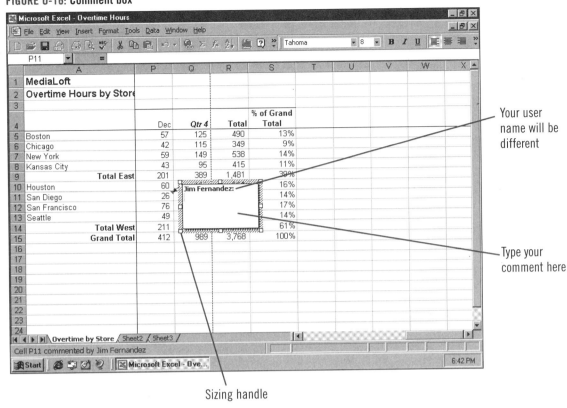

Your user name will be different

Type your comment here

Sizing handle

Excel 2000

Preview and print multiple worksheets

To preview and print multiple worksheets, press and hold down [Ctrl] and click the tabs for the sheets you want to print, then click the Preview or Print button.

In Page Preview, the multiple worksheets will appear as separate pages in the Preview window, which you can display by clicking Next and Previous.

Saving a Workbook as a Template

A **template** is a workbook that contains text (such as column and row labels), formulas, macros, and formatting you use repeatedly. Once you save a workbook as a template, it provides a model for creating a new workbook without your having to reenter standard data. Excel provides several templates on the Spreadsheet Solutions tab of the New dialog box. In most cases, though, you'll probably want to create your own template from a worksheet you use regularly. When you save a file as a template, the original workbook remains unchanged. ◄━━━ Jim plans to use the same formulas, titles, frozen panes, and row and column labels from the Overtime Hours worksheet for subsequent yearly worksheets. He will delete the extra sheets, the comments, and the data for each month, then save the workbook as a template.

Steps 1234

1. Click the **Sheet2 tab**, press **[Ctrl]**, click the **Sheet3 tab**, right-click the **Sheet3 tab**, click **Delete**, then click **OK**

2. Right-click cell **P11**, then click **Delete Comment**
   Now that you've removed the extra sheets and the comment, you'll delete the data on overtime hours. You'll leave the formulas in rows 9, 14, and 15, and in columns E, I, M, Q, R, and S, however, so that another user can simply begin entering data without having to re-create the formulas.

Trouble?

If you accidentally delete a formula, insert a copy from the appropriate adjoining cell or click the Undo button and repeat Step 3.

3. Press **[Ctrl]**, select the ranges **B5:D8**, **B10:D13**, **F5:H8**, **F10:H13**, **J5:L8**, **J10:L13**, **N5:P8**, **N10:P13**, press **[Delete]**, then click anywhere to deselect the ranges
   See Figure O-17. The hyphens in the subtotal and total rows and columns indicate that the current value of these cells is zero. The divide by zero error messages in column S are only temporary and will disappear as soon as you open the template, save it as a workbook, and begin to enter next year's data. To make subsequent template use easier, it's best to have the first data entry cell selected when you save it.

4. Scroll left to bring columns B through G into view, then click cell **B5**

5. Click **File**, click Save As, click the **Save as type list arrow**, then click **Template (.xlt)**
   Excel adds the .xlt extension to the filename (although you will not see it if your file extensions are turned off) and automatically switches to the Templates folder, as shown in Figure O-18. If you are using a computer on a network, you may not have permission to save to the Templates folder. You'll save your template to your Project Disk instead.

6. Click the **Save in list arrow**, click the drive and folder containing your Project Disk, click **Save**, close the workbook, then exit Excel
   Jim would save the template to one of his template folders. Next year, when he needs to compile the information for overtime hours, he can simply open a document based on the Overtime Hours template and begin entering data. When this new work is saved for the first time, Excel will automatically save the template as a regular workbook. The original template will remain intact.

FIGURE O-17: Preparing the template

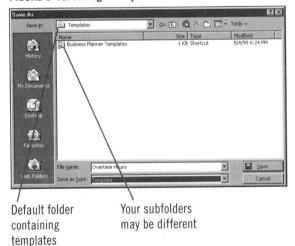

	A	L	M	N	O	P	Q	R	S	T
1	MediaLoft									
2	Overtime Hours by Store									
3									% of Grand	
4		Sep	Qtr 3	Oct	Nov	Dec	Qtr 4	Total	Total	
5	Boston		-				-	-	#DIV/0!	
6	Chicago		-				-	-	#DIV/0!	
7	New York		-				-	-	#DIV/0!	
8	Kansas City		-				-	-	#DIV/0!	
9	Total East	-	-	-	-	-	-	-	#DIV/0!	
10	Houston		-				-	-	#DIV/0!	
11	San Diego		-				-	-	#DIV/0!	
12	San Francisco		-				-	-	#DIV/0!	
13	Seattle		-				-	-	#DIV/0!	
14	Total West	-	-	-	-	-	-	-	#DIV/0!	
15	Grand Total	-	-	-	-	-	-	-	#DIV/0!	

Temporary divide-by-zero messages

Hyphens indicate value of zero

Overtime by Store

FIGURE O-18: Saving a template

Default folder containing templates

Your subfolders may be different

FIGURE O-19: New dialog box

The basic Excel workbook template

Represent subfolders in the Templates folder

Storing, applying, and modifying templates

If you're using your own computer, you may want to save your templates in one of the Templates subfolders, such as the one shown in Figure O-18. Then you can quickly open a document based on your template (that is, apply a template to a document) from the New dialog box by clicking File, clicking New, then selecting the template.

The New dialog box contains tabs containing icons for workbook templates, as shown in Figure O-19. The Spreadsheet Solutions tab in the New dialog box contains several ready-made templates you can use for business-related tasks, such as creating invoices or purchase orders. The other tabs in the New dialog box depend on which subfolders of the Templates folder you used to save your templates. For instance, if you saved a template named "Personnel" in the Other Documents subfolder, then you would see an Other Documents tab in the New dialog box, with the Personnel template as an option. To open a document based on this template, you would click it, then click OK.

To edit a template, you must use the Open command to open the template itself, change it, then save it under the same name. The changes will be applied only to new documents you create; it does not change documents you've already created using the template.

Practice

► Concepts Review

Label each element of the Excel screen shown in Figure O-20.

FIGURE O-20

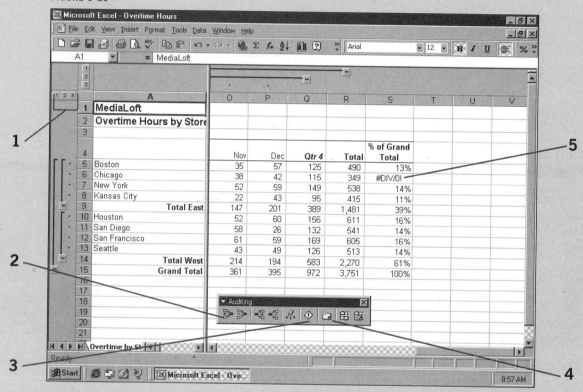

Match each term with the statement that describes it.

a. Find dialog box
b. Options dialog box
c. Auditing toolbar
d. Outlining a worksheet
e. Circular reference
f. [Shift][F9]
g. AutoFill
h. Comment

6. Contains settings for customizing Excel
7. Note that appears when you place the pointer over a cell
8. Occurs in a formula that refers to its own cell location
9. Calculates the worksheet manually
10. Automatically enters a list in a worksheet
11. Used to track errors and determine worksheet logic
12. A powerful searching tool that makes it easy to locate files
13. Allows you to display the most important columns and rows

Select the best answer from the list of choices.

14. When searching for a file, which of these characters can substitute for unknown characters in a filename?
    a. #
    b. &
    c. *
    d. !

15. You can search for a file by
    a. Name.
    b. Text within the file.
    c. Property.
    d. All of the above.

16. The _____ button locates the cells used in the active cell's formula.
    a. Trace Precedents
    b. Trace Antecedents
    c. Function
    d. Validation Circle

17. The _____ automatically hides everything in the worksheet except the most important row or rows.
    a. Column Level 1 button
    b. Row Level 1 button
    c. Trace Precedents button
    d. Outline feature

18. To create a custom AutoFill list you should first
    a. Press [Shift][F9].
    b. Click the AutoFill tab in the Edit dialog box.
    c. Drag the AutoFill handle.
    d. Select the list in the worksheet.

19. The _____ tab in the Options dialog box controls whether the Properties dialog box is displayed when you save a workbook.
    a. General
    b. Edit
    c. Properties
    d. View

▶ Skills Review

1. Find files.
a. In the Open dialog box, locate the drive that contains your Project Disk, and, if necessary, the folder where you store your Project Files.
b. If necessary, display detailed information about each file.
c. Display the files' properties.
d. Display only filenames.
e. Search for all files that begin with EX O, adding the search criterion to the criteria list.
f. Open the workbook EX O-2.
g. Save the workbook as "Cafe Budget".

2. Audit a worksheet.
a. Display the Auditing toolbar and drag it to the bottom of the worksheet.
b. Select cell E10, then use the New Comment button on the Auditing toolbar to add the comment "Does this include temporary holiday staff?" Close the Comments box, then use the pointer to redisplay the comment.
c. Select cell B10, then use the Trace Dependents button to locate all the cells that depend on this cell. (*Hint:* Click the button three times.)
d. Clear the arrows from the worksheet using the Remove All Arrows button on the Auditing toolbar.
e. Select cell B19, use the Trace Precedents button on the Auditing toolbar to find the cells on which that figure is based, then correct the formula in cell B19.
f. Select cell G6, trace the error it contains, then correct the formula.
g. Hide the Auditing toolbar, then save the workbook.
h. Practice opening and hiding the Picture toolbar.

3. Outline a worksheet.
a. Display the worksheet in outline view.
b. Use the Row Level buttons to display only the most important rows in the budget.
c. Use the Row Level buttons to display the second most important rows in the budget.
d. Add your name to the footer, then print the outlined worksheet in Landscape orientation.
e. Use the Row Level buttons to display all the rows in the budget.
f. Clear the outline from the worksheet.

4. Control worksheet calculations.
a. Open the Options dialog box and switch to manual calculation.
b. Change the figure in cell B6 to 30000.
c. Recalculate the worksheet manually using the appropriate key combination.
d. Turn off manual calculation and save the workbook.

5. Create a custom AutoFill list.
a. Select the range A4:A19.
b. Open the Custom Lists tab in the Options dialog box. Delete any custom lists except the four default day and month lists.
c. Import the selected text into the dialog box.
d. Close the dialog box.
e. On Sheet2, enter "Income" in cell A1.
f. Drag the fill handle to cell A15.

g. Select cell A1 again, and drag its fill handle to cell O1.

h. Open the Options dialog box again, and delete the list you just created.

i. Save the workbook.

6. Customize Excel.

a. Open the Options dialog box.

b. In the Edit tab, change the direction of the cell selector to "Up".

c. In the General tab, indicate that you want the Properties dialog box to appear when you save a workbook for the first time.

d. In the View tab, turn off the worksheet gridlines.

e. Close the dialog box and return to Sheet2, which is now displayed without gridlines.

f. Click the Budget tab, and notice that this worksheet is displayed with gridlines.

g. Open a new workbook.

h. Type your name in cell C5, then press Enter. Check to make sure the cell selector moves up.

i. Save the workbook to your Project Disk as "Customizing Excel", adding your name if necessary, and the comment "Sample workbook" to the Properties dialog box, then close the workbook.

j. Open the Options dialog box and change the cell selector direction back to "Down". Then turn off the Prompt for workbook properties option and close the Options dialog box.

7. Add a comment to a cell.

a. In the Budget sheet, select cell E12.

b. Open the Comment box by using the Comment command on the Insert menu.

c. Type "Does this include TV and radio spots, or only newspaper and magazine advertising? It is very important to include these."

d. Drag the resize handles on the borders of the Comment box until you can see the entire note.

e. Click anywhere outside the Comment box to close it.

f. Display the comment, and check it for errors.

g. Edit the comment in cell E12 so it ends after the word "spots", with a question mark at the end.

h. Delete the comment you added earlier in cell E10.

i. Print the worksheet and your comment in landscape orientation.

j. Change the orientation of Sheet2 to landscape and fit it to one page.

k. Preview and print both the Budget worksheet and Sheet2 at the same time.

l. Save the workbook.

8. Save a workbook as a template.

a. Delete Sheet2 and Sheet3.

b. Delete the comment in cell E12.

c. Delete the budget data for all four quarters. Leave the worksheet formulas intact.

d. Save the workbook to your Project Disk as a template, using the filename Budget Template.

e. Select cell B4 and close the template.

f. Copy the template into your Business Planner directory. (If you do not have access to the Business Planner directory, skip to Step 1.)

g. Open a document based on the template using the New command on the File menu.

h. Enter your own data for all four quarters and in every budget category.

i. Save the workbook as Cafe Budget 2.

j. Open the template using the Open command on the File menu, reformat it any way you wish, then save it.

k. Delete the copy of the template from the Business Planner directory.

l. Print and close the workbook, then exit Excel.

Excel 2000

▶ Independent Challenges

1. You are a manager at Life Skills, a nonprofit agency devoted to helping people with severe learning disabilities become proficient computer users. Your department specializes in hands-on instruction for popular personal computer (PC) programs. During the month of October, you created a check register in Excel for department expenses. Before you begin generating a November register, however, you want to check the October register for errors. In your worksheet audit, you will look for missing check numbers, miscalculated totals, and faulty formula logic. Also, you want to add comments to document the worksheet.

To complete this independent challenge:

a. Open the workbook titled EX O-3, then save it as "2000 Monthly Check Register".

b. Open the Auditing toolbar.

c. The balance in cell F16 does not reflect the RAM upgrade on 10/15/00. Use the Trace Precedents button to show the logic of the formula in F16. Once you identify the error in cell F16, edit the formula in cell F16 to subtract the RAM expense from the previous balance.

d. Due to illness, your Excel instructor taught only three hours of a six-hour course. Create a comment indicating this in cell C19.

e. Use the Trace Error button to determine the source of the problem in cell E24. Edit the formula to solve the problem, then format the cell to display a percentage with no decimal places.

f. Add your name to the worksheet footer, then save the workbook. Preview, then print the worksheet on one page and the comment on another.

g. Close the Auditing toolbar, then close the workbook, saving changes, if necessary.

2. As a manager at Life Skills, a nonprofit agency devoted to helping people with severe learning disabilities become proficient computer users, you need to keep track of your department's regular monthly expenses. Your assistant has compiled a list of fixed expenses in an Excel workbook but forgot the filename. Once you find the file using the Search tools in the Open dialog box, you want to create a custom AutoFill list containing each expense item to save time in preparing similar worksheets in the future. Finally, you will practice using manual calculation, then turn off the worksheet gridlines to make the expense data easier to read.

To complete this independent challenge:

Note: If you have access to the Microsoft Office 2000 installation disks, begin from Step a; if not, open the file EX O-4 and begin with Step b.

a. Search your Project Disk for a file with the text "printer paper" in the workbook. Search again for a file with the text "Fixed Monthly Expenses" in the workbook. Open the workbook.

b. Save the workbook as "Monthly Budget".

c. Select the cells containing the list of expense items. Then open the Options dialog box and import the list into the Custom Lists tab.

d. Close the Options dialog box and practice using the AutoFill handle to insert your list in a column in Sheet2. Insert the list a second time in a row in Sheet2.

e. Add your name to the worksheet footer, save the workbook, then preview and print Sheet2 on a single page.

f. Return to the Fixed Expenses sheet, then delete your custom list from the Options dialog box.

g. Use the Options dialog box to switch to manual calculation and to turn off the gridlines in the Fixed Expenses sheet.

h. Change the expense for printer paper to 25.00. Calculate the worksheet manually.

i. Turn on automatic calculation again, add your name to the footer, then print the Fixed Expenses worksheet.

j. Save and close the workbook.

3. Your business, Babies, Inc., helps parents find high-quality in-home childcare. In exchange for a one-time fee, you recruit and interview potential nannies, confirm references, and conduct thorough background checks. In addition, once a nanny has been hired, you provide training in child development and infant CPR. Currently, you are preparing your budget for the next four quarters. After you enter the data for each expense and income category, you will create a condensed version of the worksheet using Excel outlining tools.

To complete this independent challenge:

a. Open a new workbook, then save it as "Babies Budget".

b. Enter a title, then the following column labels: Description, 1st Qtr, 2nd Qtr, 3rd Qtr, 4th Qtr, and Total.

c. Enter the following income items: Nanny Fee, Child Development Course, and CPR Course. Subtotal the income items, then enter at least six office-expense items.

d. Subtotal the expenses. Enter expenses and income data for each quarter. Create formulas for the total column and a cash flow row (income - expenses). Format the worksheet appropriately.

e. Display the worksheet in Outline view.

f. Contract the outline to display only the subtotal and total rows, add your name to the footer, then print the outline.

g. Redisplay all the rows, then contract the outline again to eliminate the data for each quarter. Print the outline.

h. Clear the outline, then print the entire worksheet.

i. Save the workbook, and close it.

4. The MediaLoft Accounting department has asked Jim Fernandez to analyze the CD sales for the New York store for the next year. The department wants him to use the format that is currently used on the Accounting page of the MediaLoft intranet site. Jim wants to begin the analysis right away, so he decides to copy the table containing the information categories he needs directly from the site. He will then add information and a comment, then save the worksheet as a template that he can use again in the future.

To complete this independent challenge:

a. Connect to the Internet, and use Internet Explorer to go to the MediaLoft intranet site at http://www.course.com/Illustrated/MediaLoft. Click the Accounting link, then scroll until you see the table under New York Q2 Book Sales. Minimize the Internet Explorer window.

b. Open a new Excel workbook, minimize the Excel window, and arrange the Internet Explorer and Excel windows so they are next to each other.

c. Select the Sales by Category at MediaLoft New York table and drag it to cell A1 of the blank worksheet, then save the worksheet as New York Q2 Book Sales.

d. Close Internet Explorer and disconnect from the Internet.

e. Use formulas to add totals for each month and each book category, then put the totals in boldface.

f. Format the numbers in Comma format with no decimal places.

g. Change the workbook calculation from automatic to manual.

h. Change the children's book figure for April to 13,000, print the worksheet, circle the incorrect totals, then manually update the totals and return calculation to automatic.

i. On Sheet2, create a custom AutoFill list containing the book categories on Sheet1.

j. On Sheet1, add a comment to any cell, then print both Sheet1 and the comment.

k. Clear the data, the comment, and the month names from the worksheet, leaving the formulas intact, and save the workbook as a template called "New York Book Sales Template" on your Project Disk.

l. With the template still open, format the template using colors or other formatting to make it more attractive, then save your changes.

m. Close the workbook template and exit Excel.

▶ Visual Workshop

Open the workbook titled EX O-5, then click Cancel to close the dialog box warning you of a circular reference. Save the workbook as "City Zoo Animal Count" to your Project Disk. Use the auditing techniques you have learned so far to correct any errors so that the worksheet entries and formulas match Figure O-21. Make sure to include the cell comment in cell F11. Add your name to the footer, then preview and print the worksheet and comment in landscape orientation, showing row and column headings. In addition to printing the worksheet, also print the worksheet formulas on a separate sheet, showing row and column headings.

FIGURE O-21

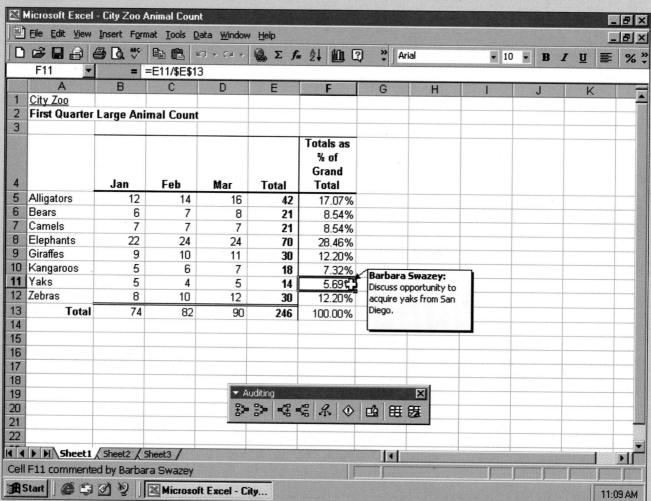

Programming
with Excel

Objectives

- ► View VBA code
- ► Analyze VBA code
- ► Write VBA code
- ► Add a conditional statement
- ► Prompt the user for data
- ► Debug a macro
- ► Create a main procedure
- ► Run a main procedure

All Excel macros are written in a programming language called Visual Basic for Applications or, simply, **VBA**. When you create a macro with the Excel macro recorder, the recorder writes the required VBA instructions for you. You can also create an Excel macro by entering the appropriate VBA instructions manually. The sequence of VBA statements contained in a macro is called a **procedure**. In this unit, you will view and analyze existing VBA code. Then you will write some VBA code on your own. You will learn how to add a conditional statement to a procedure, as well as how to prompt the user for information while the macro is running. You will also find out how to locate any errors, or bugs, in a macro. Finally, you will combine several macros into one. ✐ Alice Wegman, MediaLoft's marketing manager, has asked Jim Fernandez to create five macros to automate some of the division's time-consuming tasks.

Viewing VBA Code

Before you can write Excel macro procedures, you must become familiar with the VBA (Visual Basic for Applications) programming language. A common method of learning any programming language is to view existing code. To view VBA, you open the Visual Basic Editor, which contains a Project window, a Properties window, and a Code window. The VBA code for macro procedures appears in the Code window. The first line of a procedure, called the **procedure header**, defines the procedure's type, name, and arguments. Items displayed in blue are **keywords**, which are words recognized as part of the VBA programming language. **Comments**, which are notes explaining the code, are shown in green, and the remaining code is shown in black. You use the Editor to view or edit an existing macro procedure as well as to create a new macro procedure. ➤ Each week, MediaLoft receives a text file from the KHOT radio station containing information about weekly radio ads. Alice has already imported the text file into a worksheet but still needs to format it. Jim has begun work on a macro to automate the process of formatting this imported text file.

Steps 1 2 3 4

Trouble?

If the Virus warning dialog box shown in Figure P-1 appears, click Enable Macros. If a macro information dialog box opens informing you that Visual Basic macro modules are now edited in the Visual Basic Editor, click OK, then continue with Step 2.

1. Open the workbook titled **EX P-1**, save it as **KHOT Procedures**, then reset personalized toolbars and menus to their default state

   The KHOT Procedures workbook displays a blank worksheet. It is in this workbook that you will create and store all the procedures for this lesson.

2. Click **Tools** on the menu bar, point to **Macro**, then click **Macros**

   The Macro dialog box appears with the FormatFile macro procedure selected in the list box.

3. Click **Edit**

   The Visual Basic Editor opens and displays the FormatFile procedure in the Code window. See Figure P-2.

QuickTip

If you only see the Code window, click Tools on the menu bar, click Options, click the Docking tab, and make sure the Project Explorer and Properties options are selected.

4. Make sure both the Visual Basic window and the Code window are maximized to match Figure P-2. If the Properties or Project Explorer window is not displayed, click the **Properties Window button** 🗔, then click the **Project Explorer button** 🗔 on the toolbar

5. Examine the top three lines of comments and the first line of code beginning with Sub FormatFile ( )

   Notice that the different parts of the procedure appear in various colors. The third line of comments explains that the keyboard shortcut for this macro procedure is Ctrl+F. The keyword *Sub* in the procedure header indicates that this is a **Sub procedure**, or a series of Visual Basic statements that perform an action but do not return a value. In the next lesson, you will analyze the procedure code to see what each line does.

FIGURE P-1: Virus warning dialog box

Click here to open
workbook with the
ability to run macros

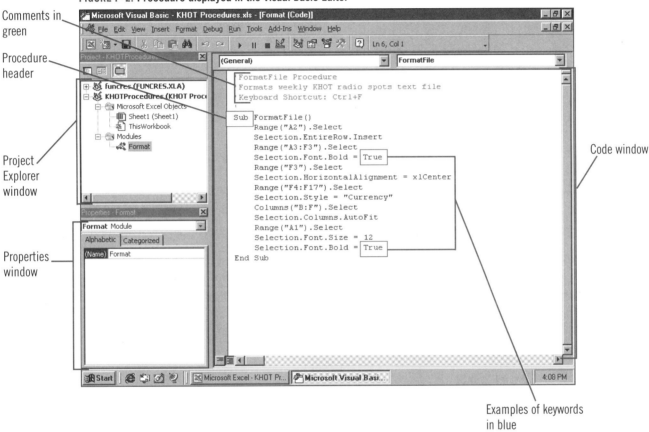

FIGURE P-2: Procedure displayed in the Visual Basic Editor

Comments in green

Procedure header

Project Explorer window

Properties window

Code window

Examples of keywords in blue

Excel 2000

Understanding the Visual Basic Editor

A **module** is the Visual Basic equivalent of a worksheet. In it, you store macro procedures, just as you store data in worksheets. Modules, in turn, are stored in workbooks (or **projects**), along with worksheets. You view and edit modules in the Visual Basic Editor, which is made up of three windows, the Project Explorer (also called the Project window), the Code window, and the Properties window. The **Project Explorer** displays a list of all open projects (or workbooks) and the worksheets and modules they contain. To view the procedures stored in a module, you must first select the module in the Project Explorer (just as you would select a file in the Windows Explorer). The **Code window** then displays the selected module's procedures. The **Properties window** displays a list of characteristics (or **properties**) associated with the module. A newly inserted module has only one property, its name.

Analyzing VBA Code

You can learn a lot about the VBA language simply by analyzing the code generated by the Excel macro recorder. The more VBA code you analyze, the easier it will be for you to write your own programming code. ◀━━ Before writing any new procedures, Jim analyzes the procedure he's already written, then opens a worksheet to which he wants to apply the formatting macro and runs the macro.

Steps

1. With the FormatFile procedure still displayed in the Code window, examine the next four lines of code, beginning with Range("A2").Select

See Figure P-3. Every element of Excel, including a range, is considered an **object**. A **range object** represents a cell or a range of cells. The statement *Range("A2").Select* selects the range object cell A2. Notice that several times in the procedure a line of code (or **statement**) selects a range, and then subsequent lines act on that selection. The next statement, *Selection.EntireRow.Insert*, inserts a row above the selection, which is currently cell A2. The next two lines of code select range A3:F3 and apply bold formatting to that selection. In VBA terminology, whether bold formatting is enabled is a value of an object's Bold property. A **property** is an attribute of an object that defines one of the object's characteristics (such as size) or an aspect of its behavior (such as whether it is enabled). The properties of an object are listed in the Properties window. To change the characteristics of an object, you simply change the values of its properties. For example, to apply bold formatting to a selected range, you assign the value True to the range's Bold property. To remove bold formatting, assign the value False.

2. Examine the remaining lines of code, beginning with Range ("F3").Select

The next two statements select the range object cell F3 and center its contents, then the following two statements select the F4:F17 range object and format it as currency. Column objects B through F are then selected and their widths set to AutoFit. Finally, the range object cell A1 is selected, its font size is changed to 12, and its Bold property is set to True. The last line, *End Sub*, indicates the end of the Sub procedure and is also referred to as the **procedure footer**.

3. Click the **View Microsoft Excel button** 🗷 on the Visual Basic Editor Standard toolbar to return to Excel

The macro is stored in the KHOT Procedures workbook. This way Jim can use it repeatedly each week after he receives that week's data. You will open the workbook containing data for January 1–7 and run the macro to format that data. You must leave the KHOT Procedures workbook open to use the macro stored there.

4. Open the workbook titled **EX P-2**, maximize if necessary, then save it as **KHOT Advertising Jan 1-7**

This is the workbook containing data you want to format.

5. Press **[Ctrl][F]** to run the procedure

The FormatFile procedure formats the text, as shown in Figure P-4.

6. Place your name in the worksheet footer, print the worksheet, then save the workbook

Now that you've successfully viewed and analyzed code and run the macro, you will learn how to write your own code.

FIGURE P-3: VBA code for the FormatFile procedure

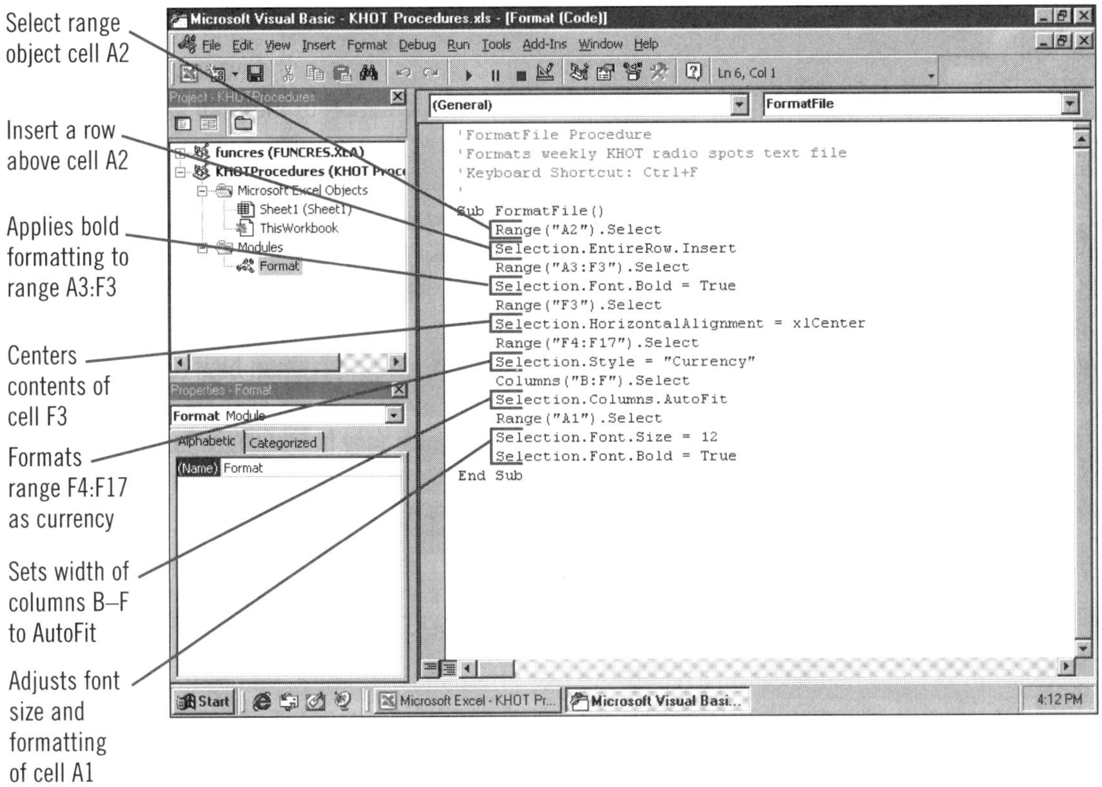

Select range object cell A2

Insert a row above cell A2

Applies bold formatting to range A3:F3

Centers contents of cell F3

Formats range F4:F17 as currency

Sets width of columns B–F to AutoFit

Adjusts font size and formatting of cell A1

```
'FormatFile Procedure
'Formats weekly KHOT radio spots text file
'Keyboard Shortcut: Ctrl+F
'
Sub FormatFile()
    Range("A2").Select
    Selection.EntireRow.Insert
    Range("A3:F3").Select
    Selection.Font.Bold = True
    Range("F3").Select
    Selection.HorizontalAlignment = xlCenter
    Range("F4:F17").Select
    Selection.Style = "Currency"
    Columns("B:F").Select
    Selection.Columns.AutoFit
    Range("A1").Select
    Selection.Font.Size = 12
    Selection.Font.Bold = True
End Sub
```

FIGURE P-4: Worksheet formatted using FormatFile procedure

Formatted title

Row inserted

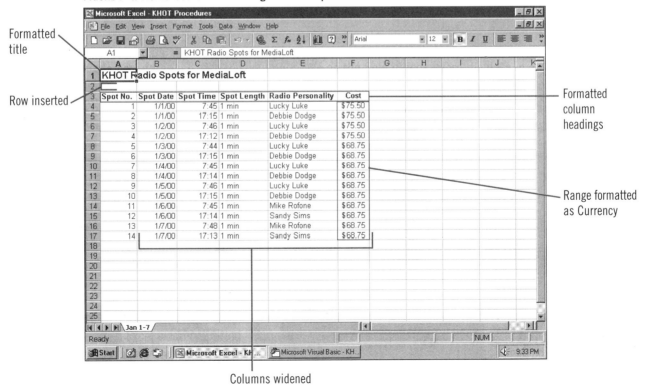

Formatted column headings

Range formatted as Currency

Columns widened

Writing VBA Code

To write your own code, you first need to open the Visual Basic Editor and add a module to the workbook. You can then begin entering the procedure code. In the first few lines of a procedure, you typically include comments indicating the name of the procedure, a brief description of the procedure, and shortcut keys, if applicable. When writing Visual Basic code for Excel, you must follow the formatting rules, or **syntax**, of the VBA programming language exactly. Even an extra space or a period could cause a procedure to fail. It is important to review the procedure based on the code you've written before you actually run it. ◄━━━ Each week, Alice asks Jim to total the cost of the radio ads. Jim decides to write a procedure that will automate this routine task.

Steps 1234

Trouble?

If the Code window is empty, verify that the workbook that contains your procedures (KHOT Procedures) is open.

1. With the Jan 1-7 worksheet still displayed, click **Tools** on the menu bar, point to **Macro**, then click **Visual Basic Editor**
   Two projects are displayed in the Project Explorer window, KHOT Procedures and KHOT Advertising Jan 1-7. KHOT Procedures is the active project; the Visual Basic title bar confirms this. The FormatFile procedure is again displayed in the Visual Basic Editor.

2. Click the **Modules folder** in the KHOT Procedures project
   You will store all of the procedures in the KHOT Procedures project.

3. Click **Insert** on the Visual Basic Editor menu bar, then click **Module**
   A new, blank module, with the default name Module1, is inserted in the KHOT Procedures workbook.

QuickTip

As you type, you may see lists of words in dropdown menus. For now, just continue to type.

4. Click **(Name)** in the Properties window, type **Total**, then press **[Enter]**
   This changes the default name to a more descriptive one. The module name ("Total") should not be the same as the procedure name (which will be "AddTotal"). Look at the code shown in Figure P-5. Notice that comments begin with an opening apostrophe and that the lines of code under "Sub AddTotal ( )" have been indented using the Tab key. When you enter the code in the next step, after you type *Sub AddTotal( )* (the procedure header) and press [Enter], the Visual Basic Editor will automatically enter *End Sub* (the procedure footer) in the Code window.

5. Click in the **Code window**, then type the procedure code exactly as shown in Figure P-5
   The lines that begin with *ActiveCell.Formula* insert the information enclosed in quotation marks into the active cell. For example, *ActiveCell.Formula = "Weekly Total:"* inserts the words "Weekly Total:" into cell E18, the active cell. The *With* clause near the bottom of the procedure is used to repeat several operations on the same object.

6. Compare the procedure code you entered in the Code window with Figure P-5; if necessary, make any corrections; then click the **Save KHOT Procedures.xls button** 🖫 on the Visual Basic Editor Standard toolbar

7. Click the **View Microsoft Excel button** 🗷 on the Visual Basic Editor Standard toolbar, use the Windows menu to display the KHOT Advertising Jan 1-7 workbook, click **Tools** on the Excel menu bar, point to **Macro**, then click **Macros**
   The Macro dialog box opens. This is where you select the macro procedure you want to run. Notice that the names of the macros have two parts. The first part ('KHOT Procedures.xls'!) indicates the workbook where the macro is stored. The second part (AddTotal or FormatFile) is the name of the procedure, taken from the procedure header.

Trouble?

If an error message appears, click Debug. Click the Reset button ■ on the Visual Basic Editor Standard toolbar to leave debug mode, correct the error by referring to Figure P-5, then repeat Steps 6–8.

8. Click **'KHOT Procedures.xls'!AddTotal** if necessary, then click **Run**
   The AddTotal procedure inserts and formats the ad expenditure total in cell F18, as shown in Figure P-6.

9. Save the workbook

FIGURE P-5: VBA code for the AddTotal procedure

Save KHOT Procedures button

Comments begin with apostrophes

Press [Tab] to indent lines

New module name

With clause repeats several operations on the same object

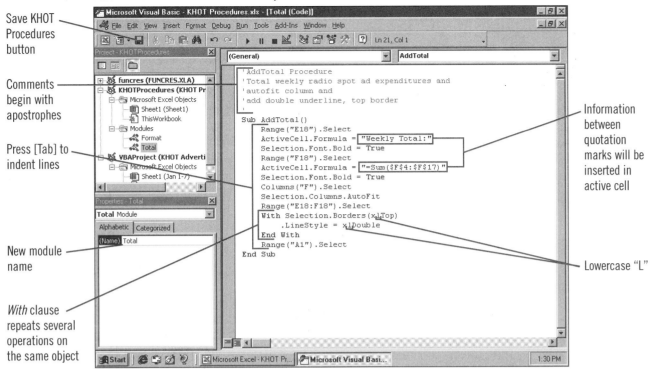

Information between quotation marks will be inserted in active cell

Lowercase "L"

FIGURE P-6: Worksheet after running the AddTotal procedure

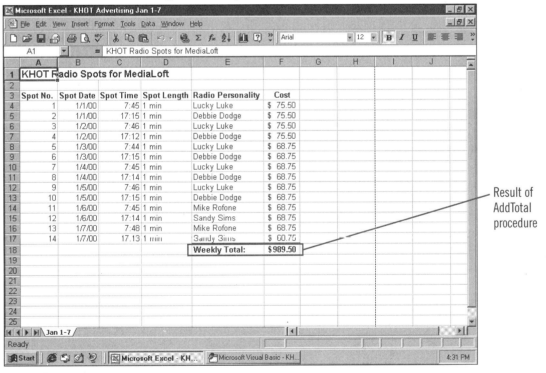

Result of AddTotal procedure

Entering code

To assist you in entering the macro code, the Editor often displays a list of words that can be used in the macro statement. Typically, the list appears after you press the . (period). To include a word from the list in the macro statement, select the word in the list, then press [Tab]. For example, to enter the *Range("E12").Select* instruction, type *Range(" E12")*, then press the . (period). Type *s* to select the Select command in the list, then press [Tab] to enter the word "Select" in the macro statement.

Adding a Conditional Statement

Sometimes, you may want a procedure to take an action based on a certain condition or set of conditions. For example, *if* a salesperson's performance rating is a 5 (top rating), *then* calculate a 10% bonus; otherwise (*else*), there is no bonus. One way of adding this type of conditional statement in Visual Basic is by using an **If...Then...Else statement**. The syntax for this statement is: "If *condition* Then *statements* Else [*elsestatements*]." The brackets indicate that the Else part of the statement is optional. ➤ Alice wants to find out if the amount spent on radio ads stays within or exceeds the $1,000 budgeted amount. Jim will use Excel to add a conditional statement that indicates this information. He starts by returning to the Visual Basic Editor and inserting a new module in the KHOT Procedures workbook.

Steps 1234

1. With the Jan 1-7 worksheet still displayed, click **Tools** on the menu bar, point to **Macro**, click **Visual Basic Editor**, verify that KHOT Procedures is the active project in the Project Explorer window, click **Insert** on the Visual Basic Editor menu bar, then click **Module**

   A new, blank module is inserted in the KHOT Procedures workbook.

2. In the Properties window click **(Name)**, then type **Budget**

3. Click in the Code window, then type the code exactly as shown in Figure P-7

   Notice the additional comment lines (in green) in the middle of the code. These extra lines help explain the procedure.

   QuickTip
   The If...Then...Else statement is similar to Excel's IF function.

4. Compare the procedure you entered with Figure P-7; if necessary, make any corrections; then click the **Save KHOT Procedures.xls button** 🖫 on the Visual Basic Editor Standard toolbar

5. Click the **View Microsoft Excel button** 🗷 on the Visual Basic Editor toolbar; click **Tools** on the menu bar; point to **Macro**; click **Macros**; in the Macro dialog box, click **'KHOT Procedures.xls'!BudgetStatus**; then click **Run**

   The BudgetStatus procedure indicates the status—within budget—as shown in Figure P-8.

6. Save your work

FIGURE P-7: **VBA code for the BudgetStatus procedure**

Elements of the If...Then...Else statement appear in blue

Module name

Type code exactly as shown

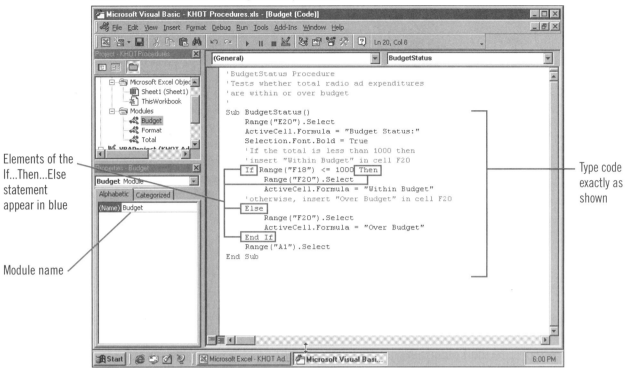

```
'BudgetStatus Procedure
'Tests whether total radio ad expenditures
'are within or over budget
'
Sub BudgetStatus()
    Range("E20").Select
    ActiveCell.Formula = "Budget Status:"
    Selection.Font.Bold = True
    'If the total is less than 1000 then
    'insert "Within Budget" in cell F20
    If Range("F18") <= 1000 Then
        Range("F20").Select
        ActiveCell.Formula = "Within Budget"
    'otherwise, insert "Over Budget" in cell F20
    Else
        Range("F20").Select
        ActiveCell.Formula = "Over Budget"
    End If
    Range("A1").Select
End Sub
```

FIGURE P-8: **Result of running BudgetStatus procedure**

Indicates status of ad budget

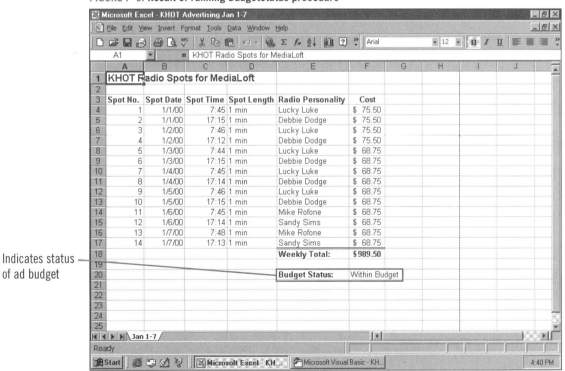

Prompting the User for Data

When automating routine tasks, you sometimes need to pause a macro to allow user input. You use VBA's InputBox function to display a dialog box that prompts the user for information. A **function** is a predefined procedure that returns a value; in this case the value returned is the information the user enters. The required elements of an InputBox function are as follows: *object*.InputBox("*prompt*"), where "*prompt*" is the message that appears in the dialog box. For a detailed description of the InputBox function, use the Visual Basic Editor's Help menu. ✐═══ Jim decides to create a procedure that will insert the user's name in the left footer area of the workbook. He'll use the InputBox function to display a dialog box in which the user can enter his or her name.

Steps

1. **With the Jan 1-7 worksheet still displayed, click Tools on the menu bar, point to Macro, click Visual Basic Editor, click Insert on the Visual Basic Editor menu bar, then click Module**

   A new, blank module is inserted in the KHOT Procedures workbook.

2. **In the Properties window, click (Name), then type Footer**

3. **Click in the Code window, then type the procedure code exactly as shown in Figure P-9**

   Like the Budget procedure, this procedure also contains comments that explain the code. The first part of the code, *Dim LeftFooterText As String*, **declares**, or defines, *LeftFooterText* as a text string variable. In Visual Basic, a **variable** is a slot in memory in which you can temporarily store one item of information. Dim statements are used to declare variables and must be entered in the following format: Dim *variablename* As *datatype*. The datatype here is "string." In this case, you plan to store the information received from the input box in the temporary memory slot called LeftFooterText. Then you can place this text in the left footer area. The remaining statements in the procedure are explained in the comment line directly above each statement.

QuickTip

To enlarge your Code window, place the mouse pointer on the left border of the Code window until it turns into ◄┃┃►, then drag the border to the left until the Code window is the desired size.

4. **Review your code for errors, make any changes if necessary, then click the Save KHOT Procedures.xls button 🖫 on the Visual Basic Editor Standard toolbar**

5. **Click the View Microsoft Excel button 🗷 on the Visual Basic Editor toolbar, click Tools on the menu bar, point to Macro, click Macros, in the Macro dialog box click 'KHOT Procedures.xls'!FooterInput, then click Run**

   The procedure begins, and a dialog box generated by the InputBox function appears, prompting you to enter your name. See Figure P-10.

QuickTip

If your macro doesn't run correctly, it may contain a spelling or syntax error. You'll learn how to correct such macro errors in the next lesson.

6. **With the cursor in the text box, type your name, then click OK**

7. **Click the Print Preview button 🔍 on the Standard toolbar**

   Although the customized footer is inserted on the sheet, notice that, due to an error, your name does *not* appear in the left section of the footer. In the next lesson, you will learn how to step through a procedure's code, line by line. This will help you locate the error in the Footer procedure.

8. **Click Close**

   This closes the Print Preview window and returns you to the Jan 1-7 worksheet.

FIGURE P-9: **VBA code for the FooterInput procedure**

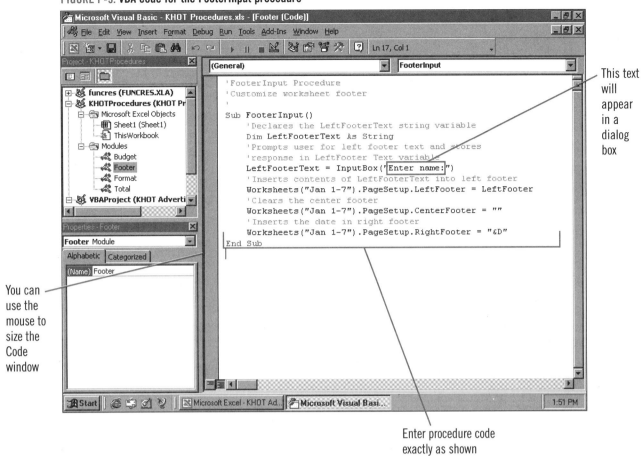

This text will appear in a dialog box

You can use the mouse to size the Code window

Enter procedure code exactly as shown

FIGURE P-10: **InputBox function's dialog box**

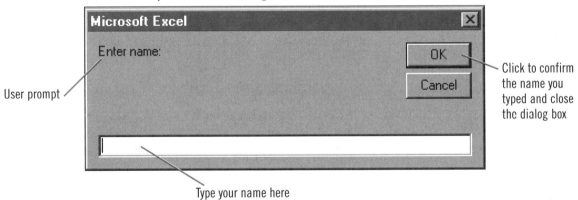

User prompt

Click to confirm the name you typed and close the dialog box

Type your name here

Debugging a Macro

When a macro procedure does not run properly, it can be due to an error, referred to as a **bug**, in the code. To assist you in finding the bug(s) in a procedure, you can use the Visual Basic Editor to step through the procedure's code, one line at a time. When you locate the error (bug), you can then correct, or **debug**, it. ✏️ Jim decides to debug the macro procedure to find out why it failed to insert his name in the worksheet's footer.

Steps

1. With the KHOT Advertising Jan 1-7 workbook still displayed, click **Tools** on the menu bar; point to **Macro**; click **Macros**; in the Macro dialog box, click **'KHOT Procedures.xls'!FooterInput**; then click **Step Into**
   The Visual Basic Editor appears with the statement selector positioned on the first statement of the procedure. See Figure P-11.

2. Press **[F8]** to step through the code
   The statement selector skips over the comments and the line of code beginning with Dim. The Dim statement indicates that the procedure will store your name in a variable named LeftFooterText. Because Dim is a declaration of a variable and not a procedure statement, the statement selector skips it and moves to the line containing the InputBox function.

3. Press **[F8]** again; with the cursor in the text box in the InputBox function dialog box, type your name, then click **OK**
   The Visual Basic Editor reappears. The statement selector is now positioned on the statement that reads *Worksheets ("Jan 1-7").PageSetup.LeftFooter = LeftFooter*. This statement inserts your name (which you just typed in the Input Box) in the left section of the footer. This is the instruction that does not appear to be working correctly.

4. If necessary, scroll right until the end of the LeftFooter instruction is visible, then place the mouse pointer I on **LeftFooter**, as shown in Figure P-12
   The last part of the InputBox function should be the variable (LeftFooterText) where the procedure stored your name. Rather than containing your name, however, the variable at the end of the procedure is empty. That's because the InputBox function assigned your name to the LeftFooterText variable, not to the LeftFooter variable. Before you can correct this bug, you need to turn off the Step Into feature.

5. Click the **Reset button** ▣ on the Visual Basic Editor Standard toolbar to turn off the Step Into feature, click at the end of the statement, then type **Text**
   The revised statement now reads *Worksheets("Jan 1-7").PageSetup.LeftFooter = LeftFooterText*.

6. Click the **Save KHOT Procedures.xls button** ▣ on the Visual Basic Editor Standard toolbar, then click the **View Microsoft Excel button** ▣ on the Visual Basic Editor toolbar

7. Click **Tools** on the menu bar, point to **Macro**, click **Macros**; in the Macro dialog box, click **'KHOT Procedures.xls'!FooterInput**; click **Run** to rerun the procedure; when prompted, type your name; then click **OK**

8. Click the **Print Preview button** ▣ on the Standard toolbar
   Your name now appears in the bottom-left section of the footer.

9. Click **Close**, save the workbook, then print your work

FIGURE P-11: Statement selector positioned on first procedure statement

Statement selector

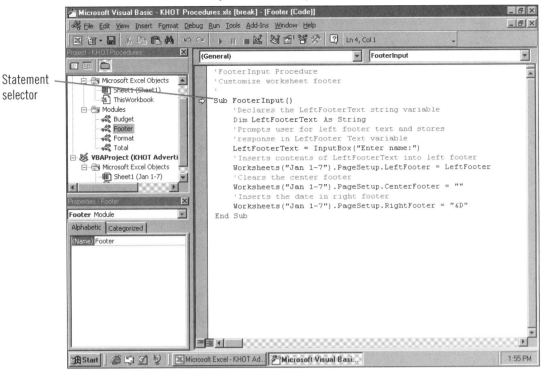

FIGURE P-12: Value contained in LeftFooter variable

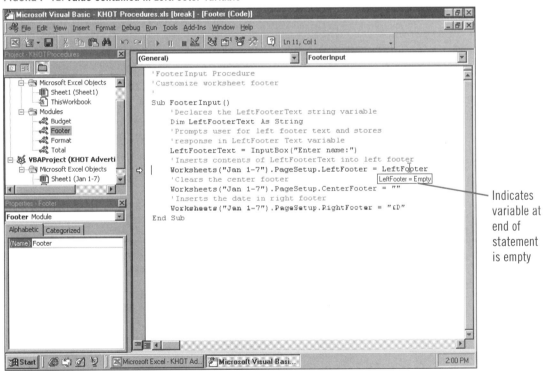

Indicates variable at end of statement is empty

Creating a Main Procedure

When you routinely need to run several macros one after another, you can save time by combining them into one procedure. The resulting procedure, which processes (or runs) multiple procedures in sequence, is referred to as the **main procedure**. To create a main procedure, you type a Call statement for each procedure you want to run. The syntax of the Call statement is Call *procedurename*, where *procedurename* is the name of the procedure you want to run. To avoid having to run his macros one after another every month, Jim decides to create a main procedure that will run (or call) each of the procedures in the KHOT Procedures workbook in sequence.

Steps 1234

1. With the Jan 1-7 worksheet displayed, click **Tools** on the menu bar, point to **Macro**, then click **Visual Basic Editor**

2. Verify that KHOT Procedures is the active project, Click **Insert** on the menu bar, then click **Module**
   A new, blank module is inserted in the KHOT Procedures workbook.

3. In the Properties window, click **(Name)**, then type **MainProc**

4. In the Code window, enter the procedure code exactly as shown in Figure P-13

5. Compare your main procedure code with Figure P-13, correct any errors if necessary, then click the **Save KHOT Procedures.xls button** 🖫 on the Visual Basic Editor Standard toolbar
   To test the new main procedure you need an unformatted version of the KHOT radio spot workbook.

6. Click the **View Microsoft Excel button** 🖾 on the Visual Basic Editor Standard toolbar, then close the KHOT Advertising Jan 1-7 workbook, saving your changes
   The KHOT Procedures workbook remains open.

7. Open the workbook titled EX P-2, then save it as **KHOT Advertising Jan 1-7 Version 2**
   In the next lesson, you'll run the main procedure.

FIGURE P-13: **VBA code for the MainProcedure procedure**

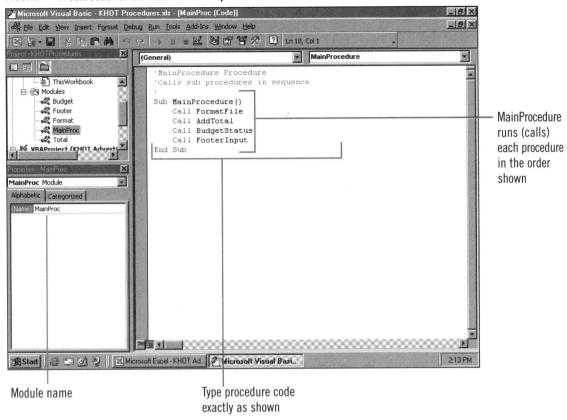

MainProcedure runs (calls) each procedure in the order shown

Module name

Type procedure code exactly as shown

Running a Main Procedure

Running a main procedure allows you to instantly run several macros in sequence. You can run a main procedure just as you would any other macro procedure—by selecting it in the Macro dialog box, then clicking Run. ✎ Jim has finished creating his main procedure and is now ready to run it. If the main procedure works correctly, it should format the worksheet, insert a budget status message, insert the ad expenditure total, and add Jim's name to the worksheet footer.

Steps 1 2 3 4

1. **With the Jan 1-7 Version 2 worksheet displayed, click Tools on the menu bar, point to Macro, and click Macros; in the Macro dialog box click 'KHOT Procedures.xls'! MainProcedure; click Run; when prompted type your name, then click OK**
   The MainProcedure runs the FormatFile, AddTotal, BudgetStatus, and FooterInput procedures in sequence. See Figure P-14. You can see the results of the FormatFile, AddTotal, and BudgetStatus procedures in the worksheet window. To view the results of the FooterInput procedure, you need to switch to the Preview window.

2. **Click the Print Preview button 🔍 on the Standard toolbar, verify that your name appears in the left footer area, then click Close**
   You could print each procedure separately, but it's faster to print all the procedures in the workbook at one time.

3. **Click Tools on the menu bar, point to Macro, then click Visual Basic Editor**

4. **In the Project Explorer window, double-click each procedure and add a comment line after the procedure name that reads "Written by [your name]"**

5. **Click File on the Visual Basic Editor menu bar, then click Print**
   The Print - KHOTProcedures dialog box opens, as shown in Figure P-15. Collectively, all procedures in a workbook are known as a project, as mentioned earlier in the unit.

6. **In the Print - KHOTProcedures dialog box, select the Current Project option button if necessary, then click OK**
   Each procedure prints on a separate page.

7. **Click the View Microsoft Excel button ▣ on the Visual Basic Editor Standard toolbar**

8. **Save the workbook and close it, close the KHOT Procedures workbook, then exit Excel**

FIGURE P-14: Result of running MainProcedure procedure

Click to verify that footer has been added

Formatting added to worksheet

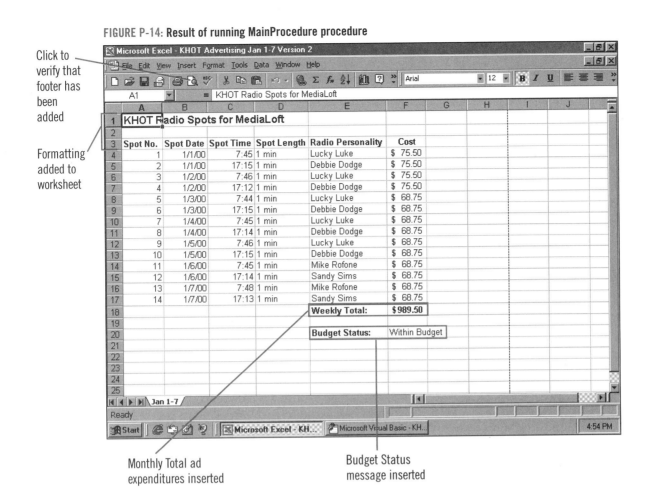

Monthly Total ad expenditures inserted

Budget Status message inserted

FIGURE P-15: Printing the macro procedures

Current Project option button

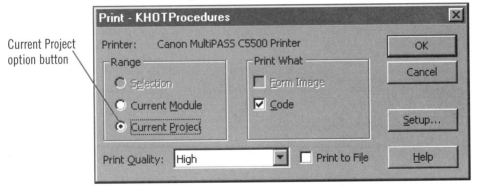

Practice

► Concepts Review

Label each element of the Visual Basic Editor screen shown in Figure P-16.

FIGURE P-16

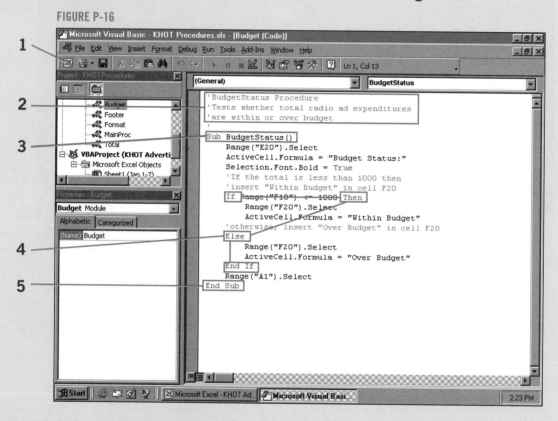

Match each term with the statement that describes it.

6. Sub procedure   **a.** Another term for a macro in Visual Basic for Applications (VBA)

7. Procedure   **b.** A procedure that returns a value

8. Keywords   **c.** Words that are recognized as part of the programming language

9. Function   **d.** A series of statements that perform an action but don't return a value

10. Comments   **e.** Descriptive text used to explain parts of a procedure

Select the best answer from the list of choices.

11. You enter the statements of a macro in
    a. The Macro dialog box.
    b. Any blank worksheet.
    c. The Properties window of the Visual Basic Editor.
    d. The Code window of the Visual Basic Editor.

12. What must you keep in mind when typing VBA code?
    a. Typographical errors can cause your procedures to fail.
    b. You can edit your code just as you would text in a word processor.
    c. The different parts of the code will appear in different colors.
    d. All of the above.

13. If your macro doesn't run correctly, you should
    a. Create an If . . . Then . . . Else statement.
    b. Select the macro in the Macro dialog box, click Step Into, and then debug the macro.
    c. Debug the macro in the worksheet window.
    d. Close the workbook and start over with a new macro.

▶ Skills Review

1. **View and analyze VBA code.**
   a. Open the workbook titled EX P-3, then save it as "Mission Medical Inc".
   b. Review the unformatted worksheet named Sheet1.
   c. Open the Visual Basic Editor.
   d. Select the ListFormat module.
   e. Insert comments in the List Format code describing what action you think each line of code will perform. (*Hint:* One of the statements will sort the list alphabetically by customer name.)
   f. Run the FormatList macro.
   g. Compare the results with the code and your comments.
   h. Save the workbook.

2. **Write VBA code.**
   a. Open Visual Basic Editor and insert a new module named "Total".
   b. Enter the Code exactly as shown in Figure P-17.
   c. Run the SalesTotal macro.
   d. Save the workbook.

FIGURE P-17

```
'SalesTotal Procedure
'Totals monthly sales
Sub SalesTotal()
  Range("F17").Select
  ActiveCell.Formula = "=SUM($F$2:$F$16)"
  Selection.Font.Bold = True
  With Selection.Borders(xlTop)
   .LineStyle = xlSingle
  End With
  Range("A1").Select
End Sub
```

3. Add a conditional statement.

a. Open Visual Basic Editor and insert a new module named "Goal".

b. Enter the procedure exactly as shown in Figure P-18.

c. Run the SalesGoal macro. If the procedure returns the message "Missed goal", the procedure worked as planned.

d. Save the workbook.

FIGURE P-18

```
'SalesGoal Procedure
'Tests whether sales goal was met
'
Sub SalesGoal()
  'If the total is >= 225000, then insert "Met Goal"
  'in cell G17
  If Range("F17") >= 225000 Then
   Range("G17").Select
   ActiveCell.Formula = "Met goal"
  'otherwise, insert "Missed goal" in cell G17
  Else
   Range("G17").Select
   ActiveCell.Formula = "Missed goal"
  End If
End Sub
```

4. Prompt the user for data.

a. Open Visual Basic Editor and insert a new module named "Header".

b. Enter the procedure exactly as shown in Figure P-19.

c. Run the HeaderFooter macro. When you encounter a runtime error, click End.

d. Save the workbook.

FIGURE P-19

```
'HeaderFooter Procedure
'Procedure to customize the header and footer
'
Sub HeaderFooter()
  'Inserts the filename in the header
  Worksheets("Sheet1").PageSetup.CenterHeader = "&F"
  'Declares the variable LeftFooterText as a string
  Dim LeftFooterText As String
  'Prompts user for left footer text
  LeftFooter = InputBox("Enter your full name:")
  'Inserts response into left footer
  Workbooks("Sheet1").PageSetup.LeftFooter = LeftFooterText
  Workbooks("Sheet1").PageSetup.CenterFooter = ""
  Workbooks("Sheet1").PageSetup.RightFooter = "&D"
End Sub
```

5. **Debug a macro.**
   a. Run the HeaderFooter macro. When you encounter a runtime error, click Debug.
   b. The statement selector is positioned on the incorrect procedure statement:
      Workbooks("Sheet1").PageSetup.LeftFooter = LeftFooterText.
      (*Hint:* Note that Workbooks, instead of Worksheets, was entered in the statement.)
   c. Change *Workbooks* in the incorrect line of code to *Worksheets*. Do the same in the two following lines of code.
   d. Rerun the HeaderFooter procedure.
   e. Check the header and footer. Notice that the procedure does not display your name in the left section of the footer.
   f. Use the Step Into feature to find the error in the code and then correct it. Make sure you leave Debugger mode by clicking the Reset button.
   g. Rerun the HeaderFooter procedure.
   h. Verify that your name now appears in the left section of the footer.
   i. Save the workbook.

6. **Create and run a main procedure.**
   a. Return to the Visual Basic Editor, insert a new module, and name it "MainProc".
   b. Enter comments that give the procedure's name (MainProcedure), and explain its purpose.
   c. Enter the following procedure header: *Sub MainProcedure ().*
   d. Enter four Call statements that will run the FormatList, SalesTotal, SalesGoal, and HeaderFooter procedures in sequence.
   e. Save the procedure and return to Excel.
   f. Open the EX P-3 workbook, then save it as Medical Mission Inc Version 2.
   g. Run the MainProcedure procedure. (*Hint:* In the Macro dialog box, the macro procedures you created will now have *'Medical Mission Inc.xls'!* as part of their names. That's because the macros are stored in the Medical Mission Inc workbook, and not in the Medical Mission Inc Version 2 workbook.)
   h. Save the Medical Mission Inc Version 2 workbook, print the worksheet, then close the workbook.
   i. Print the current project's code.
   j. Return to Excel and close any open workbooks.

▶ Independent Challenges

1. Your officemate William is on vacation for two weeks, and you have taken over his projects. The office manager, Monique, asks you to document the Excel procedure that William wrote (called DoYourThing) for the company's auditors. You have located the workbook containing the procedure; now you will document it.

To complete this independent challenge:

a. Open the workbook titled EX P-4, then save it as "Mystery Procedure".

b. Run the DoYourThing procedure, noting anything you think should be mentioned in your documentation.

c. Review the procedure in the Visual Basic Editor.

d. Document the procedure by annotating the printed code, indicating the actions the procedure performs and the objects (ranges) that are affected.

e. Print the procedures code.

f. Save and close the workbook.

2. You work in the sales office of a large automobile dealership called Auto Heaven. Each month you are required to produce a report stating whether sales quotas were met for the following five vehicle categories: compacts, sedans, sports/utility, vans, and trucks. This quarter the sales quotas for each month are as follows: compacts 50, sedans 35, sports/utility 20, vans 19, and trucks 40. The results this month (Jan 1-7) were 53, 32, 12, 25, and 35, respectively. You decide to create a procedure to automate your monthly task of determining the sales quota status for the vehicle categories. You would like the new clerk to take this task over when you go on vacation next month. Because the clerk has no previous experience with Excel, you decide to add input boxes that prompt the user to enter the actual sales results for the month.

To complete this independent challenge:

a. Create a workbook to be used as a monthly template, then save it as "Sales Quota Status".

b. Create a procedure using multiple If... Then... Else statements to determine the sales quota status for each vehicle category automatically.

c. Add input boxes to prompt the user for the actual sales data for each vehicle category. (*Hint:* You can use a combination of statements using InputBox and ActiveCell.)

d. Record a new macro called Shortcut that assigns [Ctrl]+[Q] to run the Monthly Sales macro. Insert a line on the worksheet that tells the user to press [Ctrl]+[Q] to enter sales data.

e. Test the procedure. Correct any problems.

f. Save your work, insert your name in a "Created by" line below the procedure name, then print the code.

g. Close the workbook.

3. You are an internal auditor for a large food manufacturer called Earthly Treats. You are responsible for ensuring that staff members document their Excel worksheets properly. To help the staff document their worksheets more efficiently, you decide to create two procedures. The first procedure will automate the process of displaying worksheet formulas. The second will prompt the user for his or her department name and insert that information in the footer, then print the worksheet and delete it. The company name and the date should appear in the footer as well. After you create the two procedures, you will create a main procedure to run them in sequence.

To complete this independent challenge:

a. Create a workbook, then save it as "Documentation Procedures".

b. Create a procedure that opens a new worksheet, enters "Earthly Treats Report" in cell A1, turns on formula display in the new sheet, and uses AutoFit to fit the new sheet's columns.

c. Create a procedure that creates the footer as described above. The procedure should also print the new formula sheet, then delete the new sheet as the last step. (*Hint:* You can use the Macro Recorder to create the procedure.)

d. Create a main procedure that calls the new worksheet procedure and the footer/print procedure in sequence.

e. Save, test, then debug each procedure.

f. Insert your name in a "Created by" line under the procedure name, then print the code for the current project.

g. Save your work, then close the workbook.

4. Alice Wegman, MediaLoft's marketing manager, would like to know how important the radio spots on KHOT are to MediaLoft's marketing strategy. Jim Fernandez has asked you to get a copy of the MediaLoft Advertising Campaign chart and create a formatting procedure to highlight the KHOT radio spots.

To complete this independent challenge:

a. Connect to the Internet, and go to the MediaLoft intranet site at http://www.course.com/Illustrated/MediaLoft. Click the Marketing link, then click the MediaLoft Advertising Campaigns link.

b. Select the table and drag it into a blank Excel workbook and save the workbook as "MediaLoft Ad Campaign".

c. Insert a module and create a procedure that will insert rows above and below the KHOT radio spots information row, then change the text for the radio spot row to bold and the KHOT effectiveness rating to a 14-point font.

d. Run the procedure, add your name to the workbook footer, and print the results.

e. Save the workbook and close Excel.

► Visual Workshop

Open the workbook titled EX P-5 and save it as "Big Time Audio". Create a macro procedure that will format the worksheet as shown in Figure P-20.

FIGURE P-20

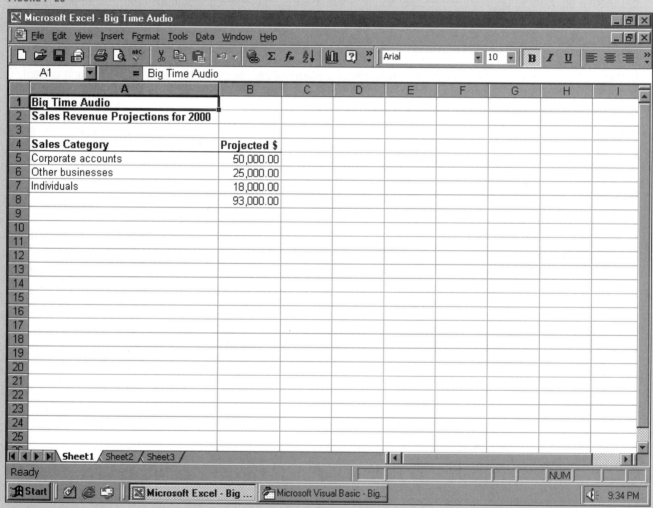

Excel 2000 MOUS Certification Objectives

Below is a list of the Microsoft Office User Specialist program objectives for Core and Expert Excel 2000 skills showing where each MOUS objective is covered in the Lessons and the Practice. This table lists the Core and Expert MOUS certification skills covered in the units in this book and in *Microsoft Excel 2000—Illustrated Introductory* (units A–H). For more information on which Illustrated titles meet MOUS certification, please see the inside cover of this book.

MOUS standardized coding number	Activity	Lesson page where skill is covered	Location in lesson where skill is covered	Practice
XL2000E.1	**Importing and exporting data**			
XL2000E.1.1	Import data from text files (insert, drag and drop)	Excel M-4	Steps 1–5	Skills Review 1, Independent Challenge 1
		Excel M-5	Clues to Use	
XL2000E.1.2	Import from other applications	Excel M-6	Steps 1–2	Skills Review 2, Independent Challenge 2
XL2000E.1.3	Import a table from an HTML file (insert, drag and drop—including HTML round tripping)	Excel M-9	Clues to Use	Independent Challenge 4
XL2000E.1.4	Export to other applications	Excel M-7 Excel M-16	Clues to Use Steps 1–9	
XL2000E.2	**Using templates**			
XL2000E.2.1	Apply templates	Excel O-17	Clues to Use	Skills Review 8, Independent Challenge 4
XL2000E.2.2	Edit templates	Excel O-17	Clues to Use	Skills Review 8, Independent Challenge 4
XL2000E.2.3	Create templates	Excel O-16	Steps 1–6	Skills Review 8, Independent Challenge 4
XL2000E.3	**Using multiple workbooks**			
XL2000E.3.1	Using a workspace	Excel F-11	Clues to Use	
XL2000E.3.2	Link workbooks	Excel F-14	Steps 1–2	Skills Review 7, Independent Challenge 4
		Excel F-7	Clues to Use	Skills Review 3
XL2000E.4	**Formatting numbers**			
XL2000E.4.1	Apply number formats (Accounting, Currency, Number)	Excel C-2 (Currency)	Step 3	Skills Review 1, Independent Challenge 2
		Excel M-4 (Currency)	QuickTip	
		Excel M-4 (Number)	Step 7	Independent Challenge 2
		Excel M-4 (Accounting)	QuickTip	Skills Review 2
XL2000E.4.2	Create custom number formats	Excel E-9	Clues to Use	Independent Challenge 1
XL2000E.4.3	Use conditional formatting	Excel C-14	Steps 1–7	Skills Review 7, Independent Challenges 2, 4

MOUS standardized coding number	Activity	Lesson page where skill is covered	Location in lesson where skill is covered	Practice
XL2000E.5	**Printing workbooks**			
XL2000E.5.1	Print and preview multiple worksheets	Excel O-15	Clues to Use	Skills Review 7
XL2000E.5.2	Use the Report Manager	Excel F-10 Excel K-7	QuickTip Clues to Use	
XL2000E.6	**Working with named ranges**			
XL2000E.6.1	Add and delete a named range	Excel B-5 (Adding) Excel B-17 (Adding) Excel K-6 (Deleting)	Clues to Use Clues to Use QuickTip	Skills Review 1, Independent Challenge 1 Independent Challenge 1
XL2000E.6.2	Use a named range in a formula	Excel B-17 Excel I-14	Clues to Use Steps 2–3	Skills Review 6
XL2000E.6.3	Use Lookup Functions (HLOOKUP or VLOOKUP)	Excel I-13 (HLOOKUP) Excel I-12 (VLOOKUP)	Clues to Use Steps 1–8	 Skills Review 5, Independent Challenge 3
XL2000E.7	**Working with toolbars**			
XL2000E.7.1	Hide and display toolbars	Excel G-16 Excel O-5	QuickTip Clues to Use	 Skills Review 2
XL2000E.7.2	Customize a toolbar	Excel G-16	Steps 1–8	Skills Review 7, Independent Challenges 1, 2
XL2000E.7.3	Assign a macro to a command button	Excel G-16	Steps 1–8	Skills Review 7, Independent Challenges 1, 2
XL2000E.8	**Using macros**			
XL2000E.8.1	Record macros	Excel G-4	Steps 1–8	Skills Review 1
XL2000E.8.2	Run macros	Excel G-6	Steps 1–8	Skills Review 2
XL2000E.8.3	Edit macros	Excel G-8	Steps 1–6	Skills Review 3
XL2000E.9	**Auditing a worksheet**			
XL2000E.9.1	Work with the Auditing toolbar	Excel O-4	Step 2	Skills Review 2, Independent Challenge 1
XL2000E.9.2	Trace errors (find and fix errors)	Excel O-4	Step 3	Skills Review 2, Independent Challenge 1
XL2000E.9.3	Trace precedents (find cells referred to in a specific formula)	Excel O-4	Step 5	Skills Review 2, Independent Challenge 1
XL2000E.9.4	Trace dependents (find formulas that refer to a specific cell)	Excel O-4	QuickTip	Skills Review 2
XL2000E.10	**Displaying and Formatting Data**			
XL2000E.10.1	Apply conditional formats	Excel C-14	Steps 2–7	Skills Review 7, Independent Challenges 2, 4

MOUS standardized coding number	Activity	Lesson page where skill is covered	Location in lesson where skill is covered	Practice
XL2000E.10.2	Perform single and multi-level sorts	Excel H-12	Steps 1–6	Skills Reviews 4, 5, Independent Challenges 1–3
		Excel H-14	Steps 1–6	Skills Review 5, Independent Challenges 1–3
XL2000E.10.3	Use grouping and outlines	Excel I-10	Steps 1–7	Skills Review 4
XL2000E.10.4	Use data forms	Excel H-6	Steps 1–8	Skills Review 2, Independent Challenge 2
XL2000E.10.5	Use subtotaling	Excel I-10	Steps 1–7	Skills Review 4, Independent Challenge 3
XL2000E.10.6	Apply data filters	Excel I-2, I-4, I-6	Steps 1–7, 1–7, 1–5	Skills Reviews 1–3, Independent Challenges 1, 3
XL2000E.10.7	Extract data	Excel I-8	Steps 1–5	
XL2000E.10.8	Query databases	Excel M-6	QuickTip	
XL2000E.10.9	Use data validation	Excel I-16	Steps 1–7	Skills Review 7, Independent Challenges 1, 3
XL2000E.11	**Using analysis tools**			
XL2000E.11.1	Use PivotTable autoformat	Excel L-12	Steps 1–8	Skills Review 6, Independent Challenges 1–4
XL2000E.11.2	Use Goal Seek	Excel K-12	Steps 1–6	Skills Review 6, Independent Challenge 3
XL2000E.11.3	Create PivotChart reports	Excel L-14	Steps 1–6	Skills Review 7, Independent Challenge 2
XL2000E.11.4	Work with scenarios	Excel K-4, K-6	Steps 1–8, 1–7	Skills Reviews 2, 3, Independent Challenges 1, 2
XL2000E.11.5	Use Solver	Excel K-14, K-16	Steps 1–8, 1–6	Skills Review 7, Independent Challenges 3, 4
XL2000E.11.6	Use data analysis and PivotTables	Excel L-1–L-12	All Steps	All Skills Reviews and Independent Challenges
XL2000E.11.7	Create interactive PivotTables for the Web	Excel N-12	Steps 1–7	Skills Review 5, Independent Challenge 3
XL2000E.11.8	Add fields to a PivotTable using the Web browser	Excel N-13	Clues to Use	
XL2000E.12	**Collaborating with workgroups**			
XL2000E.12.1	Create, edit, and remove a comment	Excel O-14 (Create)	Steps 1–6	Skills Review 7, Independent Challenge 1
		Excel O-14 (Edit)	QuickTip	Skills Review 7
		Excel O-16 (Remove)	Step 2	Skills Review 7
XL2000E.12.2	Apply and remove worksheet and workbook protection	Excel F-8	Steps 1–8, QuickTip	Skills Review 4

MOUS standardized coding number	Activity	Lesson page where skill is covered	Location in lesson where skill is covered	Practice
XL2000E.12.3	Change workbook properties	Excel F-9	Clues to Use	Independent Challenge 3
XL2000E.12.4	Apply and remove file passwords	Excel F-8 Excel N-8	Table F-1, QuickTip Steps 1–6, Clues to Use	Skills Review 3, Independent Challenge 1
		Excel N-9	Clues to Use	
XL2000E.12.5	Track changes (highlight, accept, and reject)	Excel N-6 (Highlight)	Steps 1–2, 7	Skills Review 2, Independent Challenge 1
		Excel N-6 (Accept and Reject)	QuickTip	Skills Review 2
XL2000E.12.6	Create a shared workbook	Excel N-4	Steps 1–5	
XL2000E.12.7	Merge workbooks	Excel N-7	Clues to Use	

Project Files List

To complete many of the lessons and practice exercises in this book, students need to use a Project File that is supplied by Course Technology and stored on a Project Disk. Below is a list of the files that are supplied, and the unit or practice exercise to which the files correspond. For information on how to obtain Project Files, please see the inside cover of this book. The following list only includes Project Files that are supplied; it does not include the files students create from scratch or the files students create by revising the supplied files.

Unit	File supplied on Project Disk	Location file is used in unit
Excel Unit I	EX I-1.xls	Lessons
	EX I-2.xls	Skills Review
	EX I-3.xls	Independent Challenges 1–2
	EX I-4.xls	Independent Challenge 3
	EX I-5.xls	Independent Challenge 4
Excel Unit J	EX J-1.xls	Lessons
	EX J-2.xls	Skills Review
	EX J-3.xls	Independent Challenges 1–2
Excel Unit K	EX K-1.xls	Lessons
	EX K-2.xls	Skills Review
	EX K-3.xls	Independent Challenges 1–2
	EX K-4.xls	Independent Challenge 3
Excel Unit L	EX L-1.xls	Lessons
	EX L-2.xls	Skills Review
	EX L-3.xls	Independent Challenge 1
	EX L-4.xls	Independent Challenge 2
	EX L-5.xls	Independent Challenge 3
	EX L-6.xls	Independent Challenge 4
	EX L-7.xls	Visual Workshop
Excel Unit M	EX M-1.txt	Lessons
	EX M-2.dbf	
	EX M-3.jpg	
	EX M-4.doc	
	EX M-5.xls	
	EX M-6.ppt	
	EX M-7.xls	
	EX M-8.xls	
	EX M-9.txt	Skills Review
	EX M-10.dbf	
	EX M-11.bmp	
	EX M-12.xls	
	EX M-13.ppt	
	EX M-14.xls	
	EX M-15.xls	
	EX M-16.prn	Independent Challenge 1
	EX M-17.wk1	Independent Challenge 2
	EX M-18.jpg	Visual Workshop

Unit	File supplied on Project Disk	Location file is used in unit
Excel Unit N	EX N-1.xls	Lessons
	EX N-2.xls	
	EX N-3.xls	Skills Review
	EX N-4.xls	Independent Challenge 1
	EX N-5.xls	Independent Challenge 2
	EX N-6.xls	Independent Challenge 3
Excel Unit O	EX O-1.xls	Lessons
	EX O-2.xls	Skills Review
	EX O-3.xls	Independent Challenge 1
	EX O-4.xls	Independent Challenge 2
	EX O-5.xls	Visual Workshop
Excel Unit P	EX P-1.xls	Lessons
	EX P-2.xls	
	EX P-3.xls	Skills Review
	EX P-4.xls	Independent Challenge 1
	EX P-5.xls	Visual Workshop

Glossary

Excel 2000

3-D references A reference that uses values on other sheets or workbooks, effectively creating another dimension to a workbook.

Absolute reference A cell reference that contains a dollar sign before the column letter and/or row number to indicate the absolute, or fixed, contents of specific cells. For example, the formula $A$1+$B$1 calculates only the sum of these specific cells no matter where the formula is copied in the workbook.

Active cell The current location of the cell pointer.

Address The location of a specific cell or range expressed by the coordinates of column and row; for example, A1.

Alignment The horizontal placement of cell contents; for example, left, center, or right.

Analyze To manipulate data, such as a list, with Excel or another tool.

Anchors Cells listed in a range address. For example, in the formula =SUM(A1:A15), A1 and A15 are anchors.

Area chart A line chart in which each area is given a solid color or pattern to emphasize the relationship between the pieces of charted information.

Arguments Information a function needs to create the answer. In an expression, multiple arguments are separated by commas. All of the arguments are enclosed in parentheses; for example, =SUM(A1:B1).

Arithmetic operator A symbol used in a formula, such as + or -, / or *, to perform mathematical operations.

ASCII file A text file that contains data but no formatting; instead of being divided into columns, ASCII file data are separated, or delimited, by tabs or commas.

Attribute The styling features such as bold, italics, and underlining that can be applied to cell contents.

AutoComplete A feature that automatically completes labels entered in adjoining cells in a column.

AutoFill A feature that creates a series of text or numbers when a range is selected using the fill handle.

AutoFit A feature that automatically adjusts the width of a column to accommodate its widest entry when the boundary to the right of the column selector is double-clicked.

AutoFormat Preset schemes that can be applied to format a range instantly. Excel comes with 16 AutoFormats that include colors, fonts, and numeric formatting.

AutoSum A feature that automatically creates totals using the AutoSum button.

Background color The color applied to the background of a cell.

Backsolving A problem-solving method in which you specify a solution and then find the input value that produces the answer you want; sometimes described as a what-if analysis in reverse.

Bar chart A chart that shows information as a series of (horizontal) bars.

Border The edge of a selected area of a worksheet. Lines and color can be applied to borders.

Bug In programming, an error that causes a procedure to run incorrectly.

Cancel button The X in the formula bar; it removes information from the formula bar and restores the previous cell entry.

Cell The intersection of a column and row in a worksheet.

Cell address The unique location identified by intersecting column and row coordinates.

Cell comments Notes you've written about a workbook that appear when you place the pointer over a cell.

Cell pointer A highlighted rectangle around a cell that indicates the active cell.

Cell reference The address or name that identifies a cell's position in a worksheet; it consists of a letter that identifies the cell's column and a number that identifies its row; for example, cell B3. Cell references in worksheets can be used in formulas and are relative or absolute.

Change history A worksheet containing a list of changes made to a shared workbook.

Changing cells In what-if analysis, cells that contain the values that change in order to produce multiple sets of results.

Chart A graphic representation of information from a worksheet. Types include 2-D and 3-D column, bar, pie, area, and line charts.

Chart sheet A separate sheet that contains a chart linked to worksheet data.

Chart title The name assigned to a chart.

Chart Wizard A series of dialog boxes that helps create or modify a chart.

Check box A square box in a dialog box that can be clicked to turn an option on or off.

Clear A command on the Edit menu used to erase a cell's contents, formatting, or both.

Clipboard A temporary storage area for cut or copied items that are available for pasting. See *Office Clipboard*.

Clipboard toolbar A toolbar that shows the contents of the Office Clipboard; contains buttons for copying and pasting items to and from the Office Clipboard.

Close A command that closes the file so you can no longer work with it, but keeps Excel open so that you can continue to work on other workbooks.

Code window In the Visual Basic Editor, the window that displays the selected module's procedures, written in the Visual Basic programming language.

Column chart   The default chart type in Excel that displays information as a series of (vertical) columns.

Column selector button   The gray box containing the letter above the column.

Comments   In a Visual Basic procedure, notes that explain the purpose of the macro or procedure; they are preceded by a single apostrophe and appear in green on a color monitor.

Conditional format   The format of a cell based on its value or the outcome of a formula.

Conditional formula   A formula that makes calculations based on stated conditions, such as calculating a rebate based on a purchase amount.

Consolidate   To add together values on multiple worksheets and display the result on another worksheet.

Control menu box   A box in the upper-left corner of a window used to resize or close a window.

Copy   A command that copies the content of selected cells and places it on the Clipboard.

Criteria range   A cell range containing one row of labels (usually a copy of column labels) and at least one additional row underneath it that contains the criteria you want to match.

Custom chart type   A specially formatted Excel chart.

Cut   A command that removes the cell contents from the selected area of a worksheet and places them on the Clipboard.

Data entry area   The unlocked portion of a worksheet where users are able to enter and change data.

Data form   In an Excel list (or database), a dialog box that displays one record at a time.

Data label   Descriptive text that appears above a data marker in a chart.

Data map   An Excel chart that shows information plotted on a map with symbols representing data points.

Data marker   A graphical representation of a data point, such as a bar or column.

Data point   Individual piece of data plotted in a chart.

Data series   The selected range in a worksheet that Excel converts into a graphic and displays as a chart.

Data table   A range of cells that shows the resulting values when one or more input values are varied in a formula; when one input value is changed, the table is called a one-input data table, and when two input values are changed, it is called a two-input data table.

Database   An organized collection of related information. In Excel, a database is called a list.

Debug   In programming, to correct an error in code.

Declare   In the Visual Basic programming language, to define a text string as a variable.

Delete   A command that removes cell contents from a worksheet.

Dependent cell   A cell, usually containing a formula, whose value changes depending on the values in the input cells. For example, a payment formula or function that depends on an input cell containing changing interest rates is a dependent cell.

Destination program   In a data exchange, the program that will receive the data.

Dialog box   A window that opens when more information is needed to carry out a command.

Divide-by-zero error   An Excel worksheet error that occurs when a formula attempts to divide a value by zero.

Document   To make notes about basic worksheet assumptions, complex formulas, or questionable data.

Dummy column/row   Blank column or row included at the end of a range that enables a formula to adjust when columns or rows are added or deleted.

Dynamic page breaks   In a larger workbook, horizontal or vertical dashed lines that represent the place where pages print separately. They also adjust automatically when you insert or delete rows or columns, or change column widths or row heights.

Edit   A change made to the contents of a cell or worksheet.

Electronic spreadsheet   A computer program that performs calculations on data and organizes information into worksheets. A worksheet is divided into columns and rows, which form individual cells.

Embedding   Inserting a copy of data into a destination document; you can double-click the embedded object to modify it using the tools of the source program.

Enter button   The check mark in the formula bar used to confirm an entry.

Exploding pie slice   A slice of a pie chart that has been pulled away from the whole pie to add emphasis.

External reference indicator   The exclamation point (!) used in a formula to indicate that a referenced cell is outside the active sheet.

Extract   To place a copy of a filtered list in a range you specify in the Advanced Filter dialog box.

Field   In a list (an Excel database), a column that describes a characteristic about records, such as first name or city.

Field name   A column label that describes a field.

Fill color   Cell background color.

Fill Down   A command that duplicates the contents of the selected cells in the range selected below the cell pointer.

Fill handle   A small square in the lower-right corner of the active cell used to copy cell contents.

Fill Right   A command that duplicates the contents of the selected cells in the range selected to the right of the cell pointer.

Filter   To hide data in an Excel list that does not meet specified criteria.

Find A command used to locate information the user specifies.

Floating toolbar A toolbar within its own window that is not anchored along an edge of the worksheet.

Font The typeface or design of a set of characters (letters, numbers, symbols, and punctuation marks).

Footer Information that prints at the bottom of each printed page; on screen, a footer is visible only in Print Preview. To add a footer, use the Header and Footer command on the View menu.

Format The appearance of text and numbers, including color, font, attributes, borders, and shading. See also *Number format*.

Format Painter A feature used to copy the formatting applied to one set of text or in one cell to another.

Formula A set of instructions used to perform numeric calculations (adding, multiplying, averaging, etc.).

Formula bar The area below the menu bar and above the Excel workspace where you enter and edit data in a worksheet cell. The formula bar becomes active when you start typing or editing cell data. It includes the Enter button and the Cancel button.

Freeze To hold in place selected columns or rows when scrolling in a worksheet that is divided in panes. See also *panes*.

Function A special, predefined formula that provides a shortcut for a commonly used calculation; for example, AVERAGE. In the Visual Basic programming language, a predefined procedure that returns a value.

Goal cell In backsolving, a cell containing a formula in which you can substitute values to find a specific value, or goal.

Gridlines Horizontal and/or vertical lines within a chart that make the chart easier to read.

Header Information that prints at the top of each printed page; on screen, a header is visible only in Print Preview. To add a header, use the Header and Footer command on the View menu.

Hide To make rows, columns, formulas, or sheets invisible to workbook users.

HTML Hypertext Markup Language, the format of pages that a Web browser such as Internet Explorer or Netscape Navigator can read.

Hyperlink An object (a filename, a word, a phrase, or a graphic) in a worksheet that, when you click it, will display another worksheet, called the target.

If...Then...Else statement In the Visual Basic programming language, a conditional statement that directs Excel to perform specified actions under certain conditions; its syntax is "If *condition* Then *statements* Else [*elsestatements*].

Input Information that produces desired results in a worksheet.

Input cells Spreadsheet cells that contain data instead of formulas and that act as input to a what-if analysis; input values often change to produce different results. Examples include interest rates, prices, or other data.

Insertion point Blinking I-beam that appears in the formula bar during entry and editing.

Interactive Describes a worksheet saved as an HTML document and posted to an intranet or Web site that allows users to manipulate data using their browsers.

Internet A large computer network made up of smaller networks and computers.

Intranet An internal network site used by a particular group of people who work together.

Keywords In a macro procedure, words that are recognized as part of the Visual Basic programming language.

Label Descriptive text or other information that identifies the rows and columns of a worksheet. Labels are not included in calculations.

Label prefix A character that identifies an entry as a label and controls the way it appears in the cell.

Landscape orientation A print setting that positions the worksheet on the page so the page is wider than it is tall.

Legend A key explaining how information is represented by colors or patterns in a chart.

Line chart A graph of data that is mapped by a series of lines. Line charts show changes in data or categories of data over time and can be used to document trends.

Linking The dynamic referencing of data in other workbooks, so that when data in the other workbooks is changed, the references in the current workbook are automatically updated.

List The Excel term for a database, an organized collection of related information.

Lock To secure a row, column, or sheet so that data there cannot be changed.

Logical test The first part of an IF function; if the logical test is true, then the second part of the function is applied, and if it is false, then the third part of the function is applied. In the function IF(Balance>1,000,Rate*0.05,0), the 5% rate is applied to balances over $1,000.

Macro A set of instructions, or code, that performs tasks in the order you specify.

Main procedure A procedure containing several macros that run sequentially.

Mixed reference Formula containing both a relative and an absolute reference.

Mode indicator A box located at the lower-left corner of the status bar that informs you of the program's status. For example, when Excel is performing a task, the word "Wait" appears.

Model A worksheet used to produce a what-if analysis that acts as the basis for multiple outcomes.

Module In Visual Basic, a module is stored in a workbook and contains macro procedures.

More Buttons button A button you click on a toolbar to view toolbar buttons that are not currently visible.

Mouse pointer A symbol that indicates the current location of the mouse on the desktop. The mouse pointer changes its shape at times; for example, when you insert data, select a range, position a chart, change the size of a window, or select a topic in Help.

Moving border The dashed line that appears around a cell or range that is copied to the Clipboard.

Name box The left-most area in the formula bar that shows the cell reference or name of the active cell. For example, A1 refers to cell A1 of the active worksheet. You can also get a list of names in a workbook using the Name list arrow.

Named range A range of cells given a meaningful name; it retains its name when moved and can be referenced in a formula.

Number format A format applied to values to express numeric concepts, such as currency, date, and percentage.

Object A chart or graphic image that can be moved and resized and contains handles when selected. In object linking and embedding (OLE), the data to be exchanged between another document or program.

Object Linking and Embedding (OLE) A Microsoft Windows technology that allows you to transfer data from one document and program to another using embedding or linking.

Office Assistant An animated character that appears to offer tips, answer questions, and provide access to the program's Help system.

Office Clipboard A temporary storage area shared by all Office programs that can be used to cut, copy, and paste multiple items within and between Office programs. The Office Clipboard can hold up to 12 items collected from any Office program. See also *Clipboard toolbar*.

One-input data table A range of cells that shows resulting values when one input value in a formula is changed.

Open A command that retrieves a workbook from a disk and displays it on the screen.

Order of precedence The order in which Excel calculates parts of a formula: (1) exponents, (2) multiplication and division, and (3) addition and subtraction.

Output The end result of a worksheet.

Page field In a PivotTable or a PivotChart report, a field area that lets you view data as if it is stacked in pages, effectively adding a third dimension to the data analysis.

Panes Sections into which you can divide a worksheet when you want to work on separate parts of the worksheet at the same time; one pane freezes, or remains in place, while you scroll in another pane until you see the desired information.

Paste A command that moves information on the Clipboard to a new location. Excel pastes the formula, rather than the result, unless the Paste Special command is used.

Paste Function A series of dialog boxes that lists and describes all Excel functions and assists the user in function creation.

Pie chart A circular chart that represents data as slices of pie. A pie chart is useful for showing the relationship of parts to a whole; pie slices can be extracted for emphasis. See also *Exploding pie slice*.

PivotChart report An Excel feature that lets you summarize worksheet data in the form of a chart in which you can rearrange, or "pivot," parts of the chart structure to explore new data relationships.

PivotTable report An Excel feature that allows you to summarize worksheet data in the form of a table in which you can rearrange, or "pivot," parts of the table structure to explore new data relationships; also called a PivotTable.

PivotTable list An interactive PivotTable on a Web or intranet site that lets users explore data relationships using their browsers.

Plot area The area of a chart that contains the chart itself, its axes, and the legend.

Point A unit of measure used for fonts and row height. One inch equals 72 points.

Pointing method Specifying formula cell references by selecting the desired cell with your mouse instead of typing its cell reference; this eliminates typing errors.

Portrait orientation A print setting that positions the worksheet on the page so the page is taller than it is wide.

Precedence Algebraic rules that Excel uses to determine the order of calculations in a formula with more than one operator.

Procedure A sequence of Visual Basic statements contained in a macro that accomplishes a specific task.

Procedure footer In Visual Basic, the last line of a Sub procedure.

Procedure header The first line in a Visual Basic procedure.

Print Preview A command you can use to view the worksheet as it will look when printed.

Print title In a list that spans more than one page, the field names that print at the top of every printed page.

Program Task-oriented software (such as Excel or Word) that enables you to perform a certain type of task, such as data calculation or word processing.

Programs menu The Windows 95/98 Start menu that lists all available programs on your computer.

Project In the Visual Basic Editor, the equivalent of a workbook; a project contains Visual Basic modules.

Project Explorer In the Visual Basic Editor, a window that lists all open projects (or workbooks) and the worksheets and modules they contain.

Properties In the Visual Basic Editor, the characteristics associated with a module.

Properties window In the Visual Basic Editor, the window that displays a list of characteristics, or properties, associated with a module.

Range A selected group of adjacent cells.

Range object In Visual Basic, an object that represents a cell or a range of cells.

Range format A format applied to a selected range in a worksheet.

Record In a list (an Excel database), data about an object or a person.

Refresh To update a PivotTable so it reflects changes to the underlying data.

Relative cell reference A type of cell reference used to indicate a relative position in the worksheet. It allows you to copy and move formulas from one area to another of the same dimensions. Excel automatically changes the column and row numbers to reflect the new position.

Replace A command used to find one set of criteria and replace it with new information.

Reset usage data An option that returns personalized toolbars and menus to their default settings.

Route To send an e-mail attachment sequentially to each user in a list, who then forwards it to the next user on the list.

Routing slip A list of e-mail users who are to receive an e-mail attachment.

Row height The vertical dimension of a cell.

Row selector button The gray box containing the number to the left of the row.

Save A command used to permanently store your workbook and any changes you make to a file on a disk. The first time you save a workbook you must give it a filename.

Save As A command used to create a duplicate of the current workbook with a new filename. Used the first time you save a workbook.

Scenario A set of values you use to forecast results; the Excel Scenario Manager lets you store different scenarios.

Scenario summary An Excel table that compiles data from various scenarios so that you can view the scenario results next to each other for easy comparison.

Search criterion The specification for data that you want to find in an Excel list, such as "Denver" or "is greater than 1000."

Selection handles Small boxes appearing along the corners and sides of charts and graphic images that are used for moving and resizing.

Series of labels Pre-programmed series, such as days of the week and months of the year. They are formed by typing the first word of the series, then dragging the fill handle to the desired cell.

Shared workbook An Excel workbook that several users can open and modify.

Sheet Another term used for a *worksheet*.

Sheet tab A description at the bottom of each worksheet that identifies it in a workbook. In an open workbook, move to a worksheet by clicking its sheet tab. Also known as *Worksheet tab*.

Sheet tab scrolling buttons Buttons that enable you to move among sheets within a workbook.

Sort keys Criteria on which a sort, or a reordering of data, is based.

Source list The list on which a PivotTable is based.

Source program In a data exchange, the program used to create the data you are embedding or linking.

Spell check A command that attempts to match all text in a worksheet with the words in the dictionary.

Standard chart type A commonly used column, bar, pie, or area chart in the Excel program; each type has several variations. For example, a column chart variation is the Columns with Depth.

Start To open a software program so you can use it.

Statement In Visual Basic, a line of code.

Status bar The bar at the bottom of the Excel window that provides information about various keys, commands, and processes.

Sub procedure A series of Visual Basic statements that perform an action but do not return a value.

Summary function In a PivotTable, a function that determines the type of calculation applied to the PivotTable data, such as SUM or COUNT.

Syntax In the Visual Basic programming language, the formatting rules that must be followed so that the macro will run correctly.

Table In an Access database, a list of data.

Target The location that a hyperlink displays after you click it.

Target cell In what-if analysis (specifically, in Excel Solver), the cell containing the formula.

Template A workbook containing text, formulas, macros, and formatting you use repeatedly; when you create a new document, you can open a document based on the template workbook. The new document will automatically contain the formatting, text, formulas, and macros in the template.

Text annotations Labels added to a chart to draw attention to a particular area.

Text color The color applied to the text within a cell.

Tick marks Notations of a scale of measure on a chart axis.

Title bar The bar at the top of the window that indicates the program name and the name of the current worksheet.

Toggle button A button that turns a feature on and off.

Toolbar A bar that contains buttons that give you quick access to the most frequently used commands.

Tracers In Excel worksheet auditing, arrows that point from cells that might have caused an error to the active cell containing an error.

Track To identify and keep a record of who makes which changes to a workbook.

Two-input data table A range of cells that shows resulting values when two input values in a formula are changed.

Truncate To shorten the display of a cell based on the width of a cell.

Uniform Resource Locator (URL) A unique address for a location on the World Wide Web; www.course.com is an example.

Values Numbers, formulas, or functions used in calculations.

Variable In the Visual Basic programming language, a slot in memory in which you can temporarily store an item of information; variables are often declared in Dim statements such as Dim *variablename* As *datatype*.

View A set of display or print settings that you can name and save for access at another time. You can save multiple views of a worksheet.

Visual Basic for Applications (VBA) A programming language used to create macros in Excel.

Web query An Excel feature that lets you obtain data from a Web, Internet, or intranet site and places it in an Excel workbook for analysis.

What-if analysis A decision-making feature in which data is changed and automatically recalculated.

Wildcard A special symbol you use in defining search criteria in the data form or Replace dialog box. The most common types of wildcards are the question mark (?), which stands for any single character, and the asterisk (*), which represents any group of characters.

Window A rectangular area of a screen where you view and work on a worksheet.

Workbook A collection of related worksheets contained within a single file.

Worksheet An electronic spreadsheet containing 256 columns by 65,536 rows.

Worksheet tab See *Sheet tab*.

Worksheet window The worksheet area in which data is entered.

World Wide Web A structure of documents, called pages, connected electronically over a large computer network called the Internet.

X-axis The horizontal line in a chart.

X-axis label A label describing the x-axis of a chart.

Y-axis The vertical line in a chart.

Y-axis label A label describing the y-axis of a chart.

Zoom A feature that enables you to focus on a larger or smaller part of the worksheet in Print Preview.

Index

Index

Index

Show Detail button
 on PivotTable toolbar, EXCEL L-7
Show Details button, EXCEL I-11
Show/Hide Fields button
 on PivotTable toolbar, EXCEL L-7
sizing handles
 for custom charts, EXCEL J-2
slides
 embedding Excel charts into, EXCEL M-14—15
Solver, EXCEL K-1
 setting up complex what-if analyses with,
  EXCEL K-14—15
Solver Parameters dialog box, EXCEL K-14—15,
 EXCEL K-16
Solver Results dialog box, EXCEL K-16—17
Sort Descending button, EXCEL M-6
source list
 updating, EXCEL L-10—11
source programs, EXCEL M-2
space delimited files, EXCEL M-3
Spreadsheet Property Toolbox, EXCEL N-10—11
Spreadsheet Solutions tab
 in New dialog box, EXCEL O-17
spreadsheets. See worksheets
standard chart types, EXCEL J-2
statements
 in VBA code, EXCEL P-4
stock symbols, EXCEL N-16
strings
 in VBA code, EXCEL P-10
Sub procedures, EXCEL P-2
subtotals
 creating using functions, EXCEL I-10
 creating with grouping, EXCEL I-10—11
 creating with outlines, EXCEL I-10—11
Subtotals dialog box, EXCEL I-10—11
SUM function, EXCEL L-6
 creating subtotals with, EXCEL I-10
summarizing list data, EXCEL I-14—15
summary function
 of PivotTables, EXCEL L-6—7
summary rows and columns
 outlining and, EXCEL O-6—7
SYLK files, EXCEL M-3
Symbol Lookup hyperlink, EXCEL N-16
syntax
 of VBA code, EXCEL P-5, EXCEL P-8

►T

Tab delimited files, EXCEL M-3
Table dialog box, EXCEL K-8—9, EXCEL K-10—11
tables. See Access tables; database tables; data
 tables; PivotTables
target cells
 in what-if analysis, EXCEL K-14—15
templates
 applying, EXCEL O-17
 defined, EXCEL O-16
 modifying, EXCEL O-17
 saving workbooks as, EXCEL O-16—17
 storing, EXCEL O-17
Templates folder, EXCEL O-16—17
text
 rotating, EXCEL J-14—15
text files
 delimiters in, EXCEL M-4
 importing, EXCEL M-4—5
Text Import Wizard dialog boxes, EXCEL M-4—5

three-dimensional data
 analyzing, EXCEL L-8—9
three-dimensional (3-D) charts
 rotating, EXCEL J-10—11
3-D View dialog box, EXCEL J-10—11
toolbars
 Auditing, EXCEL O-4—5
 Chart, EXCEL J-2, EXCEL J-15
 Circular Reference, EXCEL O-5
 Drawing, EXCEL J-12
 External Data, EXCEL N-16
 hiding and displaying, EXCEL O-5
 PivotTable, EXCEL L-7, EXCEL L-14
 Visual Basic Editor Standard, EXCEL P-16
 Visual Basic Standard, EXCEL P-6
Top 10 AutoFilter dialog box, EXCEL I-2
tracer arrows, EXCEL O-4—5
tracking changes
 in shared workbooks, EXCEL N-4, EXCEL N-6—7
Transition tab
 of Options dialog box, EXCEL O-13
two-input data tables, EXCEL K-10—11
TXT files, EXCEL M-3

►U

Uniform Resource Locators (URLs)
 creating hyperlinks to, EXCEL N-14—15
URLs, EXCEL N-14—15
User-defined chart types, EXCEL J-3

►V

validation, of data. See data validation
Value (y) axis, EXCEL J-6—7
Value (z) axis, EXCEL J-7
values
 looking up in a list, EXCEL I-12—13
variables
 in VBA code, EXCEL P-10
VBA, EXCEL P-1
VBA code
 adding conditional statements in, EXCEL P-8—9
 analyzing, EXCEL P-4—5
 creating main procedures, EXCEL P-14—15
 defined, EXCEL P-1
 functions in, EXCEL P-10—11
 prompting the user for data, EXCEL P-10—11
 running main procedures, EXCEL P-16—17
 syntax of, EXCEL P-5
 viewing, EXCEL P-2—3
 writing, EXCEL P-5-6
Vertical Lookup function. See VLOOKUP function
vertical split box, EXCEL O-4
View tab
 of Options dialog box, EXCEL O-13
Virus warning dialog box, EXCEL P-2, EXCEL P-3
Visual Basic Applications. See VBA
Visual Basic Editor, EXCEL P-2—3
 adding conditional statements in, EXCEL P-8—9
 code-writing aids in, EXCEL P-6
 debugging macros in, EXCEL P-12—13
 writing VBA code in, EXCEL P-5-6
Visual Basic Editor Standard toolbar, EXCEL P-16
Visual Basic Standard toolbar, EXCEL P-6
VLOOKUP dialog box, EXCEL I-12—13
VLOOKUP function, EXCEL I-12—13

►W

Web. See World Wide Web
Web browsers
 adding fields to PivotTable lists with, EXCEL N-13
 viewing interactive PivotTables in, EXCEL N-12—13
 viewing interactive worksheets in, EXCEL N-10—11
what-if analysis, EXCEL K-1—17
 complex, Solver for, EXCEL K-14—17
 data tables for, EXCEL K-8—9
 defined, EXCEL K-1
 defining, EXCEL K-2—3
 generating scenarios summary, EXCEL K-6—7
 generating Solver Answer Report, EXCEL K-16—17
 Goal Seek for, EXCEL K-12—13
 tracking with Scenario Manager, EXCEL K-4—5
 two-input data tables for, EXCEL K-10—11
wildcards
 finding files with, EXCEL O-2
WKS files, EXCEL M-3
Word Art
 in charts, EXCEL J-12—13
WordPad
 linking worksheets to, EXCEL M-12—13
workbooks
 applying and removing passwords, EXCEL N-8—9
 distributing to others, EXCEL N-2
 documenting, with comments, EXCEL O-14—15
 merging, EXCEL N-7
 on server, controlling access to, EXCEL N-2
 saving as a template, EXCEL O-16—17
 saving text files as, EXCEL M-4—5
 shared, EXCEL N-2
 setting up, EXCEL N-4—5
 tracking changes in, EXCEL N-6—7
worksheet logic, EXCEL O-4
worksheets
 auditing, EXCEL O-4—5
 embedding, EXCEL M-10—11
 enhancing, EXCEL J-1
 inserting graphic into, EXCEL M-8—9
 interactive, creating for intranet or Web,
  EXCEL N-10—11
 interactive, publishing on intranet or the Web,
  EXCEL N-2—3
 linking to another program, EXCEL M-12—13
 multiple, previewing and printing, EXCEL O-15
 navigating with hyperlinks, EXCEL N-15
 outlining, EXCEL O-6—7
 publishing on intranet or the Web, EXCEL N-2—3
 recalculating, EXCEL O-8—9
World Wide Web
 creating interactive PivotTables for, EXCEL N-12—13
 creating interactive workbooks for, EXCEL N-10—11
 customized queries on, EXCEL N-17
 managing HTML files on, EXCEL N-11
 publishing interactive workbooks and PivotTables to,
  EXCEL N-2—3
 running queries on, EXCEL N-2—3, EXCEL N-16—17

►X

XLM files, EXCEL M-3
.xlt extension, EXCEL O-16
XLT files, EXCEL M-3